1 MONTH OF
FREE
READING

at
www.ForgottenBooks.com

By purchasing this book you are eligible for one month membership to ForgottenBooks.com, giving you unlimited access to our entire collection of over 700,000 titles via our web site and mobile apps.

To claim your free month visit:
www.forgottenbooks.com/free249944

ISBN 978-0-483-98402-8
PIBN 10249944

Bibliographia Paracelsica

PARTS I.-VI.

1877-1896

FIRST SERIES

BY

JOHN FERGUSON, LL.D.

REGIUS PROFESSOR OF CHEMISTRY IN THE UNIVERSITY OF GLASGOW

Privately Printed

GLASGOW

Printed at the University Press by

ROBERT MACLEHOSE AND CO.

1896

MY interest in Paracelsus took its rise in the chemical discoveries and ideas attributed to him. It was not long, however, before I found that he was primarily and mainly a physician, and had to do with Chemistry only in so far as the science forms the necessary ground-work of pharmacy and therapeutics, of physiology and pathology. Paracelsus, conspicuous in the history of Medicine, occupies a place in that of Chemistry only incidentally; but it is such a place as a man of the first rank alone could fill, one who by the force of his ideas and personality could give a new direction to a great branch of knowledge, other than that in which his chief interest lay.

The aim of those who dealt with Paracelsus down to the year 1876 was to describe his life, to expound his opinions, and to bring some sort of system out of his bulky writings, which were all assumed to be genuine. In that year, however, Dr. Friedrich Mook asked: *Are all the writings genuine?* but before attempting an answer he was constrained to enumerate the works which pass under Paracelsus' name. In the book which he then published he gave a list of all the works and editions which he had seen, as well as of those which he had found mentioned by other writers. On perusal, Mook's work proved not quite satisfactory, and in a review of it I pointed out defects in execution and tone which had impressed me. This started me on an investigation of Paracelsus' writings which I have pursued as opportunity has offered, and the results obtained have been privately printed from time to time.

They embrace a criticism of Mook's work (Parts I. and II.); a bibliography of the editions of Paracelsus' works which I have examined (Parts I.-V.); a bibliography of the editions in English (Part III.); early lists of Paracelsus' works (Part III.); an alphabetical catalogue of Paracelsus' works mentioned by Mook and by myself (Part V.); and reprints of papers about Paracelsus (Part VI.).

The most of the matter embodied in these papers has been taken from my own collection, and, although that is not yet exhausted, I have thought that it would not be amiss to regard these six parts as forming a complete series. Two topics which I might still have considered are portraits of Paracelsus and literature relating to him, and at one time I intended to include them in this series, and made studies of them with that intent. Since, however, I acquired the Paracelsus library of the late Dr. Eduard Schubert, I have found in it so much additional material that I have refrained from printing my results till I can incorporate everything which it contains bearing on these topics. They may hereafter form parts of a new series of the *Bibliographia Paracelsica*.

THE UNIVERSITY,
GLASGOW, August 27, 1896.

ERRATA IN PART V.

Page 6, *line* 15, *insert* and *before* that.
Page 13, *line* 19, *for* Quartoze *read* Quatorze.
Page 43, *line* 20, *move* "in 89" *to the next line below*

BIBLIOGRAPHIA PARACELSICA.

AN

EXAMINATION OF

DR. FRIEDRICH MOOK'S

"THEOPHRASTUS PARACELSUS. EINE
KRITISCHE STUDIE."

PRIVATELY PRINTED

GLASGOW:
Printed at the University Press
BY ROBERT MACLEHOSE, 153 WEST NILE ST.
1877.

100 Copies printed.

IN the "Academy" for October 20, 1877, No. 285, Volume XII., p. 387, appeared a short review of Dr. Mook's work, of which the title-page runs:—"Theophrastus Paracelsus. Eine Kritische Studie von Friedrich Mook. . . . * * * Wurzburg. Verlag der J. Staudinger'schen Buchhandlung. 1876." 4to, pp. 136. The present examination, which was completed July 12, 1877, long prior to the review, contains evidence in detail of the statements made therein.

I have attempted elsewhere ("New College: Glasgow University Album. 1874. Glasgow: James MacLehose. 1874." 8vo, pp. 261-291) an estimate, in a popular form, of Paracelsus. That estimate is subject to such change, refutation, or modification as criticism and discovery may hereafter necessitate.

JOHN FERGUSON.

GLASGOW, *November 22, 1877.*

§ 1. Critical studies in the history, biography, and bibliography of science and medicine are so rare, that, when one makes its appearance, it deserves some notice. That such works are rare is not surprising. Being of no *practical* importance, they are not in demand by those skilled in the sciences, and, naturally, they excite no interest in the general public. It evinces, therefore, devotion and strength of mind amounting almost to heroism on the part of the author, to publish a work of any dimensions on such a person as Paracelsus. For three hundred years passed away from the world, the influence he may have once exerted long ago exhausted, his works all but universally believed—when they are spoken about at all—to be a farrago of boasting, nonsense, and ignorance,—is it of the least importance or interest to the modern physician or chemist to know what Paracelsus thought, or what he discovered, or whether his reputation is deserved or not ? To judge from the current of study and opinion, in these countries at least, the answer is wholly in the negative.

§ 2. But if the subject chosen by Dr. Mook is destitute of intrinsic interest for the present, it is certainly not destitute of interest as a study in comparative criticism. Few men have elicited from critics, biographers, and historians more conflicting judgments than Paracelsus By some, perhaps by most, he is denounced as a quack of the first order; by others, he is regarded as a genius, as a great reformer of medicine; and between the extremes of good and bad are to be found the intermediate estimates of less enthusiastic critics. To the curious collection of opinions exhibited by Dr. Mook, it would be easy to add those of others who have considered it their duty, and perhaps their privilege, to tilt at the supposed foe of sobriety of thought and manners. Long ago Dr. Walter Harris, Fellow of the College of Physicians, reviewed him in manner and form following :—

"*Paracelsus*, as much as he magnified himself for his great store of *Arcana*, and despised others for want of the same Pretensions, yet if we state things a little calmly, we shall find, that he did not so really promote the Honour and Glory of *Chymistry*, as he vainly boasted, or would have had the World believe. . . . He set upon *Reforming Physick*, with all the Malice, and Ill-will, with all the hatred and Contempt, that a Beast and a Sot could possibly conceive against *Sober* men, whose *Seriousness* and *Sobriety* was the greatest *Reproach*, and declaration of Enmity to his dissolute and profligate Life. . . . But know bold Wretch [*i. e.*, Paracelsus], their Names [*i. e.*, Galen's, Avicenna's, Rhasis', Montagnana's, Mesue's, &c.] will be Consecrated to after-ages, and had in good Reputation by Wise, and Sober men, when thy *Bombastick* Names shall perish and be despised, when thy frantick folly, and miserable vanity, and ill-nature, shall with thy Dust be trampled upon by all men. . . ."[1]

[1] *Pharmacologia Anti-Empirica* or a Rational Discourse of Remedies both Chymical and Galenical. . . . by *Walter Harris*, M.D. . . . *London*, 1683, 8vo, pp. 15-24. This work is dedicated to the Duke of Beaufort, and in the dedication there occurs the following :—" How Happy therefore is His *Sacred*

And so on. But for Dr. Harris having been "Physician in Ordinary to His Majesty," Charles II., and having "stated things a little calmly," as became a "physician of sense" rather than a "physician of words," one might almost suppose that he had studied in the school of the man whom he calls "this *Cacophrastus*, or foul-mouth'd railer." Even in our own day, men with a claim to encyclopædic knowledge, historic calmness, elegant language, as, for instance, Hallam, employ such critical terms as "audacious but more unworthy innovator," "mixture of fanaticism and imposture," "paradoxes so absurd and mendacious," " mystical rhapsodies;" Meryon—" rhapsody from a drunken sot," "swaggering empiricism," "mendaciously vaunted his own powers;" Pereira—" a vain, ignorant, arrogant, drunken quack, fanatic, and impostor. . . . He conferred several important benefits on medicine : he overturned Galenism, introduced chemical medicines . . .

Majesty (whom *Heaven* Preserve and Prosper) in so Wise, Faithful, and Pious a *Counsellor!* and how Happy is your *Grace* in serving a *Prince*, who *Knows* how to value justly the *Merits* of a *Subject* never so *Great*, His *Majesty* being not only in *years Superior* to all the *Kings* and *Princes* in *Europe*, but indisputably in *Wisdom* and *Capacity*. Insomuch that I have often heard very Judicious persons maintain, that if His *Majesty* had not been Born *King* of these *Realms*, he would certainly of right have claimed, and justly carried the Election before all others, who might for any kind of *Merit*, have presumed to appear Competitors. Nor is His *Sacred Majesty* only *Supream* in the *Gifts* and *Accomplishments* of *Nature*, in his *Stupendious Prudence* in the *Arts* of *Governing*, but he is pleased in his *Universal Goodness*, particularly to *Encourage* the *Profession* of *Physick ;* and it is well known, and to the *Honour* of *Physick* be it spoken, that His *Majesty* can better judge between a *Physician* of *Words*, and a *Physician* of *Sense*, between what is *Physick* in reality, and what only bears the *Name* of it, than perhaps any man of the *Faculty*." From this the reader can judge what dependence is to be placed on Dr. Harris' opinion of Paracelsus. It is curious also to observe how, in the dubious compliment with which the extract concludes, Dr. Harris unwittingly approaches Paracelsus' low estimate of the Faculty of his time.

in addition to these titles, which are given at first hand, there are numerous notes upon works and editions which have been reported from other writers, but which Mook has not himself seen, and upon those, the dates and titles of which seem to be given incorrectly by bibliographers. The list is arranged in four divisions, chronologically, and with a running number. The four divisions consist of: 1st, works published during Paracelsus' lifetime; 2nd, works published after Paracelsus' death, the date being given; 3rd, works with no date; 4th, manuscript copies of Paracelsus' works. It would have increased the value and facilitated the use of this catalogue, had there been an alphabetical list of the separate treatises, with references to the editions published in different years. This list might have been made quite short; but it would have been very handy to enable one to ascertain what editions and how many there are of any particular treatise.

§ 7. The third section contains a *résumé* and is very brief. It will be noticed more minutely below.

§ 8. If it were worth while to spend a dozen years over the bibliography of any man's works at all, and especially over those of Paracelsus, the qualities that one might expect to find in the published results would be accuracy, systematic and uniform description, quotation of all authorities that would throw light on the subject, and completeness. I consider Mook's work defective in all these qualities.

§ 9. First, *Accuracy*. What first catches one's attention is a number of literal errors and mis-spellings; for instance— *Parecelsi* (p. 65), *Paraceli* (p. 79), *painted* for *printed* (p. 113), *hochgelirten* for *hochgelehrten* (p. 120), *vnderricht* for *vnderrichtet* (p. 120), &c. Other blunders are somewhat more serious, but as they occur in dates and in cross references to the running numbers of the catalogue, they usually carry their own correction with them. The following are noticeable: No. 86 for 88 (p. 40); MDLVIII for MDLXVIII (p. 51); MDLVII for MDLXVII, and MDLVIII for MDLXVIII (p. 52); 147 for 148 (p. 64); 146 for 148 (p. 67); 140 for 141, and 141 for 142 (p. 81); 142 for 143 (p. 83); 148 for 149, and 150 for 151 (p. 84); 109 for 209 (p. 109). On p. 87 he misquotes Adelung, giving " Das Buch Paragraphorum" for " Das Buch Paragranum." At the end of the work there is a list of authorities, in which Mook says, (p. 1, note 2), " The titles of the works cited in the following will be given exactly (*genau*) in the Appendix." Many of these titles are curtailed, and are therefore not exactly given ; and there are other mistakes. Thus, on p. 77, and elsewhere, he quotes " Conrad Gesner (Bibl. von 1583)." This date, so far as I know, belongs to the " Bibliotheca institvta et collecta, primvm a Conrado Gesnero : Deinde in Epitomen redacta, . . . per Iosiam Simlerum: Iam verò . . . amplificata, per Iohannem Iacobum Frisium . . . Tigvri . . . Froschoverus, . . . M.D.LXXXIII " Fol. If this be the book meant, it has been omitted from the Index of exact Titles altogether, only the 1574 edition being referred to. In this same Index of exact Titles, Simler's "Epitome" has the date 1855 assigned to it : it ought to be 1555. In like manner he gives (p. 113) 1563 as the date of a collection of Glauber's works—an obvious but stupid misprint. The date is 1658 ; Glauber was only born about the year 1604. These mistakes arise doubtless from mere carelessness, and want of attention. To a similar cause, probably, is to be ascribed the apparent indecision of the author about the spelling of certain names and words. Thus we are favoured with *Boerhaave* (pp. 14, 15) and *Boerhave* (in Index of *exact* Titles already referred to), *Gessner* and *Gesner*, *Vosii* and *Vossii*, *Borellius* repeatedly and *Borellus* (p. 21, and Index of *exact* Titles again). Now that writer himself spells his name *Borellius* on the title-page of his "*Bibliotheca Chimica*"—(not *Chymica* as Mook inaccurately reproduces it in the Index of *exact* Titles)—and that, both in the edition of Paris, M.DC.LIV, and in the edition of Heidelberg—(not *Haidelberg* as Mook has it in the Index of *exact* Titles)--MDCLVI. Mook seems also unable to make up his mind between "unpaginirt" and "unpaginiert."

The following confusion, however, seems still more indicative of carelessness. The note to No. 79, p. 58, runs thus:

"Spachius p. 34 citirt dieses Buch [Etliche Tractatus . . . . Strassburg . . . . bey Christian Müller's Erben. Anno 1570.] mit dem Zusatz: 'apud Christianum Mylium.' Dies dürfte ein Irrthum sein. 1570 ist Christian Müller bereits todt und 1575 conf. Nr. 112 begegnen wir Christian Mylius, der wohl keine lateinische Wiederauferstehung des todten Christian Muller sein soll. Allerdings finden wir auch im gleichen Jahr wieder einen Christian Müller; aber hoffentlich ist derselbe nur ein Sohn des alten seligen Muller."

So far this is right. Under the year 1575 appear the names both of 'Christianus Mylius' (No. 112, No. 116) and 'Christian Müller' (No. 119) ['Christian Muller' also in 1574, No. 108, 109], as well as 'Muller' simply (No. 118), and in the year 1565 appears 'Christian Müller' (No. 45), who would be the senior according to the above note, and 1566

'Christianus Mylius' (No. 49). In the following note under date 1579 (p. 78), however, the author seems to have entirely forgotten the note above quoted :

"e) "De cura morbi Gallici Argent. 8° apud Christoph. Mylium." (*Athen. Rauric.* p. 172.) *Spachius* giebt an, es sei deutsch erschienen (p. 130); ebenso *Gesner* (Bibl. von 1583): [4] "Libri III de cura morbi Gallici Germanice. 8. Argentor. apud Christianum Molitorum." Wahrscheinlich, dass der Christoph. Mylius und der Christian Molitor mit unserem deutschen Christian Müller identisch sind."

That is : in 1575 *Christian Mylius* is not a Latin resurrection of *Christian Muller*; but in 1579 *Christoph. Mylius*, *Christian Molitor*, and *Christian Müller* are probably identical. To quote Mook's own words, which he applies to Marx (p. 15, note 55), "Ich kann das nur als *leichtsinniges Arbeiten* bezeichnen."

§ 10. So many misprints and mistakes in a work which ought to be scrupulously exact, beget doubts as to the accuracy of the author's statements in general, especially as to the reproduction of the titles of the books. In the few cases in which I have been able to compare the title-pages of the books with Mook's transcriptions, I have found only three (the second edition of the *Archidoxa*, Munich, 1570 ; *Etliche Tractetlein*, Munich, 1570 ; and the 1571 edition of the *Von dem Bad Pfeffers*) approximately coinciding. The others vary by Mook having omitted some portion of the title, or by his having altered the spelling. Thus Dorn's *Fascicvlvs* (No. 135 in Mook's catalogue, 1581) is not given in full, and certainly not in facsimile of the copy I have had for

[4] See remark on this date above, p. 13.

comparison. Similarly, the title-page of Bitiskius' collected edition, published at Geneva in 1658, is very much curtailed, and what is given is not exact in minute points. As Mook's transcriptions, therefore, contain what the title-pages do not contain, and as there is no indication of intended abbreviations, the transcriptions are of necessity wrong. From these cases one is left in doubt when *etc.* occurs in the course of a title, as for instance in No. 211, whether it really exists in the original, or whether it is inserted for brevity by Mook. Such doubt, of course, should never be possible in the description of a book taken from an actual copy. That all the misprints and curtailments are to be put to the author's credit cannot be avoided, for only on two or three occasions has he indicated, by the word *sic*, the existence of an original mistake in what he was transcribing. The last part of the catalogue contains the titles of twenty-eight MSS. of treatises by Paracelsus, none of which, however, are original, and most of which are late. These MSS. are preserved in the Bern, British Museum, Darmstadt, Giessen, Munich, Paris, Tubingen, and Utrecht libraries. The titles of certain of these run thus, according to Mook:

8. Archicatholik pwigr etc. of Paracelsus Archidoxes.

9. The Thendt Book of Archidoxis of Philippus Theophrastus Paracelsus.

10. The Philosophica Canons of Paracelsus.

12. Magick Archidoxis Booke's. Philippus Theophrastus Paracelsus Phisitian and Philosopher his Magik Archidoxis Bookes.

Is it likely that these titles are correct?

§ 11. Secondly, *Systematic* and *Uniform Description.* It has been already shown that the titles are not in all cases reproduced exactly. But other points are imperfect also. The pagination of the works has not been mentioned. It is true that Mook usually tells us when a book is *not* paged, or, as he puts it, 'unpaginirt,' or 'unpaginiert,' or 'ohne Seitenzahl,' and he may have thought that if it was not worth Paracelsus' trouble to count the pages, it was not worth his. But he might at least have enumerated the sheets, as he has done in the first fifteen numbers. As to the later printed books, which are undoubtedly paged, he should have given the number that the book showed. Apparently, he has not in his descriptions always made reference to woodcuts or illustrations ; but he has done so very frequently to the portraits of Paracelsus which many of the treatises contain. The size of the volumes he gives is sometimes wrong. Thus, he calls the Munich *Archidoxa*, 1570, second edition, a small-folio, 'Kleinfolio,' when both by size and signatures of the sheets it is a quarto. The place of publication has been often omitted. As for the descriptions, they are distinguished by the changes rung upon the presence or absence of place, date, printer or publisher, and pagination. From the paragraph at the top of page 38, one would almost suppose that the author has tried how many different ways of quoting the same work he could devise, so as to confuse his reader.

§ 12. Thirdly, *Authorities*. In his laudable anxiety to give all information about Paracelsus' writings as the results of his own observation, he has thrown an air of doubt over accounts of editions which he has quoted at second hand; and he frequently states that the title or date of some work given by a previous authority is erroneous, or imperfectly described, because, apparently, he has failed to see it in any of the libraries he has visited. The lists he has more frequently referred to are those of Adelung, Gesner, and Borellius, but that he has not exhausted this part of the subject is obvious from those which he has omitted. To quote Lenglet du Fresnoy's *Catalogue des Auteurs de la Philosophie Hermétique*, and Borellius' *Bibliotheca*, and to omit Graesse's *Trésor de Livres Rares*, tom. V. 4to, Dresden, 1864, is incomprehensible. Not that the list of Paracelsus' works in the *Trésor* is either complete or satisfactory in its descriptions, but it approaches perfection when compared with the *Bibliotheca* of Borellius, of whom Morhof said long ago : " Sed adeò is confusus est, ut sibi nunquam visis autoribus, quos è *Ioh. Baptist. Nazari* libro Italicè de *transmutatione metallicâ* scripto, qui syllabum illic Chemicorum quorundam congerit, excerpsit ; nonnunquam fictis & mentitis è turba Philosophorum depromptis, chartas cumulet, adeoque indiligenter libros consignet, ut somnianti excidisse potius, quàm studio aliquo scriptus liber videatur." [5] He has also omitted Gmelin's enumeration in his *Geschichte der Chemie*, Manget's list in his *Bibliotheca Scriptorum Medicorum*, and, for English translations: " A Catalogue of Chymicall Books. In Three Parts. . . . Collected by *Will. Cooper*, Bookseller, at the *Pelican* in *Little-Britain, London*. . . . Printed in the Year, 1675 ;" Lowndes' *Bibliographer's Manual*, and even Robert Watt's *Bibliotheca Britannica*. It would have been well, also, had he consulted the Catalogues of the Libraries which he was unable, or thought it not worth while, to visit. Had he, for example, referred to

[5] D. G. Morhofii, *De Metallorum Transmutatione ad . . . Joelem Langelottum . . . Epistola.* Hamburgi, M.DC.LXXIII. p. 115.

the Catalogue of the Bodleian Library, he would have seen
what might have induced him to visit that library, certainly not an obscure or inaccessible one, if he were really
earnest in having his list as perfect as practicable. But,
by scorning these aids, he has overlooked and omitted
several things, and this brings us to the last quality—

§ 13. Fourthly, *Completeness*—wherein Mook's list is
deficient. The following goes so far to completing Mook's
list. In a small collection of a dozen or fifteen of Paracelsus' works, which, without taking any special trouble, I have
been able to collate with Mook's list, I have found some
works not mentioned by him at all, and curious variations
in others. They are as follows—the number is prefixed
for convenience of reference, and they are given in the
order of their dates.

1.—1581. Fascicvlvs Paracelsicae Medicinae Veteris Et Non
   Novae, Per Floscvlos Chimicos Et Medicos, tanquam in
   compendiosum promptuarium collectus. In Qvo De Vita,
   Morte, Et Resvscitatione Rervm, De Tvenda Et conser-
   uanda sanitate, necnon expellendo morbo per instau-
   rationem virium naturalium, de præparationibus medica-
   mentorum, in vsum applicationibus ad quoscunque morbos,
   cùm internos, tùm externos. Item, de generatione
   Homunculi pygmei, ex Dampra nutrimenti sanguinis. Cvm
   Elvcidationibvs Hvivs, Aliorvmqve obscuriorum quorumcunque locorum atque dictionum inibi passim occurrentium.
   Et Indice locvpletissimo. Gerardo Dorneo Interprete.
   Cum Gratia & Priuilegio Cæsareæ Maiestatis. Impressvm
   Francoforti ad Moenvm. Anno M.D.LXXXI.

   4to, Title, Epistola, Præfatio, 1 sheet; Text, foll. 147;
   Errores [p. 1]; Index, Pp—Qq2.

Mook (No. 135) gives only an abbreviation of the above
title, as has been already mentioned in § 10.

2.—1598-1599. [Mook, No. 240, among the books without date.]
Aurei Velleris. . . . Tractatus II. . . . Rorschach am
Bodensee.

This is the second of the five parts of which the alchemical collection entitled *Aureum Vellus* consists. The first part was published in 1598 ; and, in a note at the end of the contents, it is said that for want of time the second and third parts were not ready, but would be published later in the year. As a matter of fact, Part III. bears at the end to have been printed in 1599. The fourth and fifth parts did not appear till some years later—Basel, 1604. Mook is right therefore in saying that Tractatus II. was printed probably before 1600, but he does not seem to have seen a complete copy of the collection. There are several literal errors in his transcription of the title, and only the part of it referring to Paracelsus is given.

3.—1650. A New Light of Alchymie: Taken out of the fountaine
of Nature, and Manuall Experience. To which is added a
Treatise of Svlphvr : Written by *Micheel Sandivogius : i.e.*
Anagram matically [*sic*], *Divi Leschi Genus Amo.* Also
Nine Books *Of the Nature of Things,* Written by *Paracelsvs,*
viz.

Of the { Generations / Growthes / Conservations / Life: Death } { Renewing / Transmutation / Separation / Signatures } *of Naturall things.*

Also a Chymicall Dictionary explaining hard places and words met withall in the writings of *Paracelsus,* and other obscure Authors.

All which are faithfully translated out of the *Latin* into the *English* tongue, By *J. F.* M.D.

London, Printed by *Richard Cotes,* for *Thomas Williams,* at the Bible in Little-Britain, 1650.

Small 4to. Title, Epistle, 1 sheet. Preface, 1 sheet. Text of New Light of Alchymie: pp. 147; Contents, half sheet. Of the Nature of Things: Title and Epistle, 1 sheet; Text, pp. 145. A Chymicall Dictionary: Sheets Aaa to Fff, and separate title—not paged.

Mook (1650, p. 110) merely quotes the title of the above, as given briefly by Adelung. He does not confirm its existence by any authority, though it is given by Will. Cooper, by Watt, by Lowndes, and by Graesse (who says that it is in 8vo); and though a copy of it is in the Bodleian Catalogue, a point of still greater importance. See below, No. 10 and No. 38.

4.—1652. Lexicon Chymicum. Cum Obscuriorum Verborum, et Rerum *Hermeticarum*, Tum Phrasium *Paracelsicarum*, In Scriptus ejus: Et aliorum *Chymicorum*, passim occurrentium, planam explicationem continens. Per *Gulielmum Johnsonum* Chymicum. *Londini*, Excudebat *G.D.* impensis *Gulielmi Nealand*, apud quem prostant venales sub Signo *Coronæ*, in vico vulgò vocato Duck-lane, 1652.

8vo. Title, Dedication, Præfatio, &c., A-B1. Lexicon, pp. 244. Conclusio Operis, pp. 145 [*sic*, for 245]-250.

Another edition, or rather a reprint, appeared in MDCLX. The title-page is the same. It is in 8vo, but of larger size. Twelve pages of sheet A are taken up with title, &c., as above, and the Lexicon, &c., pp. 259. Eight pages of words, previously omitted, have been added to this edition. There appeared also in this year a supplement as follows:

Lexicon Chymicum. Continens Vocabula Chymica in priore Libro omissa, multis vocabulorum Chymicorum Characteribus adjectis è *Basilio* ⁺*Valentino*, *Theophrasto Paracelso, Osvvaldo Crollio*, aliisque Authoribus Chymicis collectis. *Opera & Industria* Gulielmi Johnsoni Chymici, apud *Amen Corner*. Lib. Secundus. *Londini,* Excudebat

Medicinal Stone. *Of the* Virtues *of the* Members. *Of the* Three Principles. And Finally his Seven Books, *of the* Degrees *and* Compositions *of* Receipts, *and* Natural *Things.* Faithfully and plainly Englished, and Published by, *J. H.* Oxon.

London, Printed for *W. S.* and are to be sold by *Thomas Brewster* at the *Three Bibles* in *Pauls Church-yard.* 1660.

8vo. Title, Epistle, in all pp. 6. Text, pp. 158. [2.] 171. [1.]

Muok (No. 222) quotes the title from a copy in the British Museum. With the exception of a couple of misprints, his version agrees with the above up to the words " sold by," after which it runs " Samuel Thomson at the Bishops Head in Pauls Church-yard," with the date 1661. Will. Cooper likewise gives the date of it as 1661 ; but, at a recent sale of works on the occult sciences in London, there was a copy of this 1660 edition. I have, therefore, little doubt that there are at least two editions of this Work, if, indeed, there be not three. For, in a list of " Books sold by William Cooper" contained in *"Collectanea Chymica:* a Collection of Ten Several Treatises in Chymistry, London, 1684," 8vo, there occurs *"Paracelsus* his *Archidoxis,* 1663, 8vo." The catalogue of the Bodleian does not contain any. Watt, Lowndes, and Graesse seem to have made a mistake in the title. See below, No. 45.

9.—1667. Theatro D'Arcani del Medico Lodovico Locatelli da Bergamo ; Nel Qvale Si Tratta Dell' Arte Chimica, & suoi Arcani. *Con gli Afforismi d'Ipprocrate Commentati da Paracelso* Et l'espositione d'alcune Cifre, & Caratteri oscuri de Filosofi. Con Dve Tavole Vna de' Capitoli, & l'altra delle Cose più Notabili. In Venetia,

M. DC. LXVII.   Presso Paolo Baglioni.   *Con Licenza de'*
Superiori, Et Privilegio.

8vo. Title, &c., 1 sheet. Text, pp. 392. Tavole [pp. 22].

Mook has not quoted this work. The "characters" are from Crollius, and so far as they go are identical with those given by Johnson. (See above, No. 4.)

10.—1674. A New Light of Alchymy : Taken out of the Fountain of Nature And Manual Experience. To which is added A Treatise of Sulphur. Written by *Micheel Sandivogius : i.e.* Anagrammatically, *Divi Leschi Genvs Amo.* Also Nine Books *Of the Nature of Things,* Written by *Paracelsvs, viz.*

$$Of\ the \begin{cases} Generations \\ Growths \\ Conservations \\ Life,\ Death \end{cases} \cdot \begin{cases} Renewing \\ Transmutation \\ Separation \\ Signatures \end{cases} of\ Natural\ Things.$$

Also a Chymical Dictionary explaining hard Places and Words met withal in the Writings of *Paracelsus,* and other obscure Authors.

All which are faithfully translated out of the *Latin* into the *English* Tongue, by *J. F.* M.D.

London, Printed by *A. Clark,* for *Tho. Williams* at the *Golden Ball* in *Hosier-Lane,* 1674.

8vo. Title, Preface, Epistle, 1 sheet. Text, paged continuously to the end of the "Chymical Dictionary," pp. 351.

This is a reprint of No. 3 above, with varied spelling. It is not mentioned by Mook, nor by Will. Cooper,[6] R. Watt, Lowndes, or Graesse, nor in the Bodleian Catalogue. The translator, I presume, is Dr. John French, who appears to have been the translator of Glauber's " Philosophical

---

[6] It is quoted, however, in the list of "Books sold by William Cooper," contained in "Collectanea Chymica, London, 1684." 8vo.

Furnaces," London, 1651 ; he was the author also of "The
Art of Distillation," London, 1651 ; 2nd ed., 1653 ; 4th ed.,
1667. All of these works were, like Nos. 3 and 10, printed
for Thomas Williams.

11.—1771. Der Hermetische Nord-Stern, oder getreuer Unterricht
und Anweisung, wie zu der Hermetischen Meisterschaft zu
gelangen, nebst gutherziger Warnung und Ermahnung, wie
sich vorhero jedermann wohl zu prüfen habe, ehe er sich
unterstehe, dieser so grossen und geheimen Wissenschaft
zu unterwerfen. in fossa uniti chare ignes, heraus gegeben von
J. J. F. Sac. Cæs. Reg. M. C. A. Liebhaber des grossen
Geheimnuss und wahren Weissheit, nebst einem Anhang,
handlend von der ewigen Weissheit oder Magia, und sechs
Tractätlein Philippi Aureoli Theophrasti Bombast ab
Hochenheim.

    I. Psalterium Chymicum seu Manuale Paracelsi.

    II. De Tinctura Physica.

    III. Apocalipsis Hermetis.

    IV. Thesaurus Thesaurorum Alchimistarum.

    V. Cœlum Philosophorum.

    VI. Secretum Magicum.

Frankfurt und Leipzig, zu finden im Krausischen
Buchladen. 1771.

8vo. Title, Vorrede, Inhalt, in all pp. 8. Text, pp. 296.

Mook has not given this collection of Tracts in his
list. The editions of VI which he quotes are in Arnold's
" Ketzer-Historie," 1729, II. 445, ; and 1740, I. 1500.

Of these eleven works there are thus certainly seven which
are unknown to Mook, or at least do not appear in his list : an
eighth he gives at second hand with that air which says, " I
have not seen it, and in all probability therefore it does not
exist : but the reader may believe the authority I quote if
he feel so inclined." If these should happen to form what

Mook, speaking of some of Haeser's mistakes, terms 'ein ganzes Nest voll Unrichtigkeiten,' it is unfortunate for Mook that precisely the wanting numbers should be those to which access has been readily had ; but if there are similar defects throughout, what value can the Catalogue have ?

Instead of these being the only omissions, comparison with the lists I have already so frequently referred to shows several works, some of which he has not seen ;' while others, with which he is acquainted only by description, have doubts cast upon their very existence.

Thus Will. Cooper, besides those already referred to, mentions the following :

12.—1575. The Key of Phylosophy, the first Part, shewing the order to distil the Oyles of all manner of Gums, Spices, Seeds, Roots and Herbs, with their perfect taste, smell and virtues. Lond. 1575, 1580, & 1633. 8°.

Will. Cooper gives also the following under " Paracelsus ":

His Key of Philosophy, or The most excellent secrets of Physick and Philosophy, with the Order of Distillation of Oyls, Gums, Spices, Seeds, Roots, and Herbs, with their perfect Taste, Smell, and Virtues, and how to Calcine, Sublime, and dissolve all manner of Minerals, and how to draw forth their Oyl and Salts, Lond. 1580, & 1633. 8.

This 1580 edition seems to be larger than that of 1575, in so far as it contains apparently the Second Part of the work. This, again, appeared separately in 1596, according to Will. Cooper :

The Second part containing the ordering and preparing of all Metals, Minerals, Allumes, Salts, and such like for

Medicines both inwardly and outwardly, and for divers other uses. Lond. 1596. 8.

Watt, however, has the following:

> The first part of the Key of Philosophy. Translated by J. Hester. Lond. 1596, 8vo.

Of the 1633 edition, Will. Cooper gives the title as follows:

> The Store-house of Physical and Pholosoprical [*sic*] secrets, teaching to distil all manner of Oyls, from Gums, Spices, Seeds, Roots, Herbs, Minerals, &c, Lond. 1633. 4° (but under " Paracelsus," 12mo).

Lowndes has the following in his list of Paracelsus' works:

> The first part of the Key of Philosophie published in the Englishe Tongue, by Ihon Hester. 1580, Lond. by Richard Day, 16mo.

This is repeated by Graesse in his list; but neither gives the second part.

In the collection of Paracelsian books, already referred to, there is a small black-letter volume which I have no doubt is a copy of some edition of this work, probably 1580. It is in two parts. The first wants the title-page, so that the exact form of it and date cannot be determined. The heading of the book is, " A Trve and perfect Order to make *Oyles out of al maner of Gummes*, Spices, Seedes, Rootes, and Hearbes. Whereunto is added some of their vertues gathered out of sondrie Auctors." At the end is a note to the effect that these oils can be had " at Poules wharf at the signe of the Furnases, by one Ihon Hester, practisioner in the arte of distillations." The title-page of the Second Part runs as follows : " The Key of Philosophie. The seconde parte. *Containyng the orderyng, & preparyng* of all Metalles, Mineralles, Alumes, Salts, and such like. For Medicines both inwardly, and outwardly, and for diuers other vses. At London printed *by Richard Daie.* Cum Priuilegio." There is no pagination in either part, but the signatures run to G (112 pages). Mook does not quote " the Key of Philosophie."

13.—1590. An English translation of the ' De Morbo Gallico,' ' with all other Diseases arising and growing thereof,' London. 1590. 4.

Mook does not give this translation. Watt, who mentions it, adds, " Translated by J. Hester."

14.—1596.— According to Will. Cooper, the second part of the Key of Philosophy was published this year. See above, No. 12.

15.—1596. Phil. Aur. Th. Paracelsus his 114 Experiments and Cures, whereunto is added certain excellent and profitable works of B. G. Penotus ; also certain secrets of Isaac Hollandus concerning the Vegitable and Animal work; also the Spagyrick Antidotary for Gun-shot of Joseph Quercitanus, collected by Jo. Hester. Lond. 1596. 4°.

This edition is not mentioned by Mook, but he gives the edition which was published in 1652 (No. 214), and which is also mentioned by Will. Cooper, and by R. Watt.

16.—1633. According to Will. Cooper, an edition of the Key of Philosophy was published this year. See above, No. 12.

17.—1659. Ph. Theoph. Paracelsus his Aurora and Treasure of the Philosophers, as also the Water-stone of the wise men, describing the matter of, and manner how to attain the Vniversal Tincture. Lond. 1659. 12°.

Mook (p. 113) gives this on Adelung's authority only. It is mentioned by R. Watt, who adds, "Into English, by J. H., 8vo;" by Graesse, who also adds, "Englished by J. H.;" and, according to the catalogue, there is a copy in the Bodleian.

18.—Philosophical and Chymical Treatise of Fire and Salt. 8.

Without date, or other particulars. So far as I have noticed, it is not given by Mook.

Let us turn now to Graesse, whose account occupies five columns of his large quarto pages, and includes a considerable proportion of Mook's numbers.

19.—1565. Von ersten dreien Principiis; item zween Tractat von Lahme sammt grundlicher gewisser Kur. Auch 36 Kap. von apostematibus, ulceribus, seronibus. Deutsch d. A. v. Bodenstein. s. l. 1565. in-8°.

This resembles Mook's No. 34, taken from a copy in the British Museum, except that, according to Mook, it has no year or place ·specified, and he puts it under 1563 on account of the date of the dedication. Probably they are identical. Mook's title, however, has "LXIII. Capitul."

20 —1566. Mook, in his " Bemerkung a)" to this year, says : " In Athenae Rauricae p. 172 wird angefuhrt: 'Opus chirurgicum german. interpret. Adamo a Bodenstein. Francof. fol.' Die Bezeichnung des Druckortes mag wohl auf einem Irrthum beruhen, so dass dieses Werk identisch ist mit Nr. 51." By way of comment, the following from Graesse is interesting : " Opus chyrurgicum, vollkommene Wundartz- eney, in Truck geben durch Ad. von Bodenstein. Strassb. 1566. in-fol. (1½th. Lempeitz. 4 fl. 48 kr. Scheible.) Frcft., Feyerabend 1566. in-fol. Av. fig en bois. (5 fl 24 kr. le

même.)" The Strassburg edition is Mook's No. 51, but the Francfort edition, which he thinks a mistake, appears here with name of publisher, with woodcuts specified, and with the price in a second-hand book catalogue !

21.—1567. Mook (No. 59) gives "Philosophiae Magnae. . . . . Tractatus aliquot. . . . Gedruckt zu Cöln. . . ." Graesse, however, gives "Philosophia magna (*en allem.*). Ulm 1567. in-4°. (4 fl. Scheible.)" Are there two separate editions of this work also, or have Ulm and Cóln been mistaken by some of the printers?

22.—1567. Similarly Mook (No. 56) gives the "Astronomica et Astrologica," as printed at Coln, but Graesse at Ulm.

·3.—1567. Under the year 1568 Mook (No. 62) gives a title which I shall shorten : "Theophrasti Paracelsi Philosophiae Et Medicinae Utriusque Universae, Compendium, . . . Cum Scholiis. . . Auctore Leone Suavio I. G. P. Vita Paracelsi. Catalogus operum et librorum. . . . Basileae MDLVIII." [which, by the way, ought to be MDLXVIII., illustrating one of Mook's arithmetical misprints.] In his remarks he adds that 'as to previous Paris editions he will not doubt about their existing, and is surprised that he has met with no copy.' He refers to Bemerkung a) 1567, where Marx is quoted as giving that as the year of the Paris edition, and Bemerkung c) 1566, in which Mook infers that 1566 may have been the year, and ultimately to p. 13, note 50, which I quote at length : "Marx Anm. 56 p. 19 sagt : 'Sowie Leo Suavius Catalogus operum et librorum Paracelsi. Parisiis 1567 p. 15.' Nun ist aber *meines* Wissens zu Paris dieses Werk nicht erschienen, sondern zu Basel 1568, und darin findet sich auf der von Marx citirten Seite weiter nichts als eine lateinische Uebersetzung: 'Valentii Antrapassi Silerani Praefatio' etc., die wir soeben deutsch aufgefuhrt haben. Die Angabe von Marx scheint auf einem Irrthum zu beruhen." As a matter of fact Marx may be wrong ; but it is difficult to see how Mook arrives at his conclusion by first doubting the existence of the book Marx does quote, and then testing Marx's statement by a book he does not quote. But whatever be the state of the case as between them, the following from Graesse is interesting : "Compendium cum scholiis in libros IV ejd. de vita longa, plenos mysteriorum, parabolarum, aenigmatum. Vita Paracelsi. Catalogus operum et librorum auct. J. Suavio. Paris. 1567. in-8°. (2 fl. 24 kr. Scheible.)"

24.—1568. Mook (p. 54, Bemerkung c)) gives, on the authority of Gesner : 'De praeparatione Ellebori, item de perforata. Liber editus a Bodensteinio.' In German. Graesse has the following : 'Declaration zu bereiten Hellebori in sein Arcanum dadurch Infectiones der vier Elemente ausgetrieben werden. Basel 1568. in-8°." See below, No. 36.

25.—1572. Of No. 95, "Drey herrliche Schrifften . . . . vom geist des lebens vnd seiner krafft, . ." which Mook says was printed at Basel in 1572, Graesse mentions an edition printed at Augsburg in 1572, in 8vo, as well as the Basel edition.

26.—1574. Graesse has the following: "Onomastica II. I Philosophicum, medicum, synonymum ex variis vulgaribusque linguis. II Theoph. Parac. h. e. earum vocum, quarum in scriptis ejus solet usus esse, explicatio. Argent. p. Bernh. Jobinum 1574. in-8°. (490 pp.) Ce livre diffère d'un autre intit. *Onomasticon : . . . . durch Ad. v. Bodenstein. Basel, Petrus Perna* 1575. in-8°. (31 pp.) [Mook, No. 114] et d'un second par L. Thurneissen, intitulé : *Onomasticum und Interpretatio über die fremden und unbekannten Worter, Namen* etc. *welche in den Schriften Theophr. Par. gefunden werden. s. l. ni d.* in-8°. (1 fl. 12 kr. Scheible.) Il existe aussi un *Dictionarium . . . . a G. Dorneo coll. Frcft.* 1583. in-8°." [Mook, No. 142.] Neither Jobinus' nor Thurneissen's work is given by Mook.

27.—1576. 'Von den Kranckheiten, so den Menschen der Vernunfft naturlich berauben. . . . Strassburg, 1576. 8°."

[Mook, No. 120.] Graesse gives this edition, and also Basel 1576. in-4°, and adds "(1 fl. 12 kr. Scheible)," but whether this refers to both editions or only to the Strassburg one may be questioned—probably only to the latter.

28.—1580. Graesse mentions the Key of Philosophy. See above, No. 12.

29.—1586. Graesse mentions, as published at Basel in this year in 8vo, an edition of "Das Buch Paragranum darin die Philosophie, Astronomie, Alchemie und Virtus, auf welche Theophr. Medizin fundirt ist, tractirt werden ; item von Aderlassens, Schrepfens und Purgirens rechtem Gebrauch. Deutsch d. Ad. von Bodenstein." He mentions also the Basel edition of 1589, in 4to, which Mook (p. 87) quotes from Adelung, where, however, he puts 'Paragraphorum' for 'Paragranum.' Mook does not refer to this 1586 edition.

30.—1588. Mook mentions on the authority of Spachius : "Pandora, id est, tractatus de lapide etc. Basileae . . . . 8°. Deutsch." Graesse gives it more in detail with price : "Pandora : das ist die edelste Gab Gottes oder der werde vnd heils. Stein d. Weysen, mit welchem die alten Philosophi, aus Theophr. Paracelsus Metallen aus Gewalt des Fewrs verbess : sammpt allen Krankheiten jnnerlich vnnd äusserlich haben vertrieben. Basel 1588. in-8°. Av. de cur. fig. en bois. (20 gr. Lempeitz.) "

31.—1596. Graesse mentions the English translation of the "115 cures and experiments," which is not given by Mook. See above, No. 15. Graesse says it is "in-8°."

32.—1632. Graesse gives : "Wahrhaffte Beschreibung einer Prophecey was es mit dem jetzigen Krieg—für eine Endschaft gewinnen. s. l. 1632. in-4°." This does not appear in Mook's list under this year.

33.—1647. Graesse gives : "Zween Tractat von der signatura aller Erdgewachse was man nehmlich aus ihrem Geruch,

Geschmack, Gestalt etc. judiciren soll. Nürnb. 1647. in-8°. (1 fl. 12 kr. Scheible.)" This confirms its existence, but it is not given by Mook.

34.—Graesse quotes an edition of the *Archidoxa* in Latin by " Ad. Schröter : *Crac. s. d.* in-4°. (2 fl. 24 kr. Scheible)." This edition is not given by Mook in his list of books without date, but he has apparently assigned it to the year 1569 on the strength of the date of Schroter's dedicatory epistle (Mook, No. 73).

35.—Graesse gives the following : " De meteoris liber unus, it. de matrice, de tribus principiis, et quaedam astron. et astrologiae fragmenta. Bas. s. d. in-8°. ib. 1569. in-8°. (1 fl. 48 kr. Scheible.)" In a note he adds : " Ses fragments d'astronomie se réunissent aussi à son *Liber de praesagiis* etc. *Bas.* 1569. in-8°." Mook (No. 243) gives the edition without date, and on page 62, Bemerkung a), remarks, on the authority of Gesner, that the book very likely belongs to 1570. He also gives (No. 72) *De praesagiis . . . Fragmenta*, Basil, 1569, but says nothing about the 1569 edition of the " De Meteoris," a copy of which Graesse seems to have met with in Scheible's Catalogue. Under the year 1575, Bemerkung b), he quotes the " De Meteoris . . . Basil " on the authority of Spachius.

Whether these works exist or not is a question ; but since they have been enumerated by a respectable authority, they should not have been omitted, while others, on doubtful authority, have been included.

Let us turn to the Catalogue of the Bodleian Library, the titles from which I shall shorten.

36.— 1568. Præparationis ellebori . . . declaratio. Basil, 8vo. This Mook has not seen, as he gives it, 1568, Bemerkung c), on the authority of Gesner. See above, No. 24.

37.—1582. Pandora. Basil, 8vo. There is no mention by Mook of this work under this year.

38.—1650. Nine Books of the Nature of Things, &c. London, 4to. This is given by Mook on Adelung's authority. See above, No. 3.

39.—1657. Philosophy Reformed, &c. Not given by Mook at all. See above, No. 7.

40.—1659. Paracelsus, his Aurora, by J. H. London, 8vo. This is given by Mook on Adelung's authority. See above, No. 17.

41.— 1697. Arcana philosoph'a; or chymical secrets by John Headrich. London, 8vo.

42.—There is also a copy of J. Hester's "114 Experiments and Cures," without place and date. Not mentioned by Mook. See above, No. 15.

These, with other nineteen enumerated by Mook, are contained in the Bodleian Library.

In addition to the articles already quoted, Watt refers to Erastus and some other writers on Paracelsus. I select the following, which are not given by Mook.

43.—1578. Demosterion, sive ccc. Aphorismi, Continentes summam Doctrinæ Paræcelsæ [sic, Watt]. Paris, 8vo. By Roche de Bailli or Bailliff.

44.—1583. De Naturæ Luce Physica, ex Genesi desumpta, justa [sic] sententiam Theophrasti Paracelsi Tractatus. Franc. 12mo. By G. Dorn.

45.—1661. His Paradoxes. London, 12mo. Is this a misprint for "Archidoxis"? It is repeated by Lowndes and by Graesse. See above, No. 8.

46.—1669. Opera Omnia. Genev. 3 tom. fol.

47.—1675. Liquor Alcahest, or a Discourse of that immortal dissolvant of Paracelsus and Helmot [*sic*]. Lond. 8vo. By James Pynophilas Astell.

48.—Lastly, Watt and Lowndes give the following : " Joyfull Newes out of Helvetia, from Theophr. Paracelsum, declaring the ruinate Fall of the Papall Dignitie : also a Treatise against Vsurie. By Stephen Batman. Lond. for John Allde, 1575. 8vo." This is probably a translation of Paracelsus' explication of the Pictures at Nuremberg, which are said to be a satire upon Rome.

§ 14. I have not thought it necessary to collate Mook's list with Adelung's, or with Gmelin's or Borellius', but I have little doubt differences and omissions would be found. So far as I have seen, Mook does not intentionally misrepresent any authority, or omit any item, but that he has overlooked, at the lowest estimate, some twenty treatises, which have been quoted above, not from recondite, but from a few common authors, besides seven or eight others which have been described from actual copies, is a curious instance of the vanity of human efforts, however long and well sustained, to attain perfection. It is true that the books are not, any of them, of first-rate importance, but the question is one of drawing up a complete list of the works ascribed to Paracelsus—not of their intrinsic value. How many besides the above have escaped the author's notice I do not profess to say, but it is to be hoped there are not many.

§ 15. But the most disappointing part of the work is the third section, which contains what Mook calls the " Schluss-Resumée." The criteria of genuineness having been enunciated, and the works having been enumerated, the only thing remaining for Mook to do was to apply the criteria to the works. Let us see his conclusions.

1. There being no original manuscripts, the first criterion cannot be applied. It *is* singular, as Mook says, that all the MSS. which seem to have existed at the end of the sixteenth century should have entirely disappeared.

2. The works printed in Paracelsus' lifetime are genuine. These include numbers 1 to 14 in Mook's list, but comprehend only 11 separate treatises, of which 5 are medical, and 6 contain "prognostications." Mook claims the credit —and, justly, so far as I know—of having brought to light several of these writings, the existence of which had been overlooked by previous writers. He enters into a long and, it seems to me, irrelevant explanation of the character of these prognostications, which he thinks were not actual prophecies, but rather reflections upon the state of politics at the time, and attempts to forecast to what future events they might give rise. He also takes occasion to point out the futility of Marx's tests, by applying them to these 14 genuine works.

3. According to the third criterion, comparison of Huser's reprints with the genuine works (or with originals) must decide whether Huser's statements are trustworthy or not. This leads to a vindication of Huser from the suspicions of later critics, Marx and Wolf, by quoting Huser's account of the occasion of his making a collected edition. This is long, and also to some extent irrelevant ; and, after all, it is only inferentially that one finds out that, according to Mook's experience, Huser and the originals agree. Mook says that if we compare the works of

Paracelsus' lifetime with Huser's reprints, and with what Huser says about the sources he made use of, he believes himself justified in the conclusion that there is absolutely no reason to throw doubt of any kind upon Huser's trustworthiness. Hence—

4. Whatever Huser says he took "ex Manuscripto Theophrasti" must be considered as really emanating from Paracelsus. This, however, is obviously subject to the condition that with every desire on Huser's part to ·be accurate, he may have unwittingly made mistakes. At any rate, Mook informs us in one or two cases only, for example No. 127, what Huser has taken from original sources; so that we must have Huser's editions and repeat a great part of Mook's work to ascertain what he himself lays down as the leading subject of his investigation, and what he ought to have stated clearly as the result of his labours.

5. The fifth and last criterion—"those writings are genuine which, tried by the previous tests, bear undoubted marks of authorship, both as regards matter and form"— Mook admits is the one which gives greatest scope for critical skill, and he says "I leave it to future critics, as an undivided harvest." Precisely the works about which there may be a difficulty have been left without the criteria, upon which Mook has laid so much stress, being applied to settle whether they are genuine or not. Besides the first 14 numbers, Mook, so far as I have noticed, has expressed a favourable opinion respecting two only, and an unfavourable opinion respecting four. It is much to be regretted that after all the time spent, and all the opportunities Mook had of comparing the different editions, the dis-

crimination of the true from the spurious works, which in Mook's own judgment is the gist of the whole question, should not have become practically a whit easier or more satisfactory than it was before.

§ 16. To sum up. The Title is a misnomer. The monograph is not a critical study of Paracelsus; it is a bibliographic study of his works, to which some might possibly deny the epithet "critical." Whatever it meant to do, it hardly gives a criticism of the editions, certainly not a critical estimate of the works, or of Paracelsus either as a man, physician, chemist, or author. It is incomplete in numbers; incomplete in descriptions; it contains many typographical errors. If Marx and Haeser have sinned against the canons of textual criticism, Mook has broken the laws of bibliography, in that he has not given the titles of many of the books complete. Mook's work is not so accurate and unprejudiced, as that, when he affirms another writer to be probably in error, that writer is to be believed in error, on his authority solely. Were I engaged in the study of Paracelsus' works, I should use this catalogue, but where Mook differed from others, I should have no confidence in the former being certainly right, and the latter wrong. The book as regards its main purpose is a failure, but it must in fairness be acknowledged that the amount of information about Paracelsus' works, gathered by direct personal inspection, is extraordinarily great, and if it were only as reliable as it is elaborate, the book would form one of the most valuable of recent additions to medical and chemical bibliography. What it requires is a thorough revision to remove inaccuracies and fill up defects, and one's opinion of the author would certainly rise if he could contrive to criticise his predecessors' facts or inferences, without gratuitous and futile attempts at satire and ridicule. When the book has been thus amended, and when it tells us what are the genuine writings of Paracelsus, and what the spurious, which are passed off under his name, it should be welcome to every one interested in the subject.

GLASGOW:
Printed at the University Press
BY ROBERT MACLEHOSE, 153 WEST NILE STREET.

BIBLIOGRAPHIA PARACELSICA.

AN

EXAMINATION OF

DR. FRIEDRICH MOOK'S

"THEOPHRASTUS PARACELSUS. EINE
KRITISCHE STUDIE."

PART II.

GLASGOW:
Printed at the University Press
BY ROBERT MACLEHOSE, 153 WEST NILE ST.
1885.

100 Copies printed.

THE former part of this *Examination*, which was printed in 1877, completed the criticism of Mook's study, so far as I myself was concerned, and I had no intention, at that time, of ever recurring again to the subject. As it might have been urged, however, that I had personally inspected only eleven of Paracelsus' works, and that that was too small a number whereon to found a general and adverse criticism, I felt bound—when opportunity placed a larger number of the books at my disposal—to avail myself of them to confirm my previously expressed opinion. Hence the appearance of this second part.

JOHN FERGUSON.

UNIVERSITY OF GLASGOW,
August, 1885.

except in that of the British Museum. Any one who desires to pursue the subject in detail would certainly have to work in that collection, where there is a large representation of Paracelsus' writings.

49.—1536. Prognostica|tio Ad Vigesimvm Qvar-|tum annum duratura, per eximium Doctorem | Theophraftum Para-celfum, Ad illuftriffimum | ac potentiffimū principem Ferdinandum, Ro-|man. Regem femper Auguftum &c̄. Archidu-|cem Auftriæ &c̄. confcripta. Anno xxxvi. |

Marcvs Tativs ad | Lectorem.

Si cupis Aftrorum fataleis fcire meatus,
Arcanisq́; fimul miftica uerba notis.
Quid facra uenturos promittant fydera in annos,
Et quod portendunt, spesúe, metusúe fiet.
Humanas pariter quo terrens omine menteis
Nos moneat clemens ad pia facta Deus.
Concitus Aethereo Doctor Thepraftus (sic) *ab œftro,*
Diuite mirandis hæc docet ore modis.
Vt caueant, queifcunq; malum, mala fata minantur,
Quamuis hic nullum nominet ille uirum.

Cum gratia & priuilegio Cæfareæ ac Regiæ Maieft. ne quis |
imprimat fine permifsione pœna 20. *marcarum auri puri.*

Small 4to. Signatures A-F. Ai, Title; Aij-Aiv, Præfatio; B-Eiv contain the 32 emblems and accompanying text; Fi to Fiij, Expositio brevis Prognosticationis. Fiv (wanting) contains verses and colophon.

In Mook's transcription (No. 10) there are several in-accuracies. He has *semder* for *semper,* and after *Austriæ* he omits *&c̄. conscripta.* In the seventh line of the verses he reads *Theophrastus ab astro,* which is all wrong; in the ninth line *quie scunque* for *queiscunque,* and in the privilege *ut quis* for *ne quis.* He has altered the punctuation in four places, and has substituted without any system *u* for *v*, and *v* for *u* of the original.

As the copy I have had before me wants the last leaf containing *M. Tatii ad Germaniam Exhortatio* and the colophon, I am unable to say whether Mook's transcription is accurate or not. The colophon which he gives is as follows :—

> *Excusum Augustae Vindelicorum, per Henricum Steyner, xxvi Augusti, An. MDXXXVI.*

This tract was reprinted some forty years later, but without date. Mook, who mentions it (No. 241) says that it contains the best set of the woodcuts he knows. There was a copy of it in the Beckford Library (*Catalogue* [1883], Part iii. No. 409). Mook does not allude to the fact that it reappeared in the *Lectiones* of Wolfius, printed in 1600, and in the *Reformir-Spiegel des weltlichen Bapsts* of Joannes de Hyperiis, printed in 1620. These will be referred to below.

In the British Museum $\left(\frac{1395. \text{h. } 47}{1}\right)$ there is a copy of this work the title of which differs both from that above given and from that of the undated edition (Mook's No. 241). It is as follows :—

> Prognostica| tio ad vigesimvm qvar-| tum vſq ; annum duratura, per eximium dūm | ac Doctorem Paracelſum, Ad illuſtriſſimum | ac potentiſſimū principem Ferdinandum, Ro-| man. Regem ſemper Auguſtum &c̄. Archidu-| ćem Auſtriæ &c̄. conſcripta. Anno xxxvi. |

> Marcvs Tativs ad | Lectorem. Same as that quoted above.

> Small 4to. Sigs. A-Fiii. Fiv wanting.

This is probably a mere variation and not a separate edition.

50.—1560. Generosi Omniqve in Scie*ntiarvm Genere Exper*tifsimi uiri, Theophrafti Paracelfi ab Hohenheim, philofophiɇ & utriufq; medicinæ Doctoris clarifsimi, Libri quatuor De uita longa.

Diligentia Et Opera Adami à Bodenstein recogniti, nûncq; primùm in lucem æditi [sic]. Ανέχȣ καὶ ἀπέχȣ. *Anno* M.D.LX.

Small 8vo. Title, Epistola Nuncupatoria, ff. 10, not numbered. Text, pp. 78, followed by a blank leaf.

In the title as given by Mook (No. 22) there are minor differences, such as the omission of contractions and the substitution of a period for a comma after *clarissimi*. The last sentence however runs thus :—

Diligentia et opera recogniti nuncque primum in lucem editi Adami a Bodenstein. Basileae.

Here the order is altered, the Greek omitted, and *Basileae* added ; has this been done gratuitously by Mook, or were there two issues of the book? If so, Mook has not seen a copy of the issue now described.

51.—1563. Medicorvm Et Philosophorvm Svmmi, Avreoli Theophrafti Paracelfi, Eremitæ, Iibri (*sic*) quinque de caufis, fignis & curationibus morborum ex Tartaro vtilifsimi. *Opera Et Indvstria Nobilis Viri Adami A Bodenstein, in lucem propter commune commodum microcofmi iamiam primum hoc tempore quod Theophrastus ante multos annos præuidit fore veritati confonum publicati.* Ανέχȣ καὶ ἀπέχȣ.

Basileae, Per Petrum Pernam. 1563.

Small 8vo. Title, Epistola Dedicatoria from Adam Bodenstein to Cosmo de Medici, ff. 8. Text, pp. 265. Errata, pp. 2, not numbered, followed by 5 blank pages.

Mook (No. 36) again makes alterations. For the mis-print *Iibri* he substitutes the correction *Libri;* alters the punctuation, and puts *publicari* for *publicati.* Among minor changes must be noticed that of *i* to *j*, of *v* to *u* and of *u* to *v*.

52.—1564. Des Hocherfarnen vnd Hochgelehrten Herrn Theophrafti Paracelfi von Hohenheim, beider Artzney Doctoris, Phisophiae (*sic*) ad Athenienfes, drey Bücher. Von vrsachen vnd Cur Epilepfiæ, das ist, des Hinfallenden siechtagen, vor in Truck nie aussgangen. Item, Vom vrsprvng, Cur oder heilung der contracten glidern, jetzt newlich auss des Theophrafti selbst eigner Handtschrift trewlich an tag geben. Gedruckt zu Coln, Durch die Erben Arnoldi Byrckmanni. Anno 1564. Mit Keis. Maiest. Gnad vnd Freyheit.

Small 4to. Title (in red and black) A1; Philosophia, A2-K4. Text ends on K4 recto: Reliqua, fi quæ deerant, defiderabantur. On the reverse is the shield, with the words: Pax viuis, requies æterna fepultis. Von dem Hinfallenden Siechtagen &c., a-l2. Vom vrsprung ... der contracten glidern ... l3-q3. On the reverse of q3 is the epitaph on Paracelsus printed in capitals, below which is the coat of arms and legend repeated. q4 is wanting. Does it contain a portrait of Parcelsus? The volume contains in all ff. 103.

Mook (No. 39) corrects the misprint into *Philosophiae*. For *Cur oder heilung* he reads *Cur und heilung;* for *eigner Handtschrift* he substitutes *eigne Handtschrifft*, and omits all after *Byrckmanni*. The copy Mook saw contained no portrait; at all events while he mentions the coat of arms he does not allude to any portrait, or to the leaf q4.

53.—1564. Des Hochgelerten vñ Hocherfarnen Herren Theophrafti Paracelfi von Hohenheim, beider Artzney Doctoris, etliche tractaten vor in Truck nie ausskommen.

Vom Podagra vnd seinen speciebus.
Vom Schlag.
Von der Fallender sücht.

Von der Daubsücht oder vnsinnigkeit.
Vom Kaltenwehe.
Von der Colica.
Von dem Bauchreissen.
Von der Wassersücht.
Vom Schwinen oder Aridura.
Vom Schwinen oder Schwindsücht Hectica.
Von Farbsüchten.
Von Würmen.
Vom Stullauff.

Gedruckt zu Cöln, Durch die Erben Arnoldi Byrck-manni. Anno 1564. Mit Keis. Maiest. Gnad vnd Freyheit.

Small 4to. Title, on the reverse of which the epitaph and shield; Ermanung zum Leser; Valentij Antrapassi Silerani Prologus, ff. 4. Text, pp. 167.

For *fallender* Mook (No. 41) reads *fallenden*, makes changes in spelling and punctuation and omits the date and privilege clause, though in other cases he quotes both.

54.—1564. Holtzbüchlein Des theuren, Hocherfarnen, von Gott hochgelehrten, weisen Theophrasti Paracelsi, Darinnen gründtlich der recht nutz vnd gebrauch des Frantzosen holtzes, sampt allem miszuerstand, verderbung, falschem schein, vnd jrrsal der vermainten artzet, reichlich würt angezaigt, trewlich ausz seinen Büchern durch einen trewen liebhaber der Artzeneyen zusamen gelesen. Item, ein nutzlicher Tractat, von dem Vitriol, vnd seiner tugendt.

Getruckt zu Strassburg bey Christian Müller. 1564.

Small 8vo, no pagination. Signatures A-C. A1 Title, on the reverse the epitaph; Aij-vij, Toxites' Dedication; Aviij-Bij, To the Christian Reader. Biij-C1 recto, Text; C1 verso to Cvij, von dem Vitriol; Cvij verso and Cviij blank.

Except for substituting a small for a capital *d* in the word *Darinnen* and spelling *zusamen* with two *m's*, Mook

(No. 42) has actually managed to quote this title correctly and in full, including the date!

55.—[1566.] *Theophrasti* | Paracelsi | Philosophiae | et Medicinæ, vtri- | *vsqve vniversæ,* | Compendivm, | Ex optimis quibuſque eius libris: | Cum ſcholiis in libros IIII. eiuſdē | *De Vita Longa,* | Plenos myſteriorum, parabolarum, | ænigmatum. | *Auctore Leone Suauio I.G.P.* | Vita Paracelsi. | Catalogus operum & librorum. | Cum Indice rerum in hoc opere ſingularium.

> Parisiis | In ædibus Rovillii, via Iacobæa, |
> Sub ſigno Concordiæ. |
> *Cvm Privilegio Regis* | [No date.]

Small 8vo; signatures in fours. Contains pp. 376 numbered; 21 not numbered; 3 blank. The following is a complete collation.

p. 1. Title, enclosed in an ornamental scroll border.

p. 2. Privilege.

p. 3. Leo Svavivs Nobili Viro Renato Peroto Cenomanensi. S. ends p. 6; dated : Lutetiæ VIII. Idus Sext. Anno M.LXVI (*sic*).

p. 7. Praefatio Leonis Svavii de Avtoris Vita et Operibvs.

p. 12. Erasmus to Paracelsus.

p. 17. Epitaph.

p. 18. Valentii Antrapassi Silerani Praefatio.

p. 22. Catalogvs eorvm quæ hoc opere continentur....Vnà cum eiuſdem Paracelſi effigie | ad viuum, vt ipſe curauit, expreſſa.

p. 23. Compendium begins.

p. 81. *Ph. Theophrasti* Paracelsi De Vita longa Libri IIII. Portrait of Paracelsus. Below are the words :

> Effigies Paracelsi, et Apophtegma.
> Alterivs non sit. qvi svvs esse potest.

p. 82. Morellus' epigram in Greek.

p. 83. Gillii Pinavtii è Græco Latinvm Epigramma.

p. 84. Valentinvs de Retiis de operibvs Paracelsi ad lectorem.

p. 85. Catalogvs.

p. 87. Leo Svavivs in Catalogvm.

p. 88. Elenchvs Capitvm Librorvm Qvatvor Th. Paracelsi de Vita Longa.

p. 89. De Vita longa begins, ends p. 152.

p. 153. Leo Svavivs I.G.P. Io. Capellæ Pariſienſi Archiatro Regio Sal., ends p. 158.

p. 159. Additional Works of Paracelsus.
p. 160. Blank.
p. 161. Præfatio Leonis Svavii I.G.P. In fua Scholia, ends p. 178.
p. 179. Scholia begin.
p. 376. Scholiorum Leonis Suauii I.G.P. in lib. IIII. Ph. Theophrafti Paracelfi De vita longa. Finis.
  *i*a. Index Rervm et verborvm Singvlarivm Hvivs Operis, ends
***₁*b*
***ii*a. Catalogvs Avtorvm Huius operis, ends ***iii*a, followed by
Errores aliqvot Infigniores Operarum.
***₁iii*b* and iv blank.

The copy—a very fine one—from which the preceding
has been taken is in the British Museum (1032. d. 1) and
it is the only one in that or any public library which has
been consulted in compiling the present list. Exception
has been made in its favour for several reasons.

1. Mook did not see it, and the present description therefore may fill a gap in Paracelsian bibliography.

2. The editor, Gohory, was a singular person, and his
works are worth remembering, for their curiosity and great
rarity.

3. The date of the first edition has caused Mook some
trouble. He knew only the 1568 edition (see No. 60 below),
and on the strength of it as well as from contempt for
Marx has all but refused (p. 13, note 50) to admit the
existence of a Paris edition of 1567, cited by Marx. How
fallacious Mook's argument is was pointed out before
(*Bibliographia Paracelsica*, 1877, No. 23), and it was shown
by a quotation from Graesse that on this occasion Marx
might possibly be correct. The 1566 edition Mook has
relegated to a note (p. 48, Bem. c), where it is quoted on
Adelung's authority.

4. After describing the 1568 edition Mook adds: "Was
vorausgegangene Pariser Ausgaben betrifft, so will ich

an deren Existenz nicht zweifeln und wundere mich nur, dass ich noch kein Exemplar, deren es gewiss noch geben müsste, aufgefunden habe." One can sympathise with Mook's wonder—for there is this copy in the British Museum, which, from his numerous allusions to it, Mook presumably visited. How did he miss it? Further, if he did not feel warranted in denying the existence of previous Paris editions, why did he not moderate the vehemence of his correction of Marx in the note already quoted?

5. The portrait contained in this edition is one of the earliest, if it be not actually the first, of Paracelsus.

56.—1567. Astronomica et Astrologica, Des Edlen, Hochge-
lährten, Wolerfahrenen Herren, Doctor Avreoli Theophrasti
von Hohenhaim, Paracelsi genandt, &c. Opuſcula aliquot,
jetzt erst in Truck geben, vnd nach der Vorred verzeichnet.
Optima ſunt, Pietas, Modus, & Cognoſce teipſum. Cum
Gratia & Priuilegio Imperiáli. Getruckt zu Cöln, bey
Arnoldi Byrckmans Erben, Anno 1567.
    Small 4to. Title, Vorrede, ff. 8. Text, pp. 235.
Innehalt, p. 236 (misnumbered 235). Erratula, epitaph,
shield and portrait of Paracelsus, 2 leaves, not numbered.
Colophon, after the Erratula: Zu Coln truckts Gerhart
Vierendunck, in verlägung Arnoldi Birckmans Erben.
Followed by a coat of arms.

In Mook's version of this title (No. 56) there is the spelling *Wolerfarenen;* after *Truck geben* the words *vnd nach der Vorred verzeichnet* are omitted. Mook puts *etc.* instead of & between *Modus* and *Cognosce;* omits the privilege clause, and the date. The portrait in Mook's copy comes after the preface and according to his description is different from that in mine. Have there been two issues of this work also? See also *Bibliographia Para-celsica,* 1877, No. 22.

57.—1567. Defs hocherfahrnesten Medici Aureoli Theophrasti
Paracelsi schreyben, von den kranckheyten, so die vernunfft
berauben, als da sein S. Veyts Thantz, Hinfallender
fiechtage, Melancholia vnd Vnsinnigkeit, &c. sampt jhrn
warhafften curen.

Darzu auss gemeldts Authoris Büchern gethan sein
etliche lustige vnd nutzbare Process, Administrationes vnd
würckungen dess Vitriols vnd Erdenhartzes, in rechter
treuw publiciert, durch Adamum von Bodenstein. Ανέχȣ
καὶ ἀπέχȣ. Innhalt vnd frucht dieses Buchs wird in der
ersten Vorrede ordenlich (*sic*) begriffen. *Cum gratia
& priuilegio.* Anno M.D.LXVII.

Small 4to. Title and Bodenstein's preface, ff. 4. Paracelsus' preface, A1. Text, A1 verso-O1. The volume
contains ff. 57 in all, not numbered.

Mook, No. 57. For *jhrn* he writes *jhre*, and omits all
between the Greek motto and the date, which he gives in
Arabic numerals. In this transcription he keeps *v* at the
beginning of the words as in the original, and does not
change them to *u* as in other cases. This proves that the
changes he has made in No. 36 (see above No. 51) are not
unintentional.

58.—1567. Theophrasti Paracelsi von Hohenheim, beyder Artzney
Doctor (*sic*) &c. Von der Bergsucht oder Bergkranckheiten
drey Bücher, inn dreyzehen Tractat verfast vnnd beschriben
worden. Dariñen begryffen vom vrsprung vnd herkomen
derselbigen kranckheiten, sampt jhren warhafftigen Preseruatiua vnnd Curen.

Allen Ertz vnnd Bergleüten, Schmeltzern, Probierern,
Müntzmaiftern, Goldschmiden, vnnd Alchimisten, auch
allen denē so inn Metallen vnd Mineralien arbayten, hoch
nutzlich, tròstlich vnnd notturfftig. Mit Röm. Kay.
Maiest. freyheit. Anno Domini 1567.

Small 4to. Title (red and black), Epistle, ff. 7, not
numbered; f. 8, blank. Text, ff. 62. Register, Qij verso—

Qiv recto. Colophon : Getruckt zu Dilingen durch Se-
baldum Mayer.

In this Mook (No. 58) again makes errors and arbitrary
changes : *Von* he gives for *vom vrsprung; Preservativa*
for *Preseruatiua,* and omits the privilege clause and date.

59.—1567. Des Hochgelertĕ vnd Hocherfahrnen Herren Theo-
phrasti Paracelsi von Hohenheim, beyder Artzeney Doc-
toris, etliche Tractaten, zum ander mal in Truck aussgangen.
Vom Podagra vnd seinen speciebus.
Vom Schlag.
Von der Fallender Sucht.
Von der Daubsucht oder vnsinnigkeit.
Vom Kaltenwehe.
Von der Colica.
Von dem Bauchreissen.
Von der Wassersucht.
Vom Schwinen oder Aridura.
Vom Schwinen oder Schwindtsucht, Hectica.
Von Farbsuchten.
Von Würmen.
Vom Stullauff.
Item newlich hinzu getruckt : Von den Podagrischen
Kranckheiten, vnd auch was jn anhengig ein *Fragmentum.*
Gedruckt zu Cöln, Durch die Erben Arnoldi Birckmanni.
Anno 1567. Mit Keis. Maiest. Gnad vnd Freiheit.
Small 4to. Title, Ermanung, Prologus, ff. 4. Text,
pp. 270 (nominal), followed by Register, 1 page, and
epitaph with shield, 1 page. Reverse is blank. Portrait
of Paracelsus on reverse of the Title. The pagination is
most irregular, but the signatures run from A to Ooij
inclusive.

In this title Mook (No. 60) again gives variations : *Von
der fallenden sucht,* for *fallender; Schwindsucht,* for
Schwindtsucht; je anhengig for *jn anhengig.* The privilege
clause is omitted.

60.—1568. Theophrasti Paracelsi Philosophiae et Medicinae
Vtrivsqve Vniversae, *Compendivm, Ex optimis quibufque
eius libris:* Cum fcholijs in libros IIII. eiufdem De Vita
Longa, Plenos myfteriorum, parabolarum, ænigmatum.
Auctore Leone Suauio I.G.P. Vita Paracelsi. Catalogus
operum & librorum. *Cum Indice rerum in hoc opere
fingularium.* Basileae, M.D.LXVIII.

Small 8vo. Pp. 334. Epistola, ff. 5. Index, ff. 9. Apologia G. Dorn, ff. 15. Typographus Leoni Suavio, ff. 3.
Colophon : Basileae, Per Petrvm Pernam.

For once Mook (No. 62) would have been accurate, had
he not given the date as MDLVIII. and changed *v* to *u*,
i to *j*, and *j* to *i*.

This is the reprint of No. 55, above, which appeared at
Paris. In that edition the Epistola is misdated M.LXVI. In
this one it is dated simply LXVI.

61.—1568. Libellvs Theophrafti Paracelsi Vtrivsqve Medicinae
Doctoris, De *Vrinarum ac pulfuum iudicijs: tum de Phy-
fionomia quantum medico opus eft.* Accessit de Morborvm
Phyfionomia Fragmentum. Argentinae Typis Samuelis
Emmelij. Anno M.D.LXVIII.

Small 8vo. Title, Praefatio, ff. 7, not numbered ; f. 8
blank. Text, ff. 42, followed by 2 blank leaves.

Mook's date (No. 63) is MDLVIII. The rest is accurate,
except the change of *v* to *u* and *j* to *i*. In this title
initial *i* is left, whereas in No. 51 above it is changed.

62.—s.a. Philosophiae Magnae Avreoli Philippi Theophrasti
Paracelsi, Helvetij, ab Hohenhaim, Philofophorum atq;
Medicorum omnium facilè principis, Collectanea quaedam :
quorum fummarium poft Apologiam inuenies. *Per Gerardvm* Dorn E Germanico Ser*mone, quanto familiarius
clariusq́; fieri debuit, Latinè reddita.* Basileae, Apvd
Petrvm Pernam.

Small 8vo. Title, Praefatio, Apologia, Elenchus, pp. 13, not numbered; followed by 3 blank pages. Epistles and Text, pp. 248. Index, pp. 6, not numbered.

Mook omits from *quorum* to *inuenies*, and has a few slight alterations of punctuation and spelling. He gives this book among those without date, No. 245, but in a note under date 1569 identifies it with one of a similar title mentioned by Gesner and concludes that the present volume was really printed in 1568.

63.—1570. Philippi Theophrasti Paracelsi von Hohenhaim, et- liche Tractetlein zur Archidoxa gehörig.

1. Von dem Magneten, vnnd seiner wunderbarlichen tugend, in allerley kranckheiten sehr nützlich zuge- brauchen.

2. De occulta Philofophia, darinnen tractirt wird De Confecrationibus. De Coniurationibus. De Caracteribus. Von allerley erscheinungen im schlaff. Von den jrrdischen Geistern oder Schrötlein. Von der Imagination. Von den verborgnen Schätzen. Wie der mensch vom Teuffel besessen wird. Wie man den bösen Geist von den besessenen leuten ausstreiben sol. Von dem Vngewitter.

3. Die recht weiss zu Administrirn die Medicin, von Theophrasti aigner hand gezogen.

4. Von vilerley gifftigen Thiern, wie man jhnen das gifft nemen, vnd tödten sol.

Mit Röm: Kay: May: freiheit nit nachzudrucken. Ge- druckt zu München, bey Adam Berg. Anno M.D.LXX.

4to. Signatures A—I3. (ff. 35). Portrait of Paracelsus on verso of Title.

In this title Mook (No. 83) makes several alterations; *Hohenhaym* for *Hohenhaim; administriren* for *administrirn;*

B

hochgelehrten, vnd erfarnen baider artzney Doctorem
Philippum Theophrastum Paracelsum. Cum Priuilegio
Cæfareo ad decennium. Getruckt zu Strassburg, bey
Christian Müller. M.D.LXXI.

Small 8vo. Signatures A-D7.

Colophon, beneath a woodcut of a man holding an
arrow : Getruckt zu Strassburg, am Kornmarckt, bey
Christian Müller. CK *M.D.LXXI.*

Mook (No. 94) omits the privilege clause and the date
and says nothing about the device at the end and the
colophon. In this title he has not changed initial *v* to *u*.

68.—1573. Philippi Avreoli Theophrasti Paracelsi Bombast Ere-
mitae, Svmmi Inter Germanos Medici & Philofophi.
Chirvrgia Magna, *in duos tomos digesta. Tomvs Primvs,*
continens

> *De Vvlnerib. et Fractvris.* Lib. III.
> *De Vlceribvs.* Lib. III.
> *De Tvmoribvs et Apertvris.* Lib. VII.
> *Nunc recens à* Iosqvino Dalhemio Ostofranco Medico
> Latinitate donata.
>   *Cum gratia & Priuilegio Cæfar. Maiestat. ad annos fex.*
>   Argentorati. *M.D.LXXIII.*

Small folio in sixes. Title, Perna's Address, Paracelsus'
Prefaces, Ramus De Paracelso, in all ff. 6. Text pp. 223,
1 blank. Index : Sigs. V-X8.

Aureoli Philippi Theophrasti Paracelsi Svmmi Philofophi
& Medici Chyrurgiæ Magnæ Tomvs Secvndvs. *Continens*
De Tumoribus, Puftulis, & Vlceribus Morbi Gallici Lib.
X. De Curatione & Impofturis Morbi Gallici Lib. octo.
*Qvibvs Insvnt Eivsdem Authoris Anatomia. Chyrvrgia
Minor, &c.* Omnia à Iosqvino Dalhemio Hietichtavvio
Ostrofranco Germano Latinitate Donata. *Anno Salvtis*
M.D.LXXIII.

Small folio, in sixes. Title leaf, and pp. 250. Index :
Sigs. Yy-aaa6.

In the first volume Mook (No. 101) writes *vulneribus* in full and omits the privilege clause. In the second volume he writes *VIII.* for *octo*, *Chirurgia* for *Chyrvrgia*, adds also *Argentorati* which is not in my copy, omits all before *Tomvs*, and all after *Minor*, &c.

69.—1573. Aureoli Philippi Theop. Paracelsi Chyrvrgia Minor, Qvam Alias Bertheoneam Intitvlavit.

> *Cvi Etiam Seqventes Tractatus accefferunt,eiusdem authoris.*
> De Apoftematibus, Syronibus, & Nodis.
> De cutis apertionibus.
> De vulnerum & vlcerum curis.
> De Vermibus, Serpentibus, &c. ac maculis à natiuitate ortis.
> *Ex Versione Gerardi Dorn.*
> Cum Gratia & Priuilegio Cæf. Maieft.
> *Anno Salvtis* M.D.LXXIII.
> Small folio, in sixes. Title leaf, and pp. 263. Index, pp. 5, not numbered.

According to his common practice Mook (No. 102) omits the privilege clause and date. But he inserts the place, *Argentorati*, which is not in my copy. He writes *acesserunt* for *accesserunt* and *Chirurgia* for *Chyrvrgia*.

70.—1577. Avrora Thesavrvsqve Philosophorvm, Theophrafti Paracelfi, Germani Philofophi, & Medici præ cunctis omnibus accuratifsimi. *Accefsit* Monarchia Phyfica per Gerardvm Dornevm, in defenfionem Paracelficorum Principiorum, à fuo Præceptore pofitorum. Præterea *Anatomia uiua Paracelfi, qua docet autor præter fectionem corporum, & ante mortem, patientibus effe fuccurrendum.* 15 : 77. Basileae.

> Small 8vo, pp. 63.

Mook (No. 125) has *acuratissimi; Basil.* for Basileae; and adds *apud Quarinum*, which is not in my copy. What

may have led Mook to make this statement is that the
device on the title page is a palm tree with the words on
either side "Palma Gvar." In any case the name is
Guarinus not *Quarinus*. For the English translation see
No. 108 below.

71.—1581. Congeries Paracelsicæ Chemiæ de Transmvtationibvs
Metallorum, ex omnibus quæ de his ab ipfo fcripta reperire
licuit hactenus. *Accessit Genealogia Mineralium, atq; metallorum omnium, eiufdem autoris.* Gerardo Dorneo interprete. Francofvrti Apud Andream Wechelum, M.D.LXXXI.
    Small 8vo. Title, Epistola, Præfatio, pp. 1-29. Text,
pp. 29-277. On the last page [278] is the colophon :
Francofvrti Excvdebat Andr. Wechelvs, Anno Salvtis
M.D.LXXXI.

Mook (No. 134) has copied this correctly, omitting the
date, and making the usual literal alterations. This tract
was reprinted in *Theatrum Chemicum*, vol. I. 1602, 1613,
1659, and by Manget, *Bibliotheca Chemica Curiosa*, 1702,
vol. II. pp. 423-463. Not one of these reprints is referred
to by Mook.

72.—1582. Pandora, Das ist, Die Edleste Gab Gottes, oder der
Werde vnnd Heilsamme Stein der Weisen, mit welchem
die alten Philosophi, auch Theophraftus Paracelfus, die
vnuolkom̃ene Metallen, durch gewalt des Fewrs verbessert :
sampt allerley schadliche vnd vnheilsame Kranckheiten,
jnnerlich vnd eusserlich haben vertrieben.
    Ein Guldener Schatz, welcher durch einen Liebhaber
diser Kunst, von seinem Vntergang errettet ist worden, vnnd
zu nutz allen Menschen, fürnemlich den Liebhabern der
Paracelsischen Artzney, erst jetz in Truck verfertiget.
    Getruckt zu Basel. Anno M.D.LXXXII.
    8vo. Title and preface, ff. 8. Text, pp. 309. Curious
Woodcuts. Colophon : Getruckt zu Basel, bey Samuel
Apiario.

This very rare alchemical treatise is not mentioned by Mook, though there is a copy in the Bodleian Library. Under date 1588, however, he quotes an edition of it, on the authority of Spachius. Compare for both editions *Bibliographia Paracelsica*, 1877, Nos. 30 and 37, and below No. 116 for the reprint of 1706.

73.—1583. *De* Natvræ Lvce Physica, ex Genesi Desvmpta, Iuxta fententiam Theophrasti Paracelsi, Germani Philofophi ac Medici præ cunctis excellentiffimi, Tractatvs. *Cui annexa est modefta quædam admonitio ad* Thomam Erastvm *Germanum etiam Philofophum atque Medicum, de retractandis calumnijs, & conuitijs in Paracelfum & fuos perperam ac immeritò datis in lucem per quatuor Tomos, De noua Medicina.* Gerardo Dorneo autore. *Francoforti,* Apud Chriftophorum Coruinum. *M.D.LXXXIII.*

Small 8vo. Pp. 431. Errata e1 verso. Index Rervm et Verborvm e2—e8.

This book is not in Mook's list. As it is not really by Paracelsus Mook is justified in excluding it, but it has been added here because referred to by Watt. See *Bibliographia Paracelsica*, 1877, No. 44.

74.—1584. Avreoli Theophrasti Paracelsi De fummis Naturæ myfteriis Commentarij tres, *À Gerardo Dorn conuerfi, multóque quàm antea fideliter characterifmis & marginalibus exornati, auctique.* Quorum nomina fequens pagella dabit. Basileae, Ex Officina Pernæa Per Conr. Vvaldkirch, cɪɔ ɪɔ xxcɪv.

Small 8vo. Title, Epistola Dedicatoria, ff. 8. On the verso of last leaf is a portrait of Paracelsus—with his left hand on the pommel of his sword. To the left of the face a coat of arms, to the right a symbol. The whole enclosed in a border, on which is printed: Effigies. Av. Ph. Theophrasti. Paracelsi. Æta. Svæ. 47. Beneath : Alterivs non sit qvi svvs esse potest. Text, pp. 173 (which is a misprint for 147); followed by pp. 10 of characters, not numbered. This volume contains : De Spiritibus Planetarum, De Occulta Philofophia, De Medicina cœlefti, fiue de fignis Zodiaci & Myfteriis eorum.

Mook (No. 143) gives this exact, but omits the date. He includes the mention of the contents, which in other cases he omits. Why has he done so on the present occasion ?

75.—1584. Commentaria in Archidoxorvm Libros X. D. Doctoris Theophrafti Paracelfi, Magni, Terquemaximi Philofophi ac Medici præ cunctis excellentiffimi : *Anteà nunquam in lucem data.* Quibus accefsit Compendium Astronomiae Magnae eiufdem autoris, in amplam Operum eius declarationem, etiam Latinè priùs nunquam editum. *Per D. Gerardvm Dornevm.* Cum locuplete Indice. *Cum gratia & priuilegio Cæfareæ Maieftatis.* Francoforti, M.D.LXXXIIII.
Small 8vo. Title, Epistola Dedicatoria, Epistola Censoria, Contents, in all, ff. 12. Text, pp. 538. Index rervm ac verborum, Ll6—Nn7. Nn8 is a blank leaf.

Mook (No. 144) has the inevitable alterations and omissions : From *Cum* to *Majestatis* and the date are dropped. The name of the place is contracted to *Francof.* Useless alteration of punctuation has made a distinct alteration in the sense : the full point after *editum* Mook omits, making it appear as if the work had never before been edited by Dorn, which is not the meaning. There are besides several unnecessary typographical changes.

76.—1589. Erster Theil Der Bücher vnd Schrifften, des Edlen, Hochgelehrten vnd Bewehrten Philosophi vnnd Medici, Philippi Theophrasti Bombast von Hohenheim, Paracelsi genannt : Jetzt auffs new auss den Originalien, vnd Theophrasti eigner Handschrifft, souiel derselben zubekommen gewesen, auffs trewlichst vnd fleissigst an tag geben : Durch Iohannem Hvservm Brisgoivm Churfurstlichen Colnischen

Rhat vnnd Medicvm. In diesem Theil werden begriffen die Bücher, welche von Vrsprung vnd herkommen, aller Kranckheiten handeln in Genere : Deren Catalogus nach der Præfation an den Leser zu finden. *Adiunctus est Index Rerum & Verborum accuratifs. & copiofifsimus.*

Getruckt zu Basel, durch Conrad Waldkirch. Anno M.D.LXXXIX.

4to. Title, Portrait, Huser's address to Archbishop Ernst of Cologne, Huser to the Reader, Linck's two poems, Contents, in all pp. 20, not numbered. Text, pp. 1-368. Register, pp. 369-426. This is followed by 1 leaf with Paracelsus' epitaph and shield, and on the reverse a device with motto : Lvcerna Pedibvs Meis Verbvm Tvvm. The titles of this and the following nine parts are printed in red and black.

With the exception of one or two very minute alterations in spelling and punctuation, Mook (No. 154) gives this title exactly as it stands. He also gives the contents in detail, but omits the pagination.

77.—1589. Ander Theil Der Bücher vnd Schrifften, . . . *to* Rhat vnnd Medicum *as in the preceding, No. 76.* Dieser Theil begreifft fürnemlich die Schrifften, inn denen die Fundamenta angezeigt werdē, auff welchen die Kunst der rechten Artzney stehe, vnd auss was Büchern dieselbe gelehrnet werde. Den Catalogum dieser Schrifften wird die vierde Pagina anzeigen. *Adiunctus est Index . . . to* M.D.LXXXIX *as in the preceding, No. 76.*

4to. Title, Portrait, Contents, pp. 1-4, not numbered. Text, pp. 5-342. Blank leaf. Register not paged, Signatures XX—DDd3, on the reverse of which are the epitaph and shield. DDd4 contains the portrait repeated—wanting in this copy.

Mook (No. 155) curtails this title, omitting all after *gelehrnet werde,* although different from the corresponding sentence in No. 76.

78.—1589. Dritter Theil Der Bücher vnd Schrifften, . . . *to* Medicvm, *as in No.* 76. Inn diesem Theil werden be-griffen deren Bücher ettliche, welche von Vrsprung, Vrsach vnd Heylung der Kranckheiten handeln in Specie. Deren Catalogum werden die sechste vnd siebende Pagina anzei-gen. *Adiunctus est Index* . . . M.D.LXXXIX. *as in No.* 76.

4to. Title, Portrait, Verses, Contents, Verses by Linck, in all pp. 8. Text, pp. 420. Register, Sigs. HHHij— XXXij. Verses by Linck, by Manlius, and the shield, XXXiij. Portrait repeated, XXXiv, with device on the reverse.

Mook (No. 156) writes *etliche* for *ettliche*, and omits all after *in Specie*.

79.—1589. Vierdter Theil Der Bücher vnd Schrifften, . . . auss den Originalien, vnnd Theophrasti eigner Handschrifft . . . *to* Medicvm, *as in No.* 76. In diesem Theil werden gleichsfals, wie im Dritten, solche Bücher be-griffen, welche von Vrsprung, Vrsach vnnd Heilung der Kranckheiten in Specie handlen : Deren Catalogum vnd Innhalt die 4. 5. vnd 6. Pagina anzeigen. *Adiunctus est Index* . . . M.D.LXXXIX. *as in No.* 76.

4to. Title, Portrait, Contents, Huser to the Reader, pp. 1-8, not numbered. Text, 9-417, on reverse of which is : Ende des Vierdten Theils Der Schrifften Theophrasti Paracelsi Von Vrsprung vnnd Heilung der Kranckheiten. Register, Sigs. GGGgij to TTTtv. On the reverse, poem by Linck, and then a leaf with the epitaph and shield, and device on the other side. The portrait is not repeated.

Mook (No. 157) omits all after *handlen*.

80.—1589. Fünffter Theil Der Bücher vnd Schrifften, des Edlen, Hochgelehrten vnd Bewehrten Philosophi vnd Medici, . . . *to* Medicvm *as in No.* 76. Wass in diesem Funfften Theil, dessgleichen in dem zugehörigen Appendice, für Bucher de Medicina Phyfica begriffen, wird auff folgenden

Paginis ordenlich (*sic*) nach ein ander angezeiget. *Ad-iuncti funt Indices Rerum & Verborum accuratifs. & copiofifs.* Dvo : *prior*, *huius* Partis, *pofterior*, Appendicis. Getruckt . . . M.D.LXXXIX.

4to. Title, Portrait, Catalogus, in all pp. 8. Text, pp. 332. Register, T5)-g5)iv. Appendix (with a contents Title), pp. 228. Errata, 1 leaf. Index, f5)-l5)iv. On the reverse is a poem by Linck.

Mook (No. 158) makes the correction *ordentlich* for *ordenlich* and stops at *angezeiget.*

81.—1590. Sechster Theil Der Bücher vnd Schrifften . . . *to* Medicvm, *as in No.* 80. In disem Tomo seind begriffen solche Bücher, in welchen dess mehrertheils von Spagyrischer Bereittung Natürlicher dingen, die Artzney betreffend, gehandelt wirt. Item, ettliche Alchimistische Büchlein, so allein von der Transmutation der Metallen tractiren. Deren aller Catalogus auff folgenden Paginis zufinden. *Index Rerum & Verborum locupletifs. & accuratifs.* Separatim *cum reliquis* Habebitvr. Getruckt . . . M.D.XC.

4to. Title, Portrait, Contents, To the Reader, in all pp. 8. Text, pp. 440. Register, kk6)-mm6)iij, followed by a leaf with the portrait and device.

Mook (No. 159) again writes *etliche* for *ettliche* and he omits the sentence *Index...habebitur.*

82.—1590. Siebender Theil der Bücher und Schrifften, . . . *to* Medicvm, *as in No.* 80. In diesem Theil sind verfasset die Bücher, in welchen fürnemlich die Kräfft, Tugenden vnd Eigenschafften Natürlicher dingen, auch der selben Bereidungen, betreffent die Artzeney, beschriben werden : Neben eingemischten sachen zur Alchimey dienstlich. Deren aller Catalogus auff folgenden Blettern ordentlich verzeichnet. *Index* . . . M.D.XC. *as in No.* 81.

4to. Title, Portrait, Contents, Three Addresses by Paracelsus, in all pp. 12. Text, pp. 439. The following page is blank. Register, signature kk7). On the reverse of the fourth leaf is the device.

Mook (No. 160) has *Bereithungen* for *Bereitdungen*, *betreffentd* for *betreffent* and stops at *dienstlich*.

83.—1590. Achter Theil der Bücher vnd Schrifften, . . . *to* Medicvm, *as in No.* 80. In disem Tomo (welcher der Erste vnter den Philosóphischen) werden solche Bücher begriffen, darinnen furnemlich die Philosophia de Generationibus & Fructibus quatuor Elementorvm beschrieben wirdt. Deren Catalogus auff folgenden Blettern ordentlich verzeichnet. *Index* . . . M.D.XC, *as in No.* 81.

4to. Title, Portrait, Verses by Linck, Contents, Preface, in all pp. 12. Text, pp. 363, following page blank. Register, pp. 6, followed by one leaf containing the epitaph, the shield, and on the reverse the device. The portrait is wanting in this copy.

Mook (No. 161) stops at *wirdt*.

84.—1590-91. Neundter Theil Der Bücher vnd Schrifften . . . *to* Medicvm, *as in No.* 80. Diser Tomvs (welcher der Ander vnter den Philosophischen) begreifft solche Bücher, darinnen allerley Natürlicher vnd Vbernatürlicher Heymligkeiten Vrsprung, Vrsach, Wesen vnd Eigenschafft, grundtlich vnd warhafftig beschriben werden: Deren Verzeichnuss auff folgenden Blettern zu finden. *Index* . . . *Separatim* . . . *Habebitvr.* . . . *as in No.* 81. Anno M.D.XCI (*sic*).

4to. Title, Portrait, Contents, To the Reader, in all pp. 6. Text, pp. 459, following page blank. Register pp. 7, and on the following page the device.

Mook (No. 162) has *Heymlichkeiten* and *wahrhafftig.* He has not noted the misprint in the date—if it be actually a misprint, and he stops at *werden.*

85.—1590. Zehender Theil Der Bucher vnd Schrifften . . . to Medicvm, *as in No.* 80. Dieser Theil (welcher der Dritte vnter den Philosophischen Schrifften) begreifft fürnemlich das treffliche Werck Theophrasti, Philosophia Sagax, oder Astronomia Magna genannt: Sampt ettlichen andern Opufculis, vnd einem Appendice, wie auff folgenden Paginis verzeichnet. *Index . . .* M.D.XC. *as in No.* 84.

4to. Title, Portrait, Contents, verses by Linck, in all pp. 8. Text, pp. 491, following page blank. Appendix (with Contents Title), pp. 275, following page blank. Register, pp. 6, then a blank leaf. After this comes a tract: Fascicvlvs Prognosticationvm Astrologicarvm: pp. 106.

Mook (No. 163) again writes *etlichen* for *ettlichen*. It may be remarked that to complete this copy of the first collected edition of Paracelsus' works is wanted the first part of the Chirurgical works, printed by Waldkirch in 1591, which was all that appeared in this form.

86.—1596. *A hundred and foureteene* Experiments and Cures of the famous Phyfitian *Philippus Aureolus Theophrastus Paracelfus; Tranfla*ted out of the Germane tongue into the Latin. Whereunto is added certaine excel*lent and profitable workes by B. G.* a Portu Aquitano. Alfo certaine Secrets of Ifacke Hollandus concerning the Vegetall and *Animall worke. Alfo the Spagericke Antidotarie for* Gunne-fhot of Iofephus *Quirfitanus. Collected by Iohn Hester.* London Printed by *Vallentine Sims* dwelling on Adlinghill at the figne of the white Swanne. 1596.

Small 4to. Title, epistle, preface, &c. A-B (ff. 8). Text: pp. 82. Title enclosed in a border.

Not in Mook. He knew only the 1652 reprint, for which see below. The present edition was quoted formerly (*Bibliographia Paracelsica*, 1877, No. 15) from Cooper. It is one of the rarest of these English tracts. There is a copy in the British Museum; how did Mook miss it?

87.—1597. Theophrastisch Vade Mecvm. Das ist: Etliche sehr nutzliche Tractat, von der warhafftigen bereittung vnd rechtem gebrauch der Chymischen Medicamenten. Durch den Achtbarn vnd Hochgelarten Herrn, Bernhardum G. Penotum, à portu S. Mariæ, Aquitanum, beider Artzney D. zu Franckenthal, erstlich in Latein heraus geben. Itzo aber allen Kunstliebendē Teutschen zu sonderbarem nutz in vnsere vernemliche Muttersprache transferiret, Durch Iohannem Hippodamum, Cherufcum. Den Inhalt aller Tractàtlein, findet man nach der Vorrede, Vnd mit einem ordentlichen Register zu Ende gesetzet.

Zu Magdeburgk bey Johan Francken, Anno 1597.

Cvm Gratia & Privilegio, &c.

4to. Title, Preface, Contents, ff. 8. Text, pp. 278 [misnumbered for 240]. Register, Hh-Ii4. Errata, Ii4 verso-Kk2. Title red and black.

It would appear as if there were distinct issues of this book in 1597; one at Eisleben, described by Mook (No. 168), and this at Magdeburg. There are differences in the title. Mook has *rechten* for *rechtem*, *sonderem* for *sonderbarem*, *Jetzo* for *Itzo*, *gesetzt* for *gesetzet*. All after this is omitted by Mook, as it was wanting in his copy, but he gives a colophon: "Gedruckt zu Eissleben durch Bartholomäum Hörnigk. Im Jahr 1597." There is nothing of this in the copy before me.

88.--1599. Avrevm Vellvs, Oder Güldin Schatz vnd Kunstkammer: Darinnen der aller furnembsten, fürtreffenlichsten, ausserlesenesten, herrlichsten vnd bewehrtesten Auctorum Schrifften Bücher, aus dem gar vhralten Schatz der vberbliebnen, verborgenen, hinterhaltenen Reliquien vnd Monumenten der AEgyptiorum, Arabum, Chaldæorum, & Affyriorum, Königen vnd Weysen. Von Dem Edlen, Hocherleuchten, furtreffenlichen, bewehrten Philosopho Salomone Trismosino (so des grossen Philosophi vnd Medici Theophrafti Paracelfi Præceptor gewesen) in sonderbare vnterschiedliche Tractetlein disponirt, vnd in das Deutsch gebracht. Sampt andern Philosophischen, alter vnnd newer Scribenten sonderbaren Tractetlein, alles zuuor niemalen, weder erhört noch gesehen, wie der ' Catalogus zuuerstehen gibt. Durch einen der Kunst Liebhabern mit grossem Kosten, Mühe, Arbeit vnd Gefahr, die Originalia vnd Handschrifften zusammen gebracht, vnd auffs trewlichst vnd fleissigst an tag geben.

Erstlich Gedruckt zu Rorschach am Bodensee, Anno M.D.XCIX.

Small 8vo. Title, red and black; on the reverse, Portrait of Paracelsus; Vorrede, Contents, a1-7 ; a8 blank. Text, pp. 1-208 (Imperfect).

Avrei Velleris Oder Der Güldin Schatz vnd Kunst-kammer. Tractatvs II. Darinn erstlich des Edlen Hochgelehrten vnd bewehrten Philosophi vnd Medici, Philippi Theophrasti, Bombasti von Hohenheim, Paracelsi genant, Fürnembste Chymische Schrifften, Tincturen vnd Process, so bisshero in keinem Truck noch nie gesehen.

Dann zum andern, dess auch Edlen vnnd fürtreffen-lichen Philosophi, Bartholomæi Korndorffers Schrifften, so viel deren an jetzo beyhanden gewesen, vnd sich zusammen der Ordnung halber gefügt, aus den Originalien in ein Volumen gebracht.

Erstlich gedruckt im F. Gottshaus S. Gallen Reichs-hoff, Rorschach am Bodensee.

Small 8vo. Title. Text, pp. 158 (Imperfect?). With woodcuts of apparatus in the text.

This is not mentioned by Mook. It is a reprint of a work which appeared in 4to in 1598 (*Bibliographia Para-celsica*, 1877, No. 2), and which Mook knew imperfectly.

89.—1600. The *Prognosticatio* (Mook Nos. 9 and 10) translated from the German into Latin by David Schram, was printed, 1600, in the *Lectiones Memorabiles* of Johannes

Wolfius, at Lauingen, Tomus Secundus, p. 484. The
woodcuts are all reversed and are more carefully finished.

This reprint of the *Prognosticatio* is not referred to by
Mook. See No. 49 above.

90.—1602. Congeries Paracelsicæ Chemiæ de Transmvtationibvs
   Metallorum. De Genealogia Mineralivm ex Paracelso.
   Reprinted in Theatrvm Chemicvm, Ursellis, MDCII.
   Vulvmen Primvm. 8vo, pp. 557-646 and 646-671.

This reprint of No. 71, above, is not quoted by Mook.
See also Nos. 98, 109, and 115.

91.—1603. Avreoli Philippi Theophrasti Bombasts von Hohenheim Paracelsi, des Edlen, Hochgelehrten, Fürtreffflich-
   sten, Weitberumbtesten Philofophi vnd Medici Opera
   Bücher vnd Schrifften, so viel deren zur Handt gebracht:
   vnd vor wenig Jahren, mit vnd auss jhren glaubwürdigen
   eigener hangeschriebenen (*sic*) Originalien collacioniert, vergliechen, verbessert: vnd durch Ioannem Hvservm Brisgoivm in zehen vnterschiedliche Theil, in Truck gegeben.
   Jetzt von newem mit vleiss vbersehen, auch mit etlichen
   bisshero vnbekandten Tractaten gemehrt, vnd vmb mehrer
   Bequemligkeit willen, in zwen vnterschiedliche Tomos vnd
   Theil gebracht, deren Begriff vnd Ordnung, nach der
   Vorrede zu finden, sampt beyder Theilen vleissigen vnd
   volkommenen Registern.
   Strassburg, In verlegung Lazari Zetzners Buchhändlers.
   Anno M.DCIII.
   Folio in sixes. Title, Huser to Archbishop Ernst,
   Huser to the Reader, Linck's verses, Contents, in all pp.
   12. Text, pp. 1127. Register, BBbvj verso-FFfviij.
   Title red and black, inside an elaborate woodcut
   border, with a portrait of Paracelsus at the top, Virgilius
   and Hermes right and left, four goddesses of the Arts,
   Cupids, architectural ornaments, and chemical apparatus.

Mook (No. 170) has *weitberuhmtesten, handgeschriebene,*

Huserum Brisgoium, and *fleissigen,* and he omits the words *vmb mehrer Bequemligkeit willen,* and *vnterschiedliche,* for no apparent reason.

92.—1603. Aureoli Philippi Theophrasti Bombasts von Hohenheim Paracelsi, des Edlen, hochgelehrten fürtreffenlichsten weitberuhmtesten Philofophi vnd Medici Opera Bücher vnd Schrifften, so viel deren zur Hand gebracht: vnd vor wenig Jahren, mit vnd auss jhren glaubwurdigen eigner Handgeschriebenen Originalien collationiert, verglichen, vnd verbessert, &c.

Ander Theyl. Darinnen die Magischen vnd Astrologischen Bücher, sampt jhren Anhangen vnd Stücken, auch von dem Philosophischen Stein handlende Tractatus, begriffen, &c. Fornen mit einem kurtzen Begriff vnd Ordnung dieses Theyls Bücher, vnd derselben Innhalt: Hinden aber mit einem durchauss vollkommenen Register vermehret.

Strassburg, In verlegung Lazari Zetzners Buchhändlers. *Anno Domini* cIɔlɔcIII.

Folio, in sixes. Fly leaf with device, Title and Contents, in all pp. 9, followed by a blank page. Text, pp. 691. Register, pp. 12, not numbered, last page blank.

Mook (No. 171) omits most of the portion before *Ander Theyl,* although it varies in spelling from that in the first part.

93.—1603. *Nobilis, Clarissimi Ac probatiffimi Philofophi & Medici, Dn. Avreoli Philippi* Theophrasti Bombast, Ab Hohenheim, Dicti Paracelsi, Operum Medico-Chimicorum Sive Paradoxorvm, Tomus Genuinus . . . Recenter Latine factus, & in vfum Affeclarum Nouæ & Veteris Philofophiæ foras datus,

A Collegio Mufarum Palthenianarum in Nobili Francofurto. *Anno M.DC.III.*

I. Tomus Genuinus Primus. *Agens de Caufsis, Origine ac Curatione Morborum in genere.*

4to. Title, Dedication, Verses, Contents, 4 leaves. Text, pp. 303.

II. Tomus Genuinus Secundus. *Tradens fundamenta, quibus veræ & genuinæ Medicinæ Ars fuperſtructa, & ex quibus folis illa addiſci poſsit.*

4to. Title, Dedication, Verses by Linck, Contents, 4 leaves. Text, pp. 272.

III. Tomus Tertius Genuinus. *Agens de Cauſsis, Origine ac Curatione Morborum in fpecie.*

4to. Title, Dedication, Contents, 2 leaves. Text, pp. 203, which is a misprint for 355.

IV. Tomus Genuinus Quartus. *Agens itidem vt Tertius de Cauſsis, Origine ac Curatione Morborum in fpecie.*

4to. Title, Dedication, Contents, 2 leaves. Text, pp. 226, which is a misprint for 326. 2 blank.

V. Tomus Genuinus Quintus. *Agens de Libris ad Medi-cinam Phyficam fpectantibus.*

4to. Title, Dedication, Preface, Acrostic, Laudation of Paracelsus, Contents, 4 leaves. Text, pp. 272. Index, Sigs. Mmmm—Ssss2. Analytical Scheme, 2 leaves.

What may be called the general part of the title has been reproduced correctly enough by Mook (No. 172) except in details of punctuation, but the special part of each has been altered to suit his convenience. The re-mainder of the translation appeared in 1605 ; I have not seen it. This section, bound in one volume and indexed, is complete in itself. The translation is made from Huser's edition 1589-90.

94.—1608. Rosarivm Novvm Olympicvm Et Benedictvm. Das ist : Ein newer Gebenedeyter Philosophischer Rosengart, Darinnen vom aller weisesten König Salomone, H. Salo-mone Trismosino, H. Trithemio, D. Theophrasto, &c. gewiesen wirdt, wie der Gebenedeyte Guldene Zweig, vnnd Tincturschatz, vom vnverwelcklichen Orientalischen Baum der Hefperidum, vormittels Göttlicher Gnaden, abzubrechen vud (*sic*) zu erlangen sey : Allen vnd jeden Filiis doctrinæ Hermeticæ, vnd D. Theophrafticæ Liebhabern zu gutem trewlich eröffnet in zwen Theilen. Pars Prima.

Iambilichus (*sic*). Quicquid habemus boni, habemus à Sole, vel ab ipfo, vel per alia.

Devs in Cœlo eft, revelans myfteria profunda & abfcondita.

Per Benedictvm Figvlvm ; Vtenhoviatem, Francum ; Poëtam L. C. Theologum ; Theofophum ; Philofophum ; Medicum Eremitam. T. M. Getruckt zu Basel, in verlegung des Autoris, Anno 1608.

Small 4to. Title, red and black, Preface, pp. [9]. Text, 1 p. not numbered and pp. 83.

Rosarii Novi Olympici et Benedicti, Pars Altera : In sich haltent ein Buch mit 32. Capiteln, Laurentii Venturæ Veneti, Medicinæ Doctoris, &c. Auss dem Latein vertiert vnnd trewlich verdolmetschet, in vnser Teutschen Sprach vor nie geschen, De Lapide Benedicto Philofophorum, &c. *Interprete* Benedicto Figulo, Vtenhoviate, Franco, Poeta L. C. Theologo; Theofopho; Philofopho, Medico, Eremita. D. T. P. D. G. N.

Getruckt zu Basel, in verlegung des Avtoris. *Anno* BeneDICtI RegIs & MagIftrI GratIæ & bonItatIs, &c.

Small 4to. Title and Preface, pp. 15, and a blank page. Text, pp. 117. Index, pp. 2, and a blank page.

In the first part Mook (No. 183) corrects the misprint *vud* into *und*, and omits the quotation from Iamblichus.

95.—1608. La Grand Chirvrgie de Philippe Aoreole Theophraste Paracelse grand Medecin & Philofophe Allemand, *Tradvite En Francois, De la verfion Latine de Iofquin d' Alhem Medecin d' Oftofranc, & illuftree d'amples annotations, auec figures de certains inftrumens propres pour remettre les membres rompus, & les contenir estans remis en forte qu'on les puiffe vifiter chacun iour. fans que l'os fe defplace.* Par M. Clavde Dariot Medecin à Beaune.

Plus vn difcours de la goutte & caufes d'icelle, auec fa
guerifon.

Item III. Traittez de la preparation des medicamens,
auec vne table pour l'intelligence du temps propre au
recueil, compofition & garde des herbes, fruits & femences.
Troisiesme Edition. A Montbeliart, par Iaqves Foillet.
cIɔIɔ Cviii.

8vo. Title, Dedication, To the Reader, Paracelsus'
Preface, ff. 8 ; Text, pp. 280 ; Indices : 3 leaves, 1
blank leaf. De la Goutte, pp. 51, including the separate
title. Trois Discours, pp. 162 (misprint for 191), including
the separate title.

Mook (No. 186) has made a sweeping curtailment of this
title. He writes *Philosoph, mombres, quon* for *qu'on* in the
original, and omits all from *Plus un discours* down to
semences. The date which he so often omits is inserted,
but in Arabic numerals, 1608, though the original is in
Roman numerals, which he uses elsewhere, on occasion.

96.—1608. *Pandora* Magnalium Naturalium Aurea et Benedicta,
De Benedicto Lapidis Philofoph. Myfterio. Darinnen Apo-
calypsis Des Hocherleuchten Aegyptischen Königs vnd
Philosophi, Hermetis Trismegisti ; von vnferm Teutschen
Hermete, dem Edlen, Hochthewrem Monarchen vnd Phil-
osopho Trifmegifto, A. Ph. Theophrasto Paracelfo &c.
Verdolmetschet : wie Auch Tinctura Phyficorum Para-
celfica, mit einer Schonen Erklerung des Auch Edlen vnd
Hocherfahrnen Philofophi, Alexandri von Süchten, Utrijus-
que Medicine D. Sampt Seiner Al. V. S angehengten 3.
Vnderschiedlichen Tractetlein, so vor nie gesehen worden,
wie auch Anderen Ejufdem materiæ Corollariis wie sie
nach der Vorredt Specifiret werden : Allen Filiis Doctrinæ
Hermeticæ Zu nutz vnd gutem Jetzo Publiciret. Durch
Benedictum Figulum ; Utenhoviatem ; Fr: P. L. C. T. T.
P. M. E. D. T. P. D. G. N.

Getruckt zu Strassburg, inn Verlegung Lazari Zetzeners 1608.

Small 8vo. Title, Preface, in all pp. 32. Text, pp. 292. Errata, p. 1, and 3 blank pages.

Mook does not mention this work of Benedictus Figulus, though he has quoted others (Nos. 94 and 113).

97.—1613. Solis e Pvteo Emergentis : sive *Dissertationis Chymio-technicæ* Libri Tres. *In quibus totius Operationis Chymicæ methodus Practica ; Materia Lapidis Philosophici, & nodus* (sic) *foluendi eius, operandique, vt & Clavis operum Paracelsi, qua abftrufa explicantur deficientia fupplentur.* Cum præfatione Chymiæ Veritatem afferente. Authore Ioanne Rhenano, Medico. *Liber primus. M.D.CXIII.*

Francofvrti. *Impenfis Antonij Hummij.*

Small 4to. Title, Dedication, and Prefatory Dissertation, in all pp. 23, and 1 blank. Text, pp. 80. Liber Secvndvs, pp. 31, and 1 blank. Liber Tertius, pp. 24. Engraved border to title, and woodcuts of furnaces and apparatus in part I. The third part contains the *Clavis operum Paracelsi.*

Quoted by Mook (p. 101, Bemerkung a), from Adelung, *Geschichte der menschlichen Narrheit*, VII. p. 363, No. 93.

98.—1613. Congeries Paracelsicae Chemiæ de Transmutationibus Metallorum. De Genealogia Mineralivm ex Paracelso.

Reprinted in Theatrvm Chemicvm, Volvmen Primvm. Argentorati, M.DC.XIII. 8vo, pp. 533-619, and 619-644.

This reprint of Dorn's collection (see above No. 71) is not referred to by Mook. Compare also Nos. 90, 109, and 115.

99.—1618. Philosophia Mystica, Darinn begriffen Eilff vnterschidene Theologico-Philofophische, doch teutsche Tractatlein, zum theil auss Theophrafti Paracelfi, zum theil auch M. Valentini Weigelii, gewesenen Pfarrherrn zu Iscopaw, bisshero verborgenen manufcriptis der Theosophischen Warheit liebhabern. An jtzo in zweyen Theilen zum Christlichen Vorschub, beyde Liechter, der Gnaden vnd der Natur, in vns zuerwecken, in offenen Truck gegeben. Deren Titul vnd Nahmen, wie ein jedes insonderheit von den Authoribus selbst genennet, die nachfolgende seite zeigen wirdt.

Getruckt zur Newstadt, vnd zu finden bey Lucas Jenis, Buchhandler. *Anno M DC.XVIII.*

Small 4to. Pp. 272.

Mook (No. 194) has made as correct a copy of the title as he seems capable of, but, nevertheless, he reads *Valentin* for *Valentini*, *Iscogaw* for *Iscopaw*, omits the sentence *Deren Titul* to *zeigen wirdt*, and reads *zu Newstadt* for *zur Newstadt*. Mook gives the contents of this collection. Four tracts bear Paracelsus' name : De Pœnitentiis ; Astronomia Olympi novi ; Theologia Cabalistica de perfecto homine in Christo Iesu, et contra ; Commentarius in Danielem Prophetam ; respecting which Mook says that the third is decidedly genuine.

100.—1618. Theophrastische Practica, Das ist, Ausserlesene Theophrastische Medicamenta, beneben eigentlicher Beschreibung derer Præparation : Auch richtigem Nutz vnd Gebrauch, Weyland durch Herren, Gerhard Dorn, in Lateinischer Sprache beschrieben, Ins Teutsch versetzt, vnd nunmehr in Druck befordert Durch Michaelem Horingium Zittavienfem, Medic. Practicum zu Hall.

Gedruckt bey Peter Schmidt, In vorlegung Michael Oelschlagers. (?) Anno MDCXVIII.

Small 8vo. Title, Vorrede, &c., Ai—iiij. Text begins Av, p. 1 and ends p. 491, which is a misprint for 492. (?) Register Ji iij—viij.

Not given by Mook.

101.—1620. In this year was published, in a small 4to volume, the *Reformir-Spiegel des weltlichen Bapsts, vñ wahren*

Antichrist zu Rom, by Joannes De Hyperiis. It is in two parts, the first of which contains a short history of the papacy; the second, magical figures and emblems, with their explanations. Among these are reproductions: 1st, of the *Prognosticatio* (No. 49 above), pp. 45-60; and, 2nd, of the so-called Nurnberg figures, pp. 1 44, which were printed in 1569 (Mook, No. 70), in 1572 (Mook, No. 97), and which are contained in the Appendix to Th. x. of Huser's edition (No. 85 above). Mook has overlooked this reprint.

102.—1623. Nvclevs Sophicvs, oder Ausslegung in Tincturam Phyficorum Theophrafti Paracelfi. Darinnen die rechte wahre Materia oder fubiectum Philofophorum Catholicum, auch dess gantzen Wercks, so wol der alten Philosophen, als dess Theophrafti newe corrigirte, rechte vnd eigentliche Præparation gezeiget wird. Sampt einem andern vnd sehr nützlichen Tractätlein Cabalistischer Weise vom lapide Philofophorum beschrieben, vnd den Veris Chymiæ ftudiofis zu gutem herfur geben Durch Liberivm Benedictvm.

Franckfurt am Mayn, bey Lvcas Jennis zu finden. Im Jahr M.DC.XXIII.

Small 8vo. Pp. 116.

Not given by Mook.

103.—1633. Princelijck Ghefchenck, Of Tractaet der Medicynen. In 't welck Natuerlijck en grondich de Loflijcke en wytberoemde Konft van Ghenefinghe, de krachten van alle Cruyderen ende ghevvaffen, als oock Gommen, Herfen, Olyen, Extracten, Wateren, gheene uyt-ghefondert. Mitfgaeders de Compofitien aller Medicamenten, en de Remedien teghens alle Krancheden, en Fenynen, die het Menfchelicke gheflacht voorvallen, verhaelt vverden, en by experientie goedt bevonden zyn. Hier is een Tractaet van de Alchymie voor de beminders Theophrasti Paracelsi by ghevoeght. Eerft befchreven Door den Hoogh-gheleerden ende Experten Medicijn Nicolaes van

Halteren, Dienaer des Godtlicken vvoorts binnen *Hornaer*.
Ende nu Tot eyghen kosten in 't licht ghebratht (*sic*) door
Iohannem à Porta. t' Amstelredam, By Ian Evertfz.
Cloppenborch, Boeckvercooper op 't Water in den ver-
gulden Bybel, tegen over te Cooren-Beurs, 1623 (1633).
Small 4to. Title, Epistle, ff. 4. Text, pp. 190.

The date may have been originally 1623, but the 2 looks
as if a 3 had been printed over it. Mook gives it under
1623.

The reproduction of the whole title by Mook (No. 205)
is so characteristic of the author's incapacity for the
mechanical—though difficult—work of accurate transcription, and it illustrates so well his views as to how a title
should be recorded for bibliographic purposes that I quote
it as it stands.

> Princelyk Gheschenck, Of Tractaet der Medicynen.   In
> 'twelck Naturlijck en grondich etc.   Hier is een Tractaet
> van de Alchymie voor de beminders Theophrasti Paracelsi
> bij ghevoegt. Eerst beschreven Door den Hooghgheleerden
> ende Experten Medicijn Nicolaes van Halteren, Ende nu
> Tot eyghen kosten in t' licht ghebracht, door Johannem a
> Porta t' Amsterdam By Jan Evertsz Cloppenborch.

Excusing the part that is omitted, comparison of the two
versions will reveal the kind of inaccuracies which pervade
almost every title as copied by Mook.

104.—1644. Theatro D'Arcani Del Medico Lodovico Locatelli
Da Bergamo; Nel Qvale Si Tratta Dell' Arte Chimica, &
luoi Arcani. *Con gli Afforifmi d'Ippocrate Commentati
da Paracelfo, & L'efpofitione d'alcune* Cifre, & Caratteri
ofcuri de Filofofi, Con Dve Tavole Vna de Capitoli, &
l'altra delle cofe più notabili. Con Privilegio Dell'
Eccell.mo Senato Di Milano, per Anni dodeci futuri. In

Milano, Per Gio. Pietro Ramellati, M.DC.XLIV. *Con licenza de' Superiori.*

8vo. Engraved Title, Woodcut Title, Printed Title, License, Dedication, Preface, Verses, Table of Chapters, in all pp. 34, not numbered. Text, pp. 456. Index, &c., pp. 24, not numbered. Both the engraved and the wood-cut title contain a full-length portrait of Paracelsus.

This is an earlier edition of the work already described (*Bibliographia Paracelsica*, 1877, No. 9), under date 1667. This edition also is not mentioned by Mook.

105.—1652. Three Exact Pieces Of Leonard Phioravant Knight, and Doctor in Physick, *Viz.* His Rationall Secrets, and Chirurgery, Reviewed and Revived. Together with a Book of Excellent Experiments And Secrets, Collected out of the Practifes of feverall Expert men in both Faculties. Whereunto is Annexed *Paracelsus* his One hundred and fourteen Experiments: With certain Excellent Works of *B. G. à Portu Aquitano.* Alfo *Ifaac Hollandus* his Secrets concerning his Vegetall and Animall Work. With *Quercetanus* his Spagyrick Antidotary for Gun-Shot. London, Printed by *G. Dawfon,* and are to be fold by *William Nealand,* at his Shop at the Sign of the Crown in *Duck-lane,* 1652.

Small 4to. pp. [8] 16 [2]. 180. [6] 106. [10] 92; [12] 75. [1 blank.]

Mook (No. 214) gives this almost correctly, but omits all after *Nealand.* This is the reprint of the edition of 1596, already described, No. 86, above.

106.—1652-53. Under this date I described formerly (*Bibliographia Paracelsica*, 1877, No. 4) Johnson's *Lexicon Chymicum*, and referred to the later reprint of 1660 as containing a supplement of words from Paracelsus and other writers previously omitted, together with certain extracts about Paracelsus' life. I have recently ascertained from an actual copy that this entire supplement appeared in 1653, uniform with the *Lexicon*. It does not however always accompany it, for I have seen two copies of the *Lexicon* without the second part.

The title of this edition of the second part is the same as that of the 1660 edition already given, except for one or two changes in spelling, and the collation is as follows : Title, Preface, Verses, 4 leaves. Lexicon Chymicum, pp. 1-8. Extracts about Paracelsus, 8 leaves. Lexicon Chymicum, pp. 9-86. Blank Leaf. Chymical characters, 6 leaves. Errata, 1 leaf. Imprimatur, 1 leaf.

107.—1658. Avr. Philip. Theoph. Paracelsi Bombast ab Hohen-heim, *Medici Et Philosophi Celeberrimi, Chemicorúmque* Principis, Opera Omnia Medico-Chemico-Chirvrgica, *Tribvs Volvminibvs Comprehensa.* Editio Novissima Et Emendatissima, Ad Germanica & Latina exemplaria accura-tiſſimè collata : Variis tractatibus & opuſculis ſummâ hinc inde diligentiâ conquiſitis, vt in Voluminis Primi Præfa-tione indicatur, locupletata : Indicibusq́ ; exactiſſimis inſtructa.

Volvmen Primvm, *Opera Medica complectens.*

Genevæ, Sumptibus Ioan. Antonij, & Samuelis De Tournes. *M.DC.LIIX.* Cvm Privilegio.

Folio in sixes. Portrait, Title, Epistle, Bitiskius' Preface, Severinus' Epistle, Contents, in all pp. 34. Text, pp. 828. Index, pp. 39, 1 blank. Title red and black.

Avreoli Philippi Theophrasti Paracelsi Bombast ab Hohenheim *Medici Et Philosophi Celeberrimi Chemi-corúmque* Principis, *Operum* Volvmen Secvndvm Opera Chemica et Philosophica Complectens, *Præfatione, Librorvm Elencho &* Indice *generali inſtructum.* Genevæ, ... Privilegio.

Folio. Title, Bitiskius' Preface, Contents, in all pp. 22. Text, pp. 718. Index, pp. 32, 2 blank. Title red and black.

Avr. Philip. Theoph. . . . *Operum* Volvmen Tertivm,

Chirvrgica Opera Complectens, Duabus Sectionibus diftincta, *Qvarvm Prior Chirvrgiam Magnam, Posterior verò* Bertheoneam *fiue* Chirvrgiam Minorem *cum Libris adiectis continet.* Extat In Vtramqve Præfatio, fingulæ Librorum Elencho & Indice generali funt inftructæ. *Genevæ,* . . . Privilegio.

Folio. Title, red and black, Bitiskius' Preface, Paracelsus' Prefaces, Contents, &c., in all pp. 12. Text, pp. 212. Index, pp. 27, 1 blank.

Bertheonea, pp. [4], 119, 1 blank. Index, pp. 7, 1 blank. Testamentum, and other miscellaneous matter, pp. 11, followed by the epitaph; this volume concludes with Roche Le Baillif's *Dictionariolvm Paracelsicvm,* pp. 13-18, followed by a blank leaf.

Mook (No. 221) quotes the title of the first volume only. He stops at *conquisitis* and puts *etc.* for what follows down to *complectens.*

108.—1659. Paracelsus His Aurora, & Treafure of the Philosophers. As alfo The Water-Stone of The Wife Men; Defcribing the matter of, and manner how to attain the universal Tincture. *Faithfully Englifhed.* And Publifhed by *J. H. Oxon. London,* Printed for *Giles Calvert,* and are to be fold at the *Black Spred Eagle,* at the Weft end of *Pauls,* 1659.

12mo. Title, To the Reader, Errata, ff.4. Text, pp. 229. Followed by a List of Books, pp. [3.]

For the original, see No. 70 above.

When the previous part of the review was written I knew of this translation only by Cooper's and Watt's references to it, and by there being a copy in the Bodleian Catalogue (*Bibliographia Paracelsica,* 1877, Nos. 17 and 40). Mook (p. 113, 1659) mentions it on Adelung's authority (VII. p. 361, No. 77). There is a copy in the British Museum. How has Mook missed it?

109.—1659. Congeries Paracelsicae Chemiae De Transmutation-
ibus Metallorum. De Genealogia Mineralium en Paracelso.
Reprinted in Theatrum Chemicum, Volumen Primum.
Argentorati, M.DC.LIX. 8vo, pp. 491-568 and 568-591.

Compare Nos. 71, 90, 98 and 115. Like the others this
reprint is not mentioned by Mook.

110.—1676. Magnalia Medico-Chymica, Oder Die höchste Artz-
ney- und Feurkünstige Geheimnisse, Wie nemlich mit dem
Circulato majori & minori oder dem Univerfal aceto mer-
curiali, und fpiritu vini tartarifato die herrlichsten Artzneyen
zum langen Leben und Heilung der unheilsamen Kranckheiten zu machen; zwar aus Paracelfi Handschrift schon
im vorigen Seculo ausgangen, aber so corrupt, dass es fast
niemand verstehen können, itzo aber aufs neue verhoch-
deutschet, und von Satz zu Satz erlautert, Nebenst bey-
gefügtem Hauptschlussel aller Hermetischen Schrifften,
Nemlich dem unvergleichlichen Tractat genannt: Offen-
stehender Eingang zu dem vormals verschlossenen König-
lichen Pallast. Dem gemeinen Nutz zum besten, und den
Curiofen zu Gefallen publiciret von Johanne Hiskia Cardi-
lucio Com. Pal. Phil. & Med. Doct.

Nürnberg, In Verlegung Wolffgang Moritz Endters, und
Johann Andreæ Endters Sel. Erben. Anno M.DC.LXXVI.

Small 8vo. Title, Preface, Comment, in all pp. 48.
Text, pp. 1-399. Errata, 400-409. Register and Errata,
pp. 30. Last page blank.

Strange to say Mook (No. 223) has contrived to give
this long title from the British Museum copy without
variation, except that he omits the date. The accuracy
is altogether phenomenal.

111.—1679. Mercurii Zweyfacher Schlangen-stab, Das ist: I.
Glücks-Ruthe zu Paracelfi Chymischem Schatz. II. Men-
ftruum feu Solvens Univerfale Philofophicum, Darinnen
das Gold fine ftrepitu, wie Eyss in warmen Wasser zer-

schmiltzt : Samt dem gantzen Philofophischen Procefs. Ulm, In Verlegung Balthasar Kühnen Seel. Wittib. 1679. Small 12mo. Pp. [4], 112.

Mook (No. 225) writes *sampt* for *samt*, and has omitted the date.

112.—1681. Lapis Vegetabilis, oder die höchste Artzney, Auss dem Wein, Auch andern Erden-Gewächsen. Sambt dem zehenden Buch der Archidoxen Philippi Theophrasti Paracelsi.

Strassburg, In verlegung Georg Andreas Dolhopff. Im Jahr M.DC.LXXXI.

Small 8vo. Pp. [4] 92.

This is not given by Mook. There is a copy in the British Museum.

113.—1682. Thesaurinella Olympica Aurea Tripartita, Das ist : Ein himmlisch güldenes Schatzkammerlein, Von vielen ausserlesenen Kleinodien zugerüstet, darinn der uhralte grosse und hochgebenedeyte Charfunckel-stein und Tinctur-schatz verborgen. In drey unterschiedliche Cellulas aussgetheilet. Allen Liebhabern der himmlischen Warheit, und Hermetischen Philosophey, so den Grund der Hochmagischen Tinctur suchen, zu gute : Wie auch zu Beförderung der edlen Alchimey anjetzo eröffnet und publicirt Durch Benedictum Figulum Utenhoviatem Franc. Poetam L. C. Theologum, Theofophum, Philofophum, Medicum, Eremitam. D. T. P. D. G. N. MDC : LXXXII. Franckfurt am Mayn, In Verlegung Georgii Wolffii Buchhändl. in Hamburg in S. Joh. Kirchen, Gedruckt durch Johann Görlin.

Small 8vo. Frontispiece, Title, Epistle, To the Reader, Contents, in all, pp. 16. Text, pp. 402.

Mook (No. 226) has *zur Beförderung* and *Alchymy;* and some variations in the punctuation. The book first appeared in 1608 (Mook No. 184), but though the only copy he quotes is in the British Museum, yet he does not give the title in full, but refers to this later edition. Did he see the Museum copy?

114.—1697. Arcana Philosophia Or, Chymical Secrets, Containing The noted and ufeful Chymical Medicines of Dr. *Wil.* and *Rich. Ruffel* Chymifts, *viz.*

I. *Species Vitæ,* alias *Univerfalis.*
II. *Tinctura Regalis,* call'd *Scorbutick,* &c.
III. *Species Coroborativa,* alias *Pleuretica.*
IV. *Species Proprietatis.*
V. *Species Minor.*
VI. A *Peftilential Cordial,* call'd his *White Cordial.*

As Also Several Curious Chymical *Proceffes* and *Spagerick* Preparations of Natural Things for the ufe of Medicin, and many other things of great ufe and vertue in *Eradicating* the most Stubborn Difeafes ; Likewife Four curious fmall Treatifes, *viz.* the I. of *Fevers,* the II. of the *Jaundies,* the III. of *Madnefs,* and the IV. of *Diarrhœas, Lientries, &c.* By the Renowned and moft Approved Dr. *Aurelius Philipus Theophraftus Paracelfus,* of *Hoheneim.* Publifh'd by *John Headrich, Philo-Chymicus,* and formerly Operator to Dr. *Richard Ruffel.*

London, Printed and Sold by *Henry Hills* in *Black-Fryers,* the Publifher, at the *Blew Ball* in *Hogsden,* over against the *Crooked Billet,* near *Shoreditch* Church, and the Bookfellers of *London, &c.* 1697.
Small 8vo. Pp. [16] 128 [8].

This book is not in Mook's list. The copy in the Bodleian was what I formerly referred to (*Bibliographia Paracelsica,* 1877, No. 41).

115.—1702. Congeries Paracelsicæ Chemiæ de Transmutationibus Metallorum. De Genealogia Mineralium ex Paracelso.
Reprinted in Manget's Bibliotheca Chemica Curiosa, Genevæ, M.DCC.II., folio. Tomus Secundus. pp. 423·454, and 454-463.

This is the last reprint of this collection. See above Nos. 71, 90, 98, and 109. It is not mentioned by Mook.

116.—1706. Joh. Michaelis Faustij, Med. Doct. Phyfici Franco-furt. Ordinarij, Academ. Leopoldino Imperialis Theophili, Compendium Alchymist. Novum, *Sive* Pandora Explicata & Figuris Jllustrata. Das ist, die Edelste Gabe Gottes, Oder Ein Guldener Schatz, Mit welchem die alten und neuen Philosophi, die unvollkommene Metall, durch Gewalt des Feuers verbessert, und allerhand schädliche und unheylsame Kranckheiten innerlich und ausserlich, durch deren Würckung, vertrieben haben. Dieser Edition wird annoch, nebst vielen Kupffern, und über 800. Philo-sophischen Anmerckungen, ein vollkomenes Lexicon Alchy-mifticum Novum, und ein vollständiges Register Rerum & Verborum, beygefüget.

Franckfurt und Leipzig, Verlegts Johann Zieger, 1706.

8vo. Engraved Title, printed Title (red and black), Pre-faces by Vogel, Faust, Reusner, in all, 2 sheets. Text, pp. 1071. Index Yyy—Llll 1. (in all pp. 194).

Lexicon, pp. 104. Summarischer Begriff, pp. 236, fol-lowed by 1 leaf.

The book should contain 19 symbolical plates.

This is a reprint of No. 72 above, to which are added copious extracts from a great variety of alchemical authors by way of elucidating the text. This reprint is not in Mook's list.

117.—1718. Eröffnete Geheimnisse Des Steins der Weisen oder Schatz-Kammer Der Alchymie, Darinnen die vortrefflichsten Schrifften derer berühmtesten alten und neuern Scribenten denen Liebhabern der Kunst dargestellet werden. Nebst vielen Kupfferstichen und andern dazu dienlichen Figuren.

. Hamburg, Bey Christian Liebezeit und Theodor Christoff Felginer, 1718.

4to. Title (red and black), Preface, Contents, 8 leaves. Text, pp. 816.

There is a portrait of Paracelsus as frontispiece.

This is a reprint of the *Aureum Vellus* of which two
editions have been previously referred to, viz., the first in
4to, 1598-99, No. 2, and the second in small 8vo, 1599,
No. 88. It is not in Mook's list.

118.—1738. Phil. Avreoli Theophrasti Paracelfi Bombaft von
Hohenheim, Welt-beruhmten *Philofophiæ* und *Medicinæ
Doctoris,* wie auch *Phyfices Profefforis Publici Ordinarii*
auf der Universität Basel, Geheimes und vollständiges
Wunsch-Hütlein, welches deutlich und gründlich anweiset,
wie nicht nur die meisten Ertze in ihre drey Principia
dergestalt zu zerlegen, dass sie so wohl in der Chymia als
Medicina sehr dienlich seyn können, sondern auch der
Philosophische Stein in kurtzer Zeit glücklich zu bereiten
sey; Aus dem wahren und rechten Manufcripto, nebst
einer Vorrede von der Ankunfft, Leben und Tod des
Auctoris, wie auch einem Register, Allen Freunden und
Untersuchern der edlen Spagyrischen Wissenschafft zum
besten, nunmehro zum öffentlichen Druck befördert worden
durch Sincerum Aletophilum, Cultorem Hermeticæ Scientiæ
Eclecticum. Erfurt, in Comiff. bey Aug. Crufio, 1738.

Small 8vo. Pp. 89. [1; Register, 6]. Symbolic frontispiece, included in the pagination. Title red and black.

Mook (No. 232) quotes this at full length, including the
date. But for one or two changes in the punctuation this
title is quoted correctly.

119.—1771. Philippi Aureoli Theophrafti Paracelfi Chymischer
Psalter, oder Philosophische Grundsätze vom Stein derer
Weisen Anno 1522. *omnia ab uno, omnia ad unum.*
Aus dem höchst seltenen lateinischen Grundtext übersetzt,
von einem Liebhaber natürlicher Geheimnisse 1771. Ber-
lin, bey dem Antiquarius Johann Friedrich Vieweg.

Small 8vo. Pp. [16] 36.

Mook (No. 238) contracts *Joh. Friedr.* Why?

120.—1791. Philippi Aureoli Theophrafti Paracelfi Chymischer Psalter, oder Philosophische Grundsätze vom Stein derer Weisen Anno 1522. *omnia ab uno, omnia ad unum.* Aus dem höchstseltenen lateinischen Grundtext übersetzt, von einem Liebhaber natürlicher Geheimnisse. Neue Auflage. Berlin, bey Friedrich Maurer, 1791.

8vo. Pp. [16] 36.

This, which seems to be actually a new edition, in whole or in part of the preceding number, is not mentioned by Mook.

121.—184–? Philippi Theophrasti Bombast von Hohenheim, Paracelsus genannt, Geheimniss aller seiner Geheimnisse, welches noch niemals wegen seiner unvergleichlichen Fürtrefflichkeit ist gemein gemacht, sondern allezeit in Geheim gehalten worden. Nach seiner eigenen Handschrift. von einem unbekannten Philosopho mitgetheilet. Nebst einem Anhang und noch mehr anderen fast unglaublich raren Curiositäten, welche noch niemals offenbar worden.

No place, publisher or date.

16mo. Pp. 75, followed by a blank page, and 4 pages of book advertisements

This is a recent cheap reprint, apparently one of Scheible's, of a book, editions of which appeared in 1746 and 1750, and possibly in 1686 and 1770. These are all quoted by Mook, but this reprint he has overlooked.

§ 2. The preceding list might be left to itself to say whether the criticism of 1877, based on eleven titles, has or has not been substantiated by other seventy. It may be as well, however, to compare the results now obtained with the former.

§ 3. The main charges brought against Mook's study were

these four—(1) want of accuracy ; (2) want of systematic
description ; (3) omission of authorities ; (4) incomplete-
ness.

§ 4. (1) *Want of Accuracy*. To the misprints formerly
enumerated (*Bibliographia Paracelsica*, 1877, § 9) might be
added others, thus: p. 13, *Petrus Ramnus* for *Petrus Ramus ;*
p. 39, *Leo S. Luavius* for *Leo Suavius ;* p. 41, Bemerkung,
Berthoneae for *Bertheoneae ;* p. 46, No. 148 for No. 136 ;
p. 104, No. 199 for No. 196. Again : on p. 3 Mook quotes
" Meiners, III. B. p. 345," but without either naming the
book or inserting this author in his so-called index of
" exact titles," and, similarly, on p. 15, " Brucker, Pars. IV
p. 646 folg.," without saying which of the two treatises
under Brucker's name in the same index he intends to be
consulted.

But the titles themselves are more than sufficient evidence
of the general inaccuracy of Mook's work. If the preceding list be analysed it will be found that there are only two
or three titles which, as given by Mook, are quite free from
typographical and other variations. I do not now allude to
the omissions and alterations which occur, but to mere differences of spelling and punctuation which are constantly
to be met with in Mook's transcriptions. However, all
that can be said against Mook on this score has been
summed up by himself (No. 125, see No. 70 above) in
the spelling of the one superlative word, *acuratissimi*.
Further proof of Mook's inaccuracy is superfluous.

§ 5. (2.) *Want of Systematic Description*. In reproduc-
ing the titles Mook had a choice of two methods. One was

to give as much of a title as would serve for the identification of any work or edition. Previous writers had tried to do this, but, according to Mook, had failed ; for he complains of the *mangelhafte titelangabe* of his predecessors, as has been already said. The other method was to give the titles in full. To this he was necessarily committed both by his criticism and by his practice. Each method is useful in its own way ; the former yields a catalogue, the latter a bibliography. Adelung and Graesse, for example, have followed the former method, and their catalogues are fairly passable. Mook has followed the second method, and his bibliography is a comparative failure. It is not meant that a particular book or edition cannot be identified by Mook's list. It can be, easily—more easily, indeed, than by any other list. What is meant is that Mook has executed his own design so irregularly that not one single title as given by him can be depended upon as representing exactly what stands in the original work. His titles are unnecessarily full for a mere catalogue ; they are not scrupulously accurate enough for a bibliography. If he thought it desirable to give the whole title, why did he depart at all from the form given by the author ? He has altered the punctuation, sometimes with an alteration of the meaning ; he has altered the spelling, usually modernising it ; he has omitted portions of the title ; he has added portions to the title ; sometimes he has given the date, sometimes he has omitted it. Some of the changes noticed in the preceding list are undoubtedly very trivial, and might have been passed over. But it is Mook himself who has set the example of literal criticism, for in one place (p. 23, note 81) he observes that the form *Basiliae* occurs instead of *Basileae.* This may be nothing else than a misprint, but, whether or not, Mook has shown by his noticing it that he was sufficiently alive to such minute differences. It is impossible, therefore, that he could be unaware of the changes that he himself has made in the course of his transcriptions.

One of the most notable irregularities is to be found in Mook's treatment of dates. Sometimes the date is given along with the title, but it is oftener omitted, and it is difficult to see what has been the guiding principle in either one case or the other. He has, too, more than once shown himself at a loss to know when a book is dated and when not. When books have no figures on them anywhere at all, he is compelled to put them in a section by themselves, though sometimes he makes a guess at their date from the printing, or the name of the printer, or some other circumstance. In consequence of his putting in the date, or missing it out, or of giving a conjectural one, Mook has left it occasionally in doubt as to whether a book is actually dated or not. He himself seems to be of opinion that a book is absolutely dated only when the year appears on the title-page. When that is not the case his difficulties begin. It is unnecessary to give instances; the following may suffice. It is to be found on p. 64, 1572, No. 95 : Drey herrliche Schrifften, etc. I quote Mook's description: "8°. Ohne Jahrzahl, Druckort und Seitenzahl. Am Ende steht: 'Getruckt zu Basel, bey Samuel Apiario MDLXXII.'" In its way that is perfect. After this, it is not surprising that a book that has only a chronogram is described as "*s. a.*," although it has found its way into the correct year. On the other hand, books undated really are put under certain years, on the strength of the date at the end of some dedicatory epistle, or of the preface. Altogether it cannot be said that Mook's treatment of dates is by any means successful and satisfactory and consistent, and the same may be said of other details as well.

§ 6. (3) *Omission of Authorities.* As I have deliberately avoided quotation from bibliographers in the present list, and have confined myself to actual copies of the books, I have nothing to add to what was said on this subject in the former part.

Mook only certifies books that he has seen, and his authorities are the copies in different libraries. He himself says that Wolfenbüttel was one of the few European libraries he did not visit. To these unvisited libraries I am inclined to add the British Museum, notwithstanding Mook's frequent references to it.

§ 7. (4) *Completeness.* Upon this point also there is no more to say than that Mook has missed more than a score of the books mentioned in the preceding. Two or three cannot fairly be considered as Paracelsian works, and Mook has correctly omitted them; others are reprints, which he ought not to have ignored; a few are quite unknown to him, and of others he knows the titles only at second hand. Some of the English books have escaped him, and this is singular; for if he had paid attention to those in the British Museum he would have filled up several blanks in his list.

§ 8. From what has now been said, it appears to me that my original conclusions are more than confirmed.

1. Mook's catalogue contains most of Paracelsus' works and editions. It is the most nearly complete that has appeared, though a considerable number have been overlooked by him.

2. It is quite possible to identify a copy of any of Paracelsus' works by Mook's description of it.

3. Though the list is nearly complete in numbers, it is imperfect and quite unreliable in its bibliographic descriptions, and it is devoid of numerical data for the comparison of copies.

We hear much of the characteristics of German research —its minuteness, its exhaustiveness, its accuracy. Mook does not think the work of Marx and Haeser distinguished by these qualities, and Mook's own work has been proved to be distinguished by their absence. Is, then, the work of Mook and his predecessors typical of that German devotion, thoroughness, and patience, which we are told we ought to copy as closely as possible? In my opinion, the only use that can be made of such a model as the work of Mook is to avoid it.

If in future I find anything more to say about Paracelsus and his books, it will be apart from special criticism of the so-called "Critical Study" of Dr. Friedrich Mook.

BIBLIOGRAPHIA PARACELSICA.

CONTRIBUTIONS

TOWARDS

A KNOWLEDGE

OF

PARACELSUS

AND

HIS WRITINGS.

PART III.

BY

JOHN FERGUSON, LL.D., F.S.A.

PRIVATELY PRINTED.

GLASGOW:
Printed at the University Press
BY ROBERT MACLEHOSE, 153 WEST NILE STREET.
1890.

100 Copies printed.

In this investigation I originally engaged with some degree of interest, inasmuch as Mook seemed to me to be criticising the errors of others with a severity, which could hardly have been excused had his own work been immaculate, but was quite indefensible when it proved on examination to abound in the very errors and defects he was complaining of. The previous parts were accordingly occupied with an enumeration of blemishes apparent in Mook's work, and with certain general conclusions deduced therefrom as to its bibliographic value.* Attention enough having been bestowed in the meantime on these matters I have turned to topics which suggested themselves to me during the earlier stages of this research as not having been taken up by Mook, and relating to which I collected material as I went along. I have considered that it may not be out of place in continuation and extension of what I have already printed to add this

* When, in 1885, the second and more detailed part was printed, I was not aware that Mook was no longer alive, otherwise one or two phrases, which I believed I was addressing to a still living author, might have been modified.

material as a contribution to Paracelsian bibliography. It has, however, become so bulky that at present I must confine myself to the following lists, and look to a future opportunity for printing other portions of my collections.

In this part are included :

I. A description of books by Paracelsus, acquired since the last part was printed.

II. A list of the works of Paracelsus in English.

III. A reprint from Leo Suavius of the first catalogues of Paracelsus' works.

IV. Corrections of my former lists and additions to them.

JOHN FERGUSON.

THE UNIVERSITY,
GLASGOW, *July*, *1889*.

PARACELSIAN BIBLIOGRAPHY

Continued.

§ 1. The following are the titles of books attributed to Paracelsus, which have come into my possession since printing Part II. of this research, and the method of description hitherto followed has been continued. The titles are brought forward now not to make further display of Mook's defects, but to increase the tale of Paracelsus' works, so far as I can, by examination of them myself ; simply, therefore, as a record of facts for reference and comparison. But, in describing a Paracelsian book it is impossible, as it is unadvisable, to overlook what Mook may have said about it, and to refrain from indicating wherein his account agrees or disagrees with the copy under consideration, and it will not fail to be observed that, as on almost every previous occasion, so on this, though Mook has described the books after personal inspection, he has done so in a strangely, almost unaccountably, inaccurate way, and thus the new titles give additional force to all that I have already said relative to the imperfections of Mook's work. In fact, with almost every fresh title, the mistakes multiply. Believing, as I did at first, that the discrepancies which I had observed, originated in carelessness and inattention, I thought it only fair to the writers with whom Mook had found fault, that the shortcomings of their critic should not be allowed to pass unchecked. Continued consideration, however, supplemented by facts about Mook personally which have only recently come to my knowledge, has led me to the different conclusion that there was some peculiarity about Mook which prevented him observing with sufficient attention to detail, or recording what he observed with sufficient precision; that, with a genuine desire and a strenuous effort to make a complete and reliable catalogue of Paracelsus' books from the books themselves, he was somehow without the capacity for carrying out his plan thoroughly. I have consequently ceased to attach significance to Mook's variations, to care to criticise them, to hold him altogether responsible for them, or to feel more than curiosity as to their extent. About their existence in a given case there need hardly be a doubt, for I believe now that the normal condition of a title as given by him is to be inaccurate, or incomplete, or both, and that should one happen to be correct, or nearly so, it is by accident, and not by any care on his part.

That this peculiarity of mind should have exercised such an influence is much to be regretted, for it has deprived Mook's work of the one important quality, accuracy.

Nothing more, however, can now be made of it, and Mook's catalogue, if it cannot be relied on for exact bibliographic comparison, is still, and will likely continue to be, indispensable as a reference list, besides being, as I have formerly remarked, the fullest that has been published up to the present time.

§ 2 :—

122.—1549. Propheceien vnd Weissagungen. Vergangne, Gegenwertige, vnd Künfftige Sachen, Geschicht vnd Zufäll, Hoher vnd Niderer Stende, Den Frommen zu ermanung vnd trost, Den Bösen zum schrecken vnd warnung, bisz zum ende, verkündende. Nemlich :

Doctoris Paracelsi,
Johan Liechtenbergers,
M. Josephi Grünpeck,
Joan. Carionis,
Der Sibyllen, vnd anderer.
Innhalt vorgestelten Registers, Auszgelegt, vnd durch Figuren angezeygt.

Small 4to, ff. 128. At the end is the date : M.D. XLIX. There is no place or printer's name. At the foot of the title-page is a vignette, representing two men ; one, to the right of the reader, has a book; the other, to the left, is holding up in his left hand a kind of astronomical circle ; both figures are pointing with the right forefinger to the sun, moon and stars in the sky. In the background are a town and a castle, and a sheet of water with a swan. In the upper left hand corner is a head with lines from its mouth, to represent the wind ; the right hand corner is filled with clouds. Besides the vignette, there are 32 symbolic figures in Paracelsus' tract; 42 in Liechtenberger's, and 14 pictures of sibyls.

Mook (No. 16) describes this book. He writes *Prophezeien, und, Vergangen, Gegenwärtige, Künnfftige*, and omits the comma before *verkündende*. As all the rest corresponds exactly with the above, I have no doubt that these are alterations of Mook's own. Paracelsus' *Prognostication* occupies leaves 2-20. Mook says it is a reprint of the German edition of 1536, omitting the dedication to Archduke Ferdinand and the epilogue. The figures are identical with those in the Latin edition of the same year (*Bibliographia Paracelsica*, Part II., 1885, No. 49).

123.—1554. Für Pestilentz. Ain seer nützlicher vnnd bewerter Tractat, der Christlichen gemayn zu nutz vnd wolfart, ausz desz weitberuembten vnd hocherfarnen Doctoris Philippi Theophrasti Paracelsi Buch gezogen. Welches Er, von diser Khranckhait beschriben. Dariñ vil vnnd manicherlay

Latwergen, Püllel, Wasser, Confect vnd Puluer, Sampt
annderñ Preseruatifen erfunnden werden. Damit sich die
Gesunden in disen geschwinden leüffen der regierenden
Pestilentz bewaren mügen : Auch, wie den Khrannckhen,
so mit disem Gebrechen behafft, soll geholffen werden &c.
Disz alles, nach ordnung jnnhalt volgunds Registers, jñ
sechs Thayl: Vormals ın Truckh nye kommen: verfertigt.
Das Büchel zu der Christlichen gemayn.
  Zu deinem nutz thue khauffen mich,
  Dañ es wirdt nit gereuen dich.
1554.
Getruckht in der Ertzbischoflichen Statt Saltzburg, durch
Hansen bauman. Mit Röm. Kö. May. Freyhait, in vier
jarñ nit nach zutruckhen.

 Small 4to. Title, red and black. On the verso is the
epitaph and the coat of arms, with the mottoes : *Pax vi-
—uis requies* | *æterna—fepultis*, and *Omne donum perfectū
a Deo,* | *Imperfectum a Diabolo.* Exhortation of brother
Egidius Karl of Saltzburg, Aa ij to Bb iij recto. On the verso
the Contents, to Cc ij verso; in all ff. 10, not numbered.
Text, ff. xxxxIII. The leaf following contains errata, and
the colophon : Getruckht in der Ertzbischoflichen Statt
Saltzburg, durch Hansen Bawman, von Rottenburg auf der
Tauber. jm̃ jar. M.D. Liiij.

 Mook (No. 20) omits the period after *Pestilentz ;* writes
vnd for *vnnd; Der* for *der ; weitberumbten* for *weitberuembten ;* omits the comma after *Er ;* writes *Kranckhait* for
Khranckhait, erfunden for *erfunnden.* Omits all from *Damit*
to *geholffen werden &c.* inclusive, and substitutes *&c.* Omits
the comma after *alles;* has *volgends* for *volgunds;* and omits
Das Büchel to *1554* inclusive, without indicating the
omission in any way, even by an *&c.*, and curtails the whole
concluding sentence about the printing. Upon Mook's
use of the sign *&c.* to denote omissions by him of part of a
title, I shall have occasion to say something under No. 124.

124.—1564. Drey Bücher, Durch den Hochgelerten Herrn Theophraſtum von Hohenheim, Paracelſum genant, beider Ertzney Doctorn, den Hochwirdigsten, Hoch vñ Ehrwirdigen, Wolgebornen, Gestrengen, Hochgelerten, Edlen, Vesten, Fürsichtigen, Ersamen, Erbarn vñ Weisen Ertzbischoffen, Bischoffen, Prelaten, Grauen, Freiherren, Ritteren, vom Adel, vnd Landtschafft des Ertzhertzogthumbs Kärnten &c. zu ehren geschriben.

Das erst Buch, die verantwortung vber etzlich verunglimpfung seiner miszgunner.

Das ander, von dem Irrgang vnd Labyrinth der Artzten, dasseyin anderē Büchern lehrnen sollen dann biszher geschehen.

Das dritt, von dem vrsprung vñ herkommem der Tartarischen kranckheiten, nach dem alten namen vom Stein, Sandt oder Griesz, auch heilung der selbigen.

Darbey ist vorm ersten Buch ein warhaffter kurtzer auszzug der Kärntischer Chronick.

Gedruckt zu Cöln, Durch die Erben Arnoldi Byrckmanni. Anno 1564.

Mit Keis. Maiest. Gnad vnd Freyheit.

Small 4to. Title, red and black. Paracelsus' address to all the dignitaries of Carinthia, dated S. Veit, August 24, 1538, a2—a4. Account of Carinthia, b1—b4. Text, pp. 292. Epitaph and coat of arms, 1 leaf, followed by a blank leaf.

The tracts are: Verantwortung, pp. 1—52. Labyrinthus Medicorum Errantium, pp. 53—135; Von den Tartarischen Kranckheiten, pp. 136—292.

Mook's variations (No. 40) may be taken in order: comma omitted after *Bücher* and after *Hohenheim ;* *genannt* instead of *genant ;* from *Wolgebornen* to *Weisen* (both included) omitted, and *&c.* substituted; from *Grauen* to *Ritteren* omitted, and *&c.* substituted; the comma after *Adel* omitted, and also after *ander ;* *lehren* instead of *lehrnen ;* comma after *Cöln* omitted; the date and privilege omitted.

Long ago (*Bibliographia Paracelsica*, 1877, p. 16) I pointed out that it was difficult to be sure when *&c.* occurred in one of Mook's titles whether it belonged to the title originally, or was used by him to indicate portions which he found it convenient to omit. In several of the following numbers examples will be given, but the present title is specially interesting. For it so happens that the original title (like No. 123) does itself contain the contraction *&c.*, yet Mook has used it also for the phrases he has left out, without considering the bibliographical confusion in which he was involving his version. For as far as he tells us all three *&c.'s* might be in the original title, or all three might have been inserted by Mook himself.

125.—1566. Das Buch, Meteororvm, des Edlen vnd Hochgelerten Herrn Avreoli Theophrasti von Hohenheim, Paracelfi genant, beider Artzney Doctoris. Item : Liber Qvartvs Paramiri de Matrice. Vor in Truck nie auszgangen. Cum gratia & Priuilegio Imperiali.

Gedruckt zu Cöln, bey Arnoldi Byrckmans Erben. Anno 1566.

Small 4to. Title, within a border, verso blank. f. [2] Portrait of Paracelsus, side face, with the superscription : Alterivs non sit. Qvi svvs esse potest. and below : Avreoli Theophrasti ab Hohenhaim. Effigies svæ ætatis 45 15 AH 38. On the reverse is the epitaph, with the shield and motto : *Pax viuis,—requies | æterna fe- —pultis.* Text of *Das Buch Meteororvm*, ff. 1—65 verso, of *Das Buch Matricis*, ff. 66—106 verso.

Mook (No. 50) has the following mistakes : the comma after *Buch* omitted ; *Meteorum* for *Meteororvm* and the comma after it omitted ; *beyder* for *beider* ; *quartus* for *Qvartvs ;* the privilege clause and *Gedruckt zu* omitted ; the comma after *Cöln* omitted ; *Byrckmann's* for *Byrckmans ;* the date omitted.

In his remarks he repeats the word *Meteorum*, and he divides the motto thus : Pax vivis—requies—æterna sepultis. This division is not only different from that in the above copy, but seems to me impossible, if the words are printed on each side of the coat of arms, in two lines as indicated by the dashes.

126.—*s. a.* [1567] *Theophrasti* Paracelsi ... Compendivm, ... Cum fcholiis in libros IIII. eiufdē *De Vita Longa*, ... *Auctore Leone Suauio I.G.P.* Vita Paracelsi. Catalogus operum & librorum. ...

Parisiis ...

Small 8vo, signatures in fours. Pp. 376, [8], [21, 3 blank].

Since describing (*Bibliographia Paracelsica*, Part II. 1885, No. 55) the British Museum copy of what I considered to be the Paris, 1566, edition of this book, I have got the present copy which introduces a new difficulty and necessitates a revision of the previous account. The two copies, except in one point, are identical throughout to the smallest detail ; they belong in fact to the same edition, so that the title-page and collation already given (No. 55) apply to this copy. The difference between the two is that in the present copy, between the close of the text on p. 376 and the *Index rerum* which follows on *i recto, there is interpolated a sheet of four leaves, having also the signature *, and containing an epistle from J(acques) G(ohory) (*i.e.* Leo Suavius): *Lodoico Sangelasio Lensaci Domino, Eqviti Torqvato, Senatori Sacri Consilii, Avgvsti Cvbicvli Præfecto, Dvci C. Virorvm Avlicorvm.* This epistle is dated at the close : Lutetiæ Cal. Ianuar. Ann. M.D.Lxvii.

At first sight it looks as if an edition had been printed about 1566, and that somewhat later this epistle had been written and had been inserted in the remainder copies, thus making it appear that there were two issues of the same edition. This explanation of the difference was so plausible that I was inclined to be content with it, until on more careful examination of the present copy I found that the Epistle of Leo Suavius to Joannes Capella, pp. 153-158, was dated at the end : Lutetiæ Parisiorum Kal. Iulii Anno 1567. Then, much to my chagrin, I afterwards ascertained that the British Museum copy contained this date also, and that I had overlooked it in my former examination of that copy, as well as in that of the Basel, 1568, reprint (No. 60). If this date be correct, it follows that the British Museum copy cannot have been printed earlier than July 1567, so that it was a mistake to assign the date 1566 to No. 55. It follows also that a Paris 1566 edition is still to discover, if such an one exist.

But after this correction is made other questions arise. What explanation is to be given of the occurrence of the letter to Sangelasius in certain copies only, and which of the sets of copies is the earlier ? I have found no distinct answer, but certain alternatives suggest themselves as possible.

There are three epistles by Leo Suavius contained in this work —:

The first to Renatus Perotus, p. 3, dated : Lutetiæ VIII. Idus Sext. Anno M.LXVI. (*sic*).

The second, to Capella, p. 153, dated : Lutetiæ Parisiorum Kal. Iulii Anno 1567.

The third, to Sangelasius (after p. 376), dated : Lutetiæ Cal. Ianuar. Ann. M.D.Lxvii.

As regards these dates, if it be assumed that there is a 1566 edition as well as one of 1567, then, the year of the second letter may be a misprint for 1566. That this is possible is obvious from the misprint in the year of the first letter, and from the misprint M.D. for M.D.XXV. on p. 13, line 24. If it be a misprint, the British Museum copy may be one of a 1566 edition, but in that case the date of the first letter is *after* that of the second letter. This also is possible, for, although the book is paged continuously from the beginning, the first letter may have been written after the second. But if the date 1567 be correct, the second letter was written eleven months after the first, and the Museum copy belongs to 1567.

But what reason is there for supposing that there is an edition of 1566 at all? It is reported by Mook (1566, Bemerkung c)) solely on the authority of Adelung (*Geschichte der Menschlichen Narrheit*, vii. p. 350, No. 29), as follows :—

Nach Adelung (VII p. 350 Nr. 29) erschien De vita longa in dem Compendium Philosophiae et Medicinae Para-celsi von Leo Suavius zu Paris in 8° in diesem Jahr. Mir ist nur die Ausgabe Basileae 1568 bekannt. Der Brief des Leo Suavius an Renatus Perotus Cenomanensis ist aller-dings datirt : Lutetiae VII Idus Sext. Anno LXVI, was für das Erscheinen in diesem Jahre sprechen würde. . . .

On referring to the passage in Adelung I find simply a list of editions of the *De Vita longa,* and the statement that it is contained in Leo Suavius' *Compendium,* Paris, 1566; but he gives no further account of it, and I have seen no other reference to it anywhere. I believe that Adelung, like myself, was misled by the date of the first letter into ascribing the book to 1566, and did not look further in the book itself for another date.

But Mook's note is of additional interest as showing that he too was inclined to the year 1566 for the Paris edition, on the ground of the date of the first letter, though his own account of the Basel edition of 1568 might have made him hesitate. For in his remarkably and unusually full collation of that edition (No. 62) he quotes as on p. 147 the dedicatory epistle of Suavius to Capella, and carefully adds that it is dated : "Lutetiae Parisiorum. Kal. July (*sic*) Anno 1567." But he does not notice that this date is eleven months after the date of the letter to Perotus, which he knew was also in the Basel edition, for he mentions it. Yet in the above note Mook does not indicate that he thinks it possible that an earlier Paris edition might contain the 1567 letter, as well as that of 1566, but trusting to Adelung has put down 1566 as a probable date.

As Adelung's statement is the only authority for a 1566 edition, and as it rests, I believe, on an imperfect examination of the book, there is no need, merely to save Adelung's accuracy, to assume actual, or to speculate about possible inaccuracy in the date of the second letter. It seems more judicious to accept the year of the second letter, 1567, as correct, and not to admit the existence of an edition of 1566, until a copy having no earlier or later date in it, has been found and described.

But whether there be a 1566 edition or not, there is still the question whether the edition of 1567 appeared at first with or without the *third* letter. To this there is no conclusive answer forthcoming ; it is, perhaps, rather more probable that the book was first issued, like the Museum copy, without the letter, which was afterwards inserted in some remaining copies, than that it contained the letter originally and was for some reason latterly issued without it. That the signature is the same as that of the sheet which follows, does not, I think, help us to either conclusion. Thus, while the fact of there being two issues is undoubted, why there should have been two remains in the meantime an unsolved bibliographical problem. In any case the third letter is subsequent to the other two, and would have been dated now January 1568. It is quite certain that the Basel edition of 1568 is subsequent to these.

This book, however, apart from its own history, is of the greatest importance as vindicating Marx's accuracy against Mook's criticism, and for this purpose it makes no difference whether or not there be a 1566 edition, so long as it can be proved that there was a Paris edition prior to that of Basel, 1568. I have referred to this matter before (*Bibliographia Paracelsica*, 1877, No. 23, and Part II., 1885, No. 55). It may be remembered that Marx, having occasion to quote Leo Suavius' catalogue of Paracelsus' works, referred to a 1567 edition of the *Compendium*. But Mook, knowing only the Basel, 1568, edition, in doubt about a previous Paris edition and refusing to accept of anything on Marx's authority, took up a quite unreasonable and indefensible position with regard to Marx's quotation. He not only tried to convict him of error because the edition of 1568 did not contain what Marx had quoted from an edition of 1567, but he even doubted altogether the existence of a 1567 edition, both because he did not know it, and more particularly because Marx had quoted it. Graesse, however, in 1864, had adduced a priced copy of this edition from Scheible, and in 1877, long before I had seen the book itself, I brought forward this quotation as proof that such an edition must almost certainly exist, and now I have given a description of two copies printed at Paris before 1568. Mook, therefore, has failed to catch Marx tripping in the date of the edition he used, and as the Basel edition of 1568, which Mook admits is the only one he knew, is quite different from that of Paris, it affords no ground whatever for the reflection he has cast upon Marx's accuracy ; it was, indeed, quite irrelevant to adduce it as a criterion at all.

There can be no doubt that on this occasion at all events Mook was wrong in his criticism of Marx. It is remarkable that it did not occur to him how improbable it was that Gohory, whose works appeared at Paris and Orleans, should have printed this one first at Basel.

But while Marx was right in the date of the edition he used, he may have made a mistake in the number of the page. On page 15 of the 1567 edition, quoted by Marx, there is an enumeration of Paracelsus' works, taken from Petrus Hassardus, but the catalogue of the works by Leo Suavius, to which Marx seems to refer, is to be found not on p. 15, but on p. 85, and I have reprinted both of these in §§ 6, 7, below. Now if Marx has here made a slip, it can be explained and may be excused. It may be a misprint; or he may have fallen into some confusion about those two enumerations; or he may have misread the number 85, which he might easily have done, for it is small and rather blurred, and anyone heedlessly or hurriedly might take it for 15. This however is not the blunder of which Mook accuses him, for, in the Basel edition of 1568, the lists appear on pages 13 and 72 respectively, and the figures are so clear as to preclude the possibility of a mistake. Marx's real error lay in quoting an edition that Mook did not know.

With the present copy the history of the book becomes more complete. It first appeared at Paris, but I am very doubtful if it was in 1566. Then came the two issues of 1567, but which was the earlier I am unable to say. The book was next reprinted at Basel (*Bibliographia Paracelsica*, Part II. 1885, No. 60). The portrait of Paracelsus was omitted, and there were added an *Apologia* by Dorn, and a letter from Perna, the printer, to Gohory, dated: Basileae, Idus Februarii, MDLXVIII.

127.—1568. De Vrinarvm Ac Pvlsvvm Ivdiciis, Theophrasti Paracelsi Heremitae Vtrivsque Medicinæ Doctoris celeberrimi Libellus, fuis Difcipulis Bafileæ, cùm ibidem publico ftipendio maxima omnium admiratione Medicinam doceret, Anno 1527. in diebus Canicularibus priuatim prælectus.

Eiufdem Phyfionomia, quantum Medico opus eft.

Omnia typis ac annotationibus vndiq; illuftrata, & in gratiam Paracelficæ Medicinæ ftudioforum nunc primum publicata.

Cum gratia & priuilegio.

Coloniae, *Apud Hæredes Arnoldi Birckmanni. Anno D.M. LXVIII.*

Small 4to, pp. 46; p. [47], errata, and colophon : Coloniae, *Typis Gerardi Virendunck.* On the title is Birckmann's device : a tree, with a bird at the foot of it, and the words : Arnold Birckman. On the reverse of the title is Paracelsus' portrait with the mottoes, and his name at the bottom.

Mook (No. 64) transcribes this title with the usual changes of *v* to *u* and *i* to *j*; he has made some slight alterations in the punctuation, and omits from *Omnia typis* to *priuilegio* and also the date.

The edition of this book printed at Strassburg in the same year was formerly described, *Bibliographia Paracelsica,* Part II., 1885, No. 61.

128.—1568. Pyrophilia Vexationvm Qve Liber. D. Phil. Theophrasti Paracelsi. *Cvi Tres Adhvc Eivsdem authoris tractatus accefferunt, quorum etiam verfa pagella Summarium indicabit.* Per Doctorem Adamum à Bodenftein ex authoris archetypo Germanico promulgati. Poftmodum per Gerardum Dorn quanto fidelius debuit, ac ratio materiæ patitur in Latinum fermonem verfi.

Basileæ, Per Petrum Pernam. 1568.

Small 8vo, pp. [5], 137. P. [138], colophon : Basileae, Per Petrvm Pernam, Anno M.D.LXVIII.

B

In this copy the word *Basileœ* has been obliterated with an ink so corrosive that it has burned through the paper. From the British Museum copy, however, I have got the name of the place and its correct spelling. On this occasion Mook (No. 66) was absolutely of no assistance, for he gives the word ·as *Basil.* which could not be correct. Mook's title otherwise differs in the most important manner from the above. He omits the phrase : *quorum etiam* . . . *indicabit,* and substitutes the following : *Primo tractatus metallorum septem. Secundo rerum naturalium tria fore principia, per demonstrationem artis igneae docetur. Tertio contracturarum origines et curae. Quarto morborum capitalium quatuor Epilepsiae, Podagrae Paralysis et Hydropisis curae.* These are short titles taken from the *Summarium.* The question arises : were there two issues or editions of this book, one with the title-page as given above, and the other with what is practically a contents-title, as given by Mook ? It is quite possible ; but I have not sufficient confidence in Mook's accuracy to accept the second title because he has so given it, and further there is strong proof against it. Mook quotes three copies of this book : one at Tübingen and one at Munich, the third in the British Museum. I have compared the last with my own copy, and they agree exactly, even to the errata. The Museum copy has not the contents-title given by Mook, and this puts him in an awkward position. If he saw the Museum copy, how did he not give the title it contains, and draw attention to the fact that it differs from his version of the title, which, if it exist at all, must be in one, at least, of the other two copies. If he did not see the Museum copy, how did he ascertain its existence ? It could only be from the catalogue ; and if he visited the Museum why did he not examine this copy ? But if he did not visit the Museum,

why does he not say that it was one of the European
Libraries he did not visit ? Lastly, if the title, as he gives
it, does not exist in any copy, whatever claim can be put
forward for him as an accurate bibliographer is entirely
destroyed, if he could make such an addition to the title-
page of a book from its table of contents. But see " Corrections and additions," § 12.

129.—*s. a.* [about 1568 ?] Avr. Phil. The. Paracelsi Chirvrgia
Minor Qvam Alias Bertheoneam intitulauit.

Cui etiam fequentes tractatus accefferunt eiufdem authoris :
De Apoftematibus, Syronibus, & Nodis.
De Cutis apertionibus.
De Vulnerum & vlcerum curis.
De Vermibus, ferpentibus, &c. ac maculis à natiuitate ortis·
Ex verfione Gerardi Dorn.
Cum Gratia & Priuil. Caef. Maieft.
Basileae. Per Petrvm Pernam.

Small 8vo. Pp. [8], containing Title, Dorn's dedicatory
epistle to Augustus duke of Saxony, and the portrait of
Paracelsus, holding his sword, all within a florid border
having the inscription : Effigies. Av. Ph. Theophrasti.
Paracelsi. Æta. Svae. 47. and below : Alterivs non sit qvi
svvs esse potest. Text, pp. 421 ; Index, pp. [5].

As my copy is bound up with Perna's edition of the
Compendium, 1568, and as the two works have been
obviously printed about the same time, I have indicated
1568 as an approximate date. Mook (p. 62, Bemerkung
b)) quotes Gesner as assigning this book to 1570. Mook
himself, however, puts it among the undated editions (No.
247) and for once reproduces the title quite correctly, with
the exception of the comma omitted after *serpentibus,* and
the privilege clause, which is also left out.

130.—1569. De Præparationibus P. Theophrasti Paracelsi, Ab
Hohenhaim Germani, Philofophi ac Medici, omnium iudicio
abfolutifsimi : Libri duo.

Cura et induſtria, ſummaqʒ fide et integritate, qua fieri potuit, ab Adamo Schrötero, Sileſio, Philoſopho et Poëta Laureato, etcet. in lucem editi. *Cum priuilegio Cæſareo ad Septennium.*

¶ *Cracoviæ.* Ex officina Typographica Mathiæ Wirzbietæ, Anno Domini 1569.

Small 4to. Signatures A—K in fours and L in six, of which 6 is blank ; in all ff. 46, not numbered.

Mook (No. 71) reproduces this title correctly, but omits the privilege clause, and makes some changes in typography and in punctuation.

131.—1570. Expositio Vera Harvm Imaginvm Olim Nvrenbergae Repertarum ex fundatiſsimo veræ Magiæ Vaticinio deducta. Per D. Doctorem Theophraſtum Paracelſum.

Anno M.D.LXX.

Small 8vo, ff. 47. f. 48 is occupied with the picture of a monster : a woman with wings, and covered with feathers, except on the head, arms, breast and legs. The legs terminate in cloven feet, which are also winged. There are two eyes at the waist ! Under the picture is the colophon : Excuſum anno poſt Chriſtum natum, M.D.LXX. There is no place or printer mentioned. The volume contains a series of 30 symbolical pictures, No. 30 serving also as a title vignette.

This—the Wodhull Copy—came into my possession shortly after Part II. of the *Bibliographia Paracelsica* was printed, and, on looking at its very brief title, I could not help thinking that surely this at least would be given accurately by Mook. But on referring to his list (No. 78) I found that fate was still against him: he has *Nurembergae* for *Nvrenbergae* of the original, and has omitted the stop before *Per*, writing that word with a lower case p.

132.—1570. Ettliche Tractatus Des Hocherfarnen vnnd berümbt-esten Philippi Theophrasti Paracelsi, der waren Philosophi vnd Artzney Doctoris.

I. Von Natürlichen dingen.
II. Beschreibung etlicher kreütter.
III. Von Metallen.
IIII. Von Mineralen.
v. Von Edlen Gesteinen.

Cum Priuilegio Cæfareo ad decennium.

Getruckt zu Straszburg am Kornmarckt, bey Christian Müllers Erben, Anno 1570.

Small 8vo, Title, Priuilegium, Dedication by Michael Toxites to Duke Ferdinand, in all pp. 16. Text: pp. 532 [4 blank].

Mook (No. 79) spells the first word *Etliche, dingen* with a capital, IV. for IIII., and omits the privilege clause. It is in a note upon this title that Mook makes the statements about Christian Müller, the confusion in which has been already pointed out (*Bibliographia Paracelsica*, 1877, pp. 14-15).

133.—1572. Metamorphosis. Doctoris Theophrasti von Hohenheim, der zerstörten guten künsten vnnd artzney, restauratoris, gewaltigs vnnd nutzlichs schreiben. Des haupt argumenten disz Buchs, erkláret das nechstuolgende blatt. Durch Doctor Adamen von Bodenstein, den anklopffenden vnd suchenden Filijs sapientiæ zu nutz, mit allem fleisz publiciert, vnnd in Truck verfertiget.

Ανέχου καὶ ἀπέχου. M.D.LXXII.

Small 8vo. Signatures in eights, except b and z, in fours; no pagination. Title, Contents, Bodenstein's letter to Archduke Ferdinand, sig. a. Paracelsus to Hans Winckelsteiner, dated Villach, 1537, b to biij recto; Bodenstein to the reader, b iij verso to b iiij verso; Text, c to z iiij. No place or printer's name.

Mook (No. 96) omits the stop after *Metamorphosis*, and the clause *Des haupt* to *blatt.* Spells *sapientie* for *sapientiæ*, *fleisz* with a capital, and omits the date.

134.—1574. Archidoxa Philippi Theo*phrasti Bombast Paracelſi Magni*, des Hocherfahrnen vnd berúmbtesten Philosophi, vnd baider Artzney Doctoris, Zehen Bücher. *Item*,

    I.   De Tinctura Phyſicorum.

    II. Teſaurus Teſaurorum.

    III. Manuale.

    IIII. Occulta Philoſophia.

Mit allem fleisz vber alle andere Exemplar corrigiert, ergentzt, vnd mit newen annotationibus erklärt. Cum gratia & priuilegio Cæſareo.

    Getruckt zu Straszburg durch Christian Müller. 1574.

    Small 8vo. Title, Contents, Preface, and Address to the Reader, A-B iij. Text, pp. 492. Printer's device and colophon, 1 leaf. The colophon is: Getruckt zu Straszburg, durch Christian Müller, Im Jahr *M.D.LXXIIII.*

This is No. 109 in Mook's list. He has omitted the commas after *Magni*, and *Philosophi*, and has " VI. Occulta Philosophia." This, of course, is a misprint for IV., though even had it been printed IV. it would still have been a gratuitous departure from the original.

135.—1574. Theophrasti | von Hohenheim, des thew | ren, hochgelehrten vnnd er- | fahrnen Philosophi vnd | Medici, | Das sechste Buch in | der artznei. | Von den Tartarischen oder Stein | kranckheiten, das ist von allen Geschlech- | ten des Steins vnnd Podagrams, | sampt derselben heilung zwen | Tractat. | Ausz eigner handt Theophrasti abgeschrie- | ben, vnd jetzundt erst an tag gegeben | Durch M. Georgium Forberger | ausz Meissen. | 1. Thessal. 5. | Probiert alles, vnd behaltet was gut ist. | M.D.LXXIIII.

    Small 8vo. Collation: title-leaf; dedication to Hans Heinrich vom Rhein, pp. iij.-ix.; Contents, p. x.; Prologus of Valentius Antrapassus Sileranus, pp. xj-xvj. Contents of the two tractates, pp. xvij-xix.; the first tractate, pp. xx-lxj; the second tractate, pp. lxj-lxxix.; at the foot is the colophon: Gedruckt zu Basel, bey | Samuel Apiario, in verle- | gung Petri Pernæ. | Mit Röm. Keys.

May. Freyheit. | On the reverse is Apiarius' device: a bear climbing a tree to reach a bee's nest.

As this book is not included in his list by Mook, he cannot have seen it. But in his Bemerkung b) to the year 1574, he quotes from Adelung (VII. p. 347, Nr. 12) and from Gesner (*Bibl. univ.* 1583) a book which I have no doubt is the present one : "Sechstes Buch in der Arzeney von Tartarischen Krankheiten. Basel 8°." From Murr (*Neues Journal zur Literatur und Kunstgeschichte*, Leipzig, 1799, p. 281, B. II. Nr. 19) he quotes: "Von den tartarischen oder Steinkrankheiten. Basel 1574," and thinks that it may be identical with No. 106 in his list. But No. 106 is the 1574 edition of the " Labyrinthus vnd Irrgang der vermeinten Artzet," to which is added "von vrsprung vnd vrsachen des griesz, sands, vnd steins, so sich im menschen befinden, kurtzer begriff," edited by Adam von Bodenstein, quite a different treatise from the present. The title of the book quoted by Murr corresponds exactly with that now described, and not at all with Mook's No. 106. This is a specially rare edition, as, besides being unknown to Mook, it does not occur in the British Museum Catalogue. Compare No. 124 above, and Huser, 1589, vols. II. and IV., for the two tracts respectively.

136.—1585. Cyclopaedia Paracelsica Christiana. Drey Bücher von dem warē vrsprung vnd herkommen der freyen Künsten auch der Phyſiognomia, obern Wunderwercken vñ Witterungen, darinn ausz der H. Schrifft mit beständigen grund nach notturfft dargethan würt, dasz alle freye Künst, als Schreiberey, Rednerey, Rechnūg, Singkunst, Erdmesserey, Gestirnkunst, sampt der Naturkündigkeit vñ Artzneykunst, nit ausz menschlichen vermeinten erfindungen, sonder allein von Gott dem Allmächtigen, als vom reichen vberquellenden Bronnen herkoñen, dasz auch solche Künst allein bey Gott durch den Glauben gesucht, vnd inn den

Büchern Gottes vnnd seiner Diener bezeuget, vnnd gelehrt sollen werden.
Erstlichen von einem Anonymo liebhaber der warheit zufaṁen getragen vnd gestellt, vnd jetzt vbersehen, corrigiert, gebessert vnnd inn Truck verfertiget von Samuele Sidero-crate Brettano Fürstlichem Speirischen Medico zu Brüssel.

Anno M.D.LXXXV.

Small 4to. Title; dedication to Johan, bishop of Strass-burg, by Siderocrates, dated Brussels, June 22, 1583; preface, containing a short summary of the book, pp. [18]. Text of the first book, pp. 174. The second book, "Physiognomia," has a separate title and pagination: pp. [8], 122; but pp. 81-6, have been dropped, although the signatures are quite consecutive. The third book treats "von oberen Wunderwercken vnd Witterungen," and has also separate title and pagination: pp. [5] 66. The general title is printed in black and red.

In this title Mook (No. 150) reads *nicht* for *nit* and omits all from *dem Allmächtigen* to *gelehrt sollen werden*, inclusive, writing *&c.* instead. I have already pointed out that it is impossible to be sure when *&c.* is used as Mook does here, whether it forms an actual part of the title, or that something is left out. In this case comparison shows that it is no part of the title. If Mook was of opinion that it was unnecessary to reproduce the whole title he should have employed some more precise method of implying the omission. For other examples of the same defect see Nos. 123, 124, and 141.

137.—1588. Pandora: | Das ist, | Die edlest Gab | Gottes, oder der werde vnd | heilsame Stein der Weysen, mit wel- | chem die alten Philosophi, auch Theo- | PHRASTVS PARACELSVS, die vnvoll- | kommene Metallen durch gewalt des Fewrs | verbessert: sampt allerley schedliche vnd vn- | heilsame kranckheiten, jnnerlich | vnnd eusserlich haben | vertrieben. | Ein Guldener Schatz, | welcher durch einen Liebhaber | dieser Kunst, von seinem Vndergang | errettet ist worden, vnd zu Nutz allen Menschen, für- | nemlich den Liebhabern der Paracelsischen Artz- | ney, jetzt widerumb in Truck | verfertiget.

Getruckt zu Basel, | Durch | Sebastianum Henricpetri. | Small 8vo. Title):(1 ; Vorrede to Martin Rulandus by Hieronymus Reusnerus Leorinus D. Med., dated Basel 1 Septr., 1588,):(2 to 8. Text, pp. 1—266. Synonima, (a Vocabulary, or brief-explanation dictionary) pp. 267— 317. p. [318] blank. p. [319] Colophon : .Getruckt zu Basel, | Durch | Sebastianum Henricpetri. | Anno | cIɔ Iɔ xxcviii. | p. [320] printer's device : right hand from a cloud holding a hammer and bringing it down on rocks which seem to be flaming, within a scroll border.

This edition contains all the curious symbolical pictures of the preceding one, only they are not so sharp. The vocabulary is in smaller type. This is a simple reprint.

Mook (p. 84) did not see this edition but quoted it on the authority of Spachius under 1588. Compare *Bibliographia Paracelsica*, Part II. 1885, No. 72, for the 1582 edition.

138.-- 1599. Theophrasti Paracelsi Medicinae D. Labyrinthvs Medicorvm Errantivm : *In quo vniuerfa Phyfica & Medica breuiter explicatur; Medicinae vanitas & abufus notatur, & veritas rectusque vfus demonftratur.* Cui acceffit Dialogvs, De Crisi Et Catacrisi Mali Cvivsdam Medici. Nunc denuo recognitus, Notis & Indice illuftratus in lucem editus.

Hanoviæ, apud Guilielmum Antonium, MDXCIX. Small 8vo. Pp. 192. Index, pp. [7], 1 blank.

For *Medica*, Mook (No. 169) writes *Medicina;* for *explicatur*, *explicantur ;* for *vanitas, veritas;* for *Hanoviæ, Hannoviæ;* and he omits the comma after *Dialogus.* Nothing need be said of the usual typographical changes, but the preceding is a fair allowance of inaccuracies for one short title, not designedly chosen to exhibit them.

139.—1615. The translation into English of certain of Paracelsus' prognostications by James Maxwell, will be referred to among the English editions, § 4, VIII.

140.—1629. Medicina Diastatica. *hoc est* Singularis Illa Et Admirabilis ad diſtans, & beneficio mumialis transplantationis operationen & efficaciam habens, *Qvæ ipſæ* Loco Commentarii in *Tractatum Tertium De Tempore ſeu Philoſop. D. Theoph. Paracelſi*, Multa, eaⷸve ſelectisſima abſtruſioris philoſophiæ & Medicinæ arcana continet *Opera & Studio,* Andreæ Tentzelii Philoſoph. & Med. D. Archiatri Schwartzburgici.

> *Jehnæ Sumtibus Johannis Birckneri Bibliop. Anno 1629.*
> 24°. Engraved and printed titles, dedication, index, preface, in all, pp. [16]. Text, pp. 188.

In this title (No. 207) Mook's alterations are mainly typographical, diphthongs are expanded, *et* is put for *&*, and so on. Positive mistakes are small: the stop is omitted after *Diastatica;* the comma after *Multa* and after *Studio;* for *ſeu Philoſop.* he writes *ſeu Philoſoph.;* for *Jehnae* he puts *Jenæ*, and he omits the year. He calls the book 8vo, whereas the signatures are in twelves, and it is quite a small volume.

The *Medicina Diastatica* was translated into English, see below, No 143, and Mook, No. 215.

141.—1631. Les XIV. Livres Des Paragraphes De Ph. Theoph. Paracelse Bombast, Allemand, tres-grand & tres-excellent Philoſophe, & tres-celebre Docteur en la Medecine ; Prince des Medecins Hermetiques & Spagiriques.

> *Où ſont contenus en Epitome ſes ſecrets admirables, tant Phyſiques que Chirurgiques, pour la curation tres-certaine & methodique des maladies estimées incurables ; A ſçauoir la Lépre, l'Epilepſie, Hydropiſie, Paraliſie, Phtiſie, Aſthme, Diſſenterie, Gonorrhées, accidents de Matrice, Fièvres, & autres.*
> Plus vn abregé des preparations Chimiques, de tous

fimples, vegetaux, animaux, & metalliques, trouué efcript de la main de Paracelfe, auec le moyen affeuré de les adminiftrer en toutes maladies.

Vn autre Difcours . excellent du mefme Autheur, de l'Alchimie, contre les erreurs & abus de la Medecine Humorale & Galenique, contenant des chofes tres-rares & vtilles.

Traduicts du latin en françois, auec explications, & annotations tres-amples. Par C. De Sarcilly, Efcuyer, fieur de Montgautier, Caunille, Culey, Canon, &c. tres-expert en la doctrine Paracelfique.

Oeuures non encor veus, & tres-neceffaires à tous Medecins, Chirurgiens, Apothiquaires, & à tous gents curieux de leur fanté.

Nihil tam ocultum, quod non aliquando reueletur.

A Paris, De l'Imprimerie de *Jean Guillemot*, ruë S. Iean de Beauuais. M.DC.XXXI.

4to. Title, Epistle to Prince Henry of Savoy, To the reader; pp. [8]. Apologetic Preface ; pp. 37. Paracelsus' Epistle : pp. [3]. Text of the Books of Paragraphs : pp. 119, following page blank. Preparation of drugs : pp. [7, 1 blank]. Of Alchemy : pp. [9, 1 blank], text, pp. 39, [1 blank]. Epitaph : pp. [2].

The title of this book is curtailed by Mook (No. 211). From *& methodique* down to *Fiévres, & autres* is omitted, and instead Mook simply puts *etc. ;* from *contenant* to *vtilles* is omitted and *etc.* is substituted ; the words *& annotations tres-amples* are omitted and *etc.* substituted, everything between *Montgautier* and *A Paris* is omitted and *etc.* is substituted, and all after *Guillemot* is omitted. Besides, there are changes in punctuation, and in typography ; the word *&* is dropped before *metalliques*, and in Mook's transcription there is the following : *Un autre Discours excellent de l'Alchimie du mesme Autheur*, which is a different arrangement from that in my own copy. This is one of the most mutilated titles which Mook has given, so far as my comparison has gone. Years before I had seen this book I had referred to it (*Bibliographia Paracelsica*, Part I., 1877, p. 16) in illustration of the doubt which Mook's method of transcription had called up as to whether the *etc.* belonged to the title originally or was introduced by Mook himself. Here again it turns out, as in No. 136, and others, that the *etc.* does not belong to the title, but is used inaccurately to signify omissions, and the same remark holds good, that if Mook thought certain titles were too long to be given in their entirety he should have chosen some other notation than *etc.* to indicate the omitted portions.

142.—1633. The Secrets of Physick and Philosophy, . . . firſt written . . . by . . . Theophraſtus Paraſelſus, and now publiſhed in the English Tongue by John Hester.

For the description of this work, see the English editions, § 4, IX.

143.—1653. Medicina Diastatica.

For the description of this work, see the English editions, § 4, XIII. The British Museum, 1036, a. 18, contains a copy.

144.—1663. Paracelſus His Archidoxis, Or, Chief Teachings; Compriſed in Ten Books, . . .
London, . . . 1663.

Here ought to be given the account of this edition of the *Archidoxes*, which I quoted formerly (*Bibliographica Paracelsica*, 1877, No. 8) from Will. Cooper, and a copy of which I have recently acquired. I have preferred, however, to insert it in the list of English translations, where it can be more easily compared with the editions dated 1660 and 1661. See § 4, XXI.

145.—1684. Aureoli Theophrafti Paracelfi kleine Hand- und Denck-Bibel, oder Einführung zu der geheimden Weiszheit und verborgenen Warheit desz Geistes Gottes und unsers Herrn Jesu Christi. Worausz zugleich desz gottseligen Autoris Glaube, Hoffnung und Liebe, wider das Vorgeben seiner Verleumder und Lästerer klärlich kan ersehen werden, Nun benebenst einem sonderbaren Tractätlein, genant, Untersuchung desz Glaubens. Jm 5. B. M. c. 11. vers. 18. (So fasset nun diese Worte zu Hertzen, und in eure Seele, und bindet sie zum Zeichen auff eure Hand, dasz sie ein stätiges Denckmal vor euren Augen seyen.) zusamt dem Haupt-Schlüssel der Paracelsischen Arcanen. Vor die Liebhaber, zum Druck befördert.

Franckfurt und Leipzig, Verlegts Andreas Luppius, Buchhändler in Nimmägen. An. 1684.

12mo. Title, Thölden's preface, Paracelsus' preface, Contents, Paracelsus' prayer, and epitaph, pp. 14. Text, pp. 284. *Haupt-Schlüssel*, or Tenth book of the *Archidoxa*. pp. [20].

The above title has been altered by Mook (No. 227) in his characteristic way. He writes *kann* for *kan; des Glaubens* for *desz Glaubens;* also omitting the stop. What follows runs thus in Mook's transcript: "Im 5. B. c. 11 vers. 18 &c." which leaves the reader completely bewildered as to what book is meant, and whether the *&c.* is part of the title or is inserted by Mook. Mook calls the bookseller *Lippius,* and repeats this spelling in his note, and he omits the date.

146.—1736. Theophrafti Paracelfi Kleine Hand und Denck-Bibel, oder Einfuhrung zu der geheimen Weisheit und verborgenen Wahrheit des Geistes GOttes und unsers HErrn JEsu Christi, Nebst einem sonderbaren Tractat, genannt, Untersuchung des Glaubens, Zu samt dem Haupt-Schlussel der Paracelsischen-Arcanen, Fur die Liebhaber aufs Neue vermehrt, und zum Druck befördert.

Muhlhausen, Bey Christoph Friderici, 1736.

8vo. Portrait and Title, Paracelsus' preface, prayer, and epitaph, pp. [16]. Text, pp. 328. Contents, pp. [8]; *Haupt-Schlüssel*, or tenth book of the *Archidoxa*, pp. [30] [2 blank]. Title red and black.

Mook's transcription (No. 231) differs in the following details: he puts a hyphen after *Hand;* writes *vnd unseres ; nebst; Zusammt*, and omits the date. I am happy, however, to be able to agree with Mook in his condemnation of the portrait of Paracelsus which precedes the title-page.

This is apparently the fourth edition of a work which is probably not by Paracelsus. The editions are: 1605 (Mook, No. 179), 1684 (see above, No. 145), 1715 (Mook, No. 228), and the present one, 1736.

II.

ENGLISH EDITIONS OF PARACELSUS' WORKS.

§ 3. In the course of these researches I have naturally taken special note of the English editions of the works of Paracelsus, and have described them whenever actual copies have come under my observation. With a few exceptions, all the works which, I believe, exist in English, have been already enumerated in the preceding general lists, but for convenience of reference I shall now bring them together and complete the account of them by adding the hitherto omitted titles. After all the total number is not large. When one considers the prominent place Paracelsus occupied in the medical world in the sixteenth, and even in the seventeenth century, the large number of works of which he is the reputed author, and the multitude of editions of them which appeared, it is surprising how few of them were translated into English. There may have been two causes for this: one, possible dislike to Paracelsus himself, his doctrines and his advocates; the other a general distaste the English had, and have even now, to translations. There does not seem to be a sufficient number of learned men, or sufficient energy and interest among the unlearned to make translation remunerative in any shape. In the case of Paracelsus the students were comparatively few and the labour of translation fell into the hands of two or three persons. John Hester, John

Howell, (?) John French or Freake, (?) W. D., H. Pinnell, R. Turner, must be considered as Paracelsus' disciples, who made some of his writings accessible to students in this country. To them the mere English reader must still repair, if he desire to have some notion of Paracelsus' views, for nothing by Paracelsus and very little about him, has appeared in this country for the last two hundred years. The student, however, will have to exercise patience, considerable patience, before he can become the gratified possessor of the little volumes. They are all extremely rare and some of them seem quite unattainable. There are, indeed, not many books of the seventeenth century so difficult to lay hands on as the translations of Paracelsus.

Besides those enumerated here which were printed, there were others, of which translations were made or making, but, so far as I know, they never saw the light as printed books. MSS. of these may survive, but I have not yet had opportunity of making a research on this subject. One cannot help regretting that Richard Russell, who by 1678 had translated two and a half out of the three volumes of Paracelsus' works, either did not live to finish his translation, or did not get the necessary encouragement to publish it. I may hereafter recur to this part of the bibliography.

In the following list I have thought it unnecessary to reprint the titles which have been given already at full length in the general catalogue, and have contented myself with referring to these. Remarks, however, have been added in all cases where I have acquired additional information since the titles were originally printed.

§ 4:—

1.—1575. The Key of Phylosophy, the first Part. London.

This is the first edition, so far as I have ascertained. There is no copy in the British Museum, and the only mention of it is by Will. Cooper, in his *Catalogue of Chymicall Books*, London, 1675, sig. C2, from whom I quoted it in *Bibliographia Paracelsica*, 1877, No. 12. It is not mentioned by Lowndes, either under "Key" or "Philosophy," or under "Hester, John," the name of the author or compiler. Watt does not quote this edition, but only that of 1596. It is not in any library catalogue which I have consulted, nor is it spoken of by either Ames or Herbert. If it exist at all, therefore, it must be of the highest degree of rarity. For other parts and other editions see under 1580, 1596, and 1633.

II.—1575. "Joyfull newes out of Heluetia, from Theophr. Paracelfum, declaring the ruinate fall of the papall dignitie; alfo a treatife againft Vfury. By Steph. Batman." Octavo.

This is given by Herbert (*Typographical Antiquities*, London, 1786, II. p. 891) under John Allde, who was the printer. From Herbert it is quoted by Watt and Lowndes, as I have already shown (*Bibliographia Paracelsica*, 1877, No. 48). It is not in the British Museum, and I have not met with a copy elsewhere.

III.—1580. "The firft part of the Key of Philofophie. Wherein is contained mofte excellent fecretes of Phificke and Philo- ˋfophie, deuided into twoo Bookes. Jn the firfte is fhewed the true and perfect order to diftill, or drawe forthe the Oiles, of all maner of Gummes, Spices, Seedes, Rootes, and Herbes, with their perfect tafte, fmell, & vertues. Jn the feconde is fhewed the true and perfect order to prepare, calcine, fublime, and diffolue all maner of mineralles, and how ye fhall drawe forthe their Oiles and Saltes, whiche are moft wonderfull in their operations, for the health of mannes bodie. Firft written in the Germaine tongue by the mofte learned Theophraftus Parafelfus (*sic*), and now publifhed

c

in the Englifh tongue by Ihon Hefter, practitioner in the Arte of diftillation. 1580. At London. Printed by Richard Day, to be fold at the long fhop at the Weft Ende of Paules." It is dedicated by the author " To the righte reuerende Father in God, and his fingular good Lord Jhon Watfon,—Bifhop of Winchester, and Prelate of the——order of the Garter." Then, an addrefs " To the reader." The firft part contains befides, D5, in eights.

" The Key of Philofophie. The feconde parte. Con-tainyng the orderyng, & preparyng of all Metalles, Miner-alles, Alumes, Salts, and fuch like. For Medicines both inwardly, and outwardly, and for diuers other vfes. At London printed by Richard Daie. Cum priuilegio." On the back begins an addrefs " To the Reader." The fignatures are continued from the firft part to G, in eights. On the laft leaf, " Well beloued Reader, I would here haue fet forthe diuers & fondry other fecretes, but that tyme would not fuffer me, the whiche ʃ meane God willing here-after to fette forthe to thy great profite & commoditie " W. H. Octavo.

This account is given by Herbert (*Typographical Antiquities*, London, 1785, I. p. 682). I omitted it when referring to the book before. Herbert's account is repeated as usual by Dibdin (*Typographical Antiquities*, London, 1819, vol. IV., p. 181). Lowndes somehow mentions only the first part as having been printed in 1580, but Cooper (*Catalogue of Chemical Books*, 1675, sig. Q4; see *Bibliographia Paracelsica*, 1877, No. 12) seems to include both parts in the title he gives. The copy of an edition printed by Richard Day, which I described under No. 12, un-fortunately wants the general title page and the pre-liminary matter, and though it has the title-page of the second part, there is no date. Unless, however, it be a copy of the edition of 1580, I do not know what it can be. At any rate it was edited by John Hester, and as far as it goes it corresponds exactly with Herbert's collation.

IV.—[1584.] "A hundred and fourtene experiments and cures of the famous Phiſition Philippus Aureolus Theophraſtus Paracelſus, Tranſlated out of the Germane tongue into Latine. Whereunto is added certaine excellent and profitable works by B. G. a Portis Aquitano *(sic)*. Alſo certaine ſecretes of Iſack Hollandus concerning the Vegetall and Animall worke. Alſo the Spagerick Antidotarie for Gunſhot of Iofephus Quirſitanus. Collected by I. H." On the back, "A briefe declaration of thoſe things which are contained in this Treatiſe." Dedicated "To the right worſhipfull Walter Raleigh Eſquier.[q]—I. Heſter. . . . An Apologeticall Preface of Maſter Barnard G. Londrada A Portu Aquitanus vnto the Booke of experiments of Paracelſus, wherein is prooued that ſick bodies ſtuffed and filled with the ſeeds of diſeaſes, can hardly be cured without Metalline Medicines: contrarie to the writings of ſome which denie that mettals (after what ſort or manner ſo euer they be prepared) may profite or helpe the nature of man. . . . B. G. Londrada *&c.* vnto the gentle reader, health." H 2, in eights; See p. 1290. Neat White letter. W. H. Octavo.

This account is also given by Herbert (*Typographical Antiquities*, London, 1790, III. pp. 1717, 1718). The book has no date, but according to Herbert's note about Sir Walter Raleigh it cannot be later than 1584; it is therefore the earliest edition of the collection, that of 1596 being probably the second. It is to the 1596 edition Herbert refers in his direction: "See p. 1290." There is no copy of this undated edition in the British Museum, but according to the catalogue, there is a copy in the Bodleian, which I could just quote in Part I., 1877, No. 42.

I have quite recently examined this copy, the description of which is as follows :—

[q] He was knighted between Decemb. 1584, and Febr. 1585. Oldys's Life of him, p. xxv.

A hundred and

fourtene   experiments   and   cures
of   the   famous   Phifition   Philip-
pus Aureolus Theophraſtus Paracel-
fus, Tranſlated out of the Germane
tongue into the Latine.
Whereunto is added certaine excellent and profita-
(*sic*) table workes by B. G. a Por-
tu Aquitano.
Alfo   certaine   fecretes   of   Ifack   Hollandus
concerning   the   Vegetall   and
Animall worke.
Alſo the Spagerick Antidotarie for
Gunſhot of Iofephus
Quirſitanus.
Collected by
I. H.

Small 8vo; neat small print; no pagination, but signatures.   Collation :—

[f. 1]   Title; on the reverse: "A brief declaration of thoſe
things which are | contained in this Treatiſe."

[f. 2]   To the right | worſhipfull, Walter | *Raleigh Esquier.* |
signed I. H.

B 1 *r*   An Apologeticall Preface of | Maſter Barnard G.
Londrada A | Portu Aquitanus vnto the Booke of experi-
| ments of *Paracelſus,* wherein is prooued that ſicke bodies
| ſtuffed and filled with the ſeeds of diſeaſes, can hardly be
| cured without Metalline Medicines: contrarie to the
wri- | tings of ſome which denie that mettals (after what |
ſort or manner ſo euer they be prepared) | may profite or
helpe the nature | of man. | Ends B 8 *v.*

B 1 *r*   *B. G. Londrada A Portu Aquitanus | vnto the gentle*
reader, health.

B 1 *v*   An hundred and 14. Expe- | *riments and cures of Philip*
| Theophraſtus Paraſelſus....   Ends B 8 *v.*

C 1 *r*   B. G. L. P. *Penotus Londrada* a portu ſan- | tæ Mariæ
Aquitanus, greeting. | .... [Then]

A Treatife of certaine particulars, whereof the firft | in-treateth of the preparation of the Markafite | of leade afwell for the tranfmutation of | Mettals, as for the alteration | of mans bodie, &c. Ends C 7 *r.*

C 7 *r*   *A Fragment out of the Theorickes | of* Io. *I | caacus* (sic) *Hollandus.*

C 8 *v*   *The order to draw forth the Quintaeffence* (sic) *of Su-| gar, collected out of the vegitable and Animall | workes of Ifack Holander. |* Ends E 4 *r.* The verso is blank.

F 1 *r*   The Spagericke Antidotarie. Ends H 2 *r.* The verso is blank.

Register : 2 ff. B 8, B 8, C 8, D 8, E 4, F 4, G 8, H 2.

It will be observed that Herbert's account differs in some small points from the present one, the most important being in the number of leaves ; he has not drawn attention to the fact that sheets E and F have only four leaves each.

v.—1590.

An excellent Treatife

teaching howe to cure the French-Pockes: with all other difeafes arifing and growing thereof, and in a manner all o-ther fickneffes.

Dravvne out of the Bookes of that learned *Doctor and Prince of Phifitians, Theo-phraftus Paracelfus.*

Compiled by the learned Phillippus Herma-nus, Phifition and Chirurgion. And now put into Englifh by Iohn Hefter in the Spagiri-call Arte, practitioner.

AT LONDON,
Printed. Anno, Dominj.
1590.

Small 4to. Title. ¶ ii. *r.* Hesters Epistle to "the Maifter Wardens, and generall Assistants of the fraternitie of Chirurgions in London," to ¶ iii. *r.* iii-*v.* To the Reader. iv. Table. Text, pp. 63. At the end of the text : Printed by Iohn Charlwood. The following page contains : Faultes escaped in the Printing. The text is in black letter, all the rest is in roman.

I quoted this book originally from Will. Cooper *(Catalogue of Chemical Books,* London, 1675, sig. Q4, *Bibliographia Paracelsica,* 1877, No. 13). Subsequently I examined the copy in the British Museum (1174, b. 4 (1)), from which I have taken the present account. The book is briefly mentioned by Herbert *(Typographical Antiquities,* London, 1786, II. p. 1101).

VI.—1596.

The first part of the Key
of Philofophie.
Wherein is contained moft excellent
fecretes of Phificke and Philofo-
phie, diuided into two
Bookes.
In the firft is fhewed the true and perfect
order to diftill, or draw forth the Oiles,
of all maner of Gummes, Spices, Seedes,
Roots and Herbs, with their per-
fect tafte, fmell and
vertues :
In the fecond is fhewed the true and perfect order to prepare, calcine, fublime, and diffolue al maner of Mineralles, and how ye fhall drawe forth their Oiles and Saltes, which are moft woonderfull in their operations, for the health of mans bodie. Firft written in the Germane tongue by the moft lear-ned Theophraftus Parafelfus (*sic*), and now publi-fhed in the Englifh tongue by IOHN
HESTER, practitioner in
the Art of disftillation
¶ Imprinted at London, by
Valentine Simmes.
1 5 9 6.

16mo, signatures in eights. Title. Hester's Epistle Dedicatorie to John Watson, Bishop of Winchester, A3-A5. Hester to the Reader, A6-A8. Verso of A8 is blank. Text of Part I., B-E5, pp. 1-57; p. 58 blank. E6, or p. 59, contains the title of Part II. as follows:

THE KEY OF
Philofophie
The fecond Part.
Containing
The ordering and preparing of all Met-
talles, Mineralles, Allumes, Saltes, and
fuch like: for medicines both inwardly
and outwardly, and for diuers other v-
fes.
Jmprinted at London by
Valentine Simmes.
1 5 9 6.

Verso blank; E7-F1 (=pp. 61-66), To the Reader. Text of Part II., F2-H8, or pp. 67-111; last page blank. Black letter, except the titles, introductions, head-lines, and headings of the sections. A copy is in the British Museum 1033. d. 2 (2).

So far as comparison is possible this is an exact reprint of the copy of R. Day's 1580 edition, omitting the advertise-ments at the end of each part. Day's edition however is more sharply printed, as usual. This work is not mentioned by Herbert or by Dibdin.

VII.—1596. A hundred and foureteene Experiments and Cures of the famous Phyfitian Philippus Aureolus Theophrastus Paracelfus; Tranflated . . . by John. Hester.

This book has been already described *Bibliographia Paracelsica*, Part II., 1885, No. 86. There is a copy in the British Museum, 778. e. 41 (1) and it is given by Herbert, *Typographical Antiquities*, London, 1786, II. p. 1290.

VIII.—1615. In this year was published a work entitled: Admirable and Notable Prophefies, vttered in former times by 24. famous Romain-Catholickes, concerning the Church of *Romes* defection, Tribulation, and reformation. *Written First In Latine, & now publifhed in the Englifh tongue, both by* Iames Maxwell *a Refearcher of Antiquities. London,* Printed by *Ed: Allde* for *Clement Knight,* and are to be fold at the holy Lambe in S. *Paules* Churchyard. *Anno Dom.* 1615.

It is a small 4to, of 10 preliminary leaves, containing the title, with an elaborate border, the dedication, a catalogue of the author's productions and the contents; pp. 164 of text, and 1 leaf of errata.

Among the prophecies are included several taken from the *Prognosticatio* of Paracelsus. They will be found in sections 12, 13, and 16 of the present work.

This can hardly be called a translation of Paracelsus, but it is the only representation in English of the *Prognosticatio,* that I know. It is not mentioned by Mook.

IX.—1633. The Secrets Of Physick and Philosophy, Divided into two Bookes: In the firft is fhewed the true and perfect order to diftill, or draw forth the Oyles of all manner of Gummes, Spices, Seedes, Roots, and Hearbs, with their perfect tafte, fmell and vertues.

In the fecond is fhewed the true and perfect order to prepare, calcine, fublime, and diffolue all manner of Minerals, and how ye fhall draw forth their oyles and Salts, which are moft wonderfull in their Operations, for the health of Mans Bodie.

Firft written in the German Tongue by the moft learned *Theophraftus Parafelfus* (sic), and *now publifhed in the Englifh Tongue,* by John Hester, Practitioner *in the Art of Distillation.*

London, Printed by *A. M.* for *William Lugger,* and are to bee fold at the Pofterne Gate at Tower Hill. 1633.

Small 12mo. Title; The Epistle Dedicatorie, from Hester to Bishop John Watson of Winchester, A3·8. To the Reader, A8-12. Text of the first part, pp. 1-99; p. 100 blank. P. 101, title of the second part, as follows: Secrets of Phisicke And Philosophie. *The fecond Booke*, Containing The ordering and preparing of all Mettalls, Mineralls, Allumes, Saltes, and fuch like, for medicines both inwardly and outvvardly, and for divers other ufes. Printed at *London* by *A. M.* for *Will. Lugger*, and are to be fold at the *Pofterne gate* at *Tower-Hill.* 1633.

P. 102 blank; To the Reader, pp. 103-115; p. 116, blank. Text of the second part, pp. 117-196. The Table: K3-K9; the colophon, K10 :—London, Printed by *A. M.* for *William Lugger*, and are to be fold at the Pofterne Gate at Tower hill. 1633. A1 is wanting in this copy.

This is a reprint of the work which appeared in 1575, 1580, and 1596, and which has been already referred to (*Bibliographia Paracelsica*, 1877, No. 12). It was unknown to Mook.

X.—1650. A New Light of Alchymie : . . . Also Nine Books of the Nature of Things, Written by Paracelsvs. . . .

This is the first edition of Sendivogius' alchemical writings and it is rare. I described it under No. 3 in Part I. 1877.

XI.—1650. Under this year Mook quotes from Adelung (*Geschichte der menschlichen Narrheit*, VII. p. 354, No. 46) an English translation of the " De Mineralibus, s. de generatione Metallorum et Mineralium und de mysteriis naturæ, London, 4°," and adds that he is unable to say whether the statement is correct or not. I have not met with such a book, though it quite possibly exists. What seems to come nearest to it is the 1657 edition of the " Chymical transmutation and generation of Metals and Minerals."

XII.—1652. Three exact pieces of Leonard Phioravant Knight, . . . whereunto is Annexed Paracelsus his One hundred and fourteen Experiments: . . .

See *Bibliographia Paracelsica*, Part II., 1885, No. 105, where the book is described, and *Notes on Books of Secrets*, Part V., where, under Fioravanti, I have endeavoured to give in detail the separate editions of the tracts collected in this reprint. To that account must now be added the undated edition, No. IV., above given. There is a copy of the 1652 edition in the British Museum, E. 642. See below, " Corrections and additions."

XIII.—1653. *Medicina Diaſtatica* Or Sympatheticall Mumie: *Containing*, Many myſterious and hidden Secrets In *Philosophy* and *Physick*.

By the {
Conſtruction
Extraction
Transplantation
and *Application*
} of *Microcoſmical* & *Spiritual* Mumie.

Teaching the *Magneticall* cure of Diſeaſes at Diſtance, &c.

Abſtracted from the Works of Dr. *Theophr. Paracelsvs :* By the labour and induſtry of *Andrea Tentzelius*, Phil. & Med. *Tranſlated out of the Latine* By Ferdinando Parkhurst, Gent.

Η ὃϑσα πάντα, καὶ κομίζεται φύσις.

London, Printed by *T. Newcomb* for *T. Heath*, and are to be ſold at his Shop in *Ruſſell-ſtreet*, neer the *Piazza's* of *Covent-Garden*, 1653.

16mo. Title, Epistle Dedicatory, Epistle to the Reader, Verses, Table, pp. [24], Text, pp. 128.

This title is given by Mook (No. 215) from the copy in the British Museum. There are some slips in copying, as usual : no comma after *Containing*; instead of *Microcosmical & Spiritual*, Mook writes *Microcosmical et Spiritual*, a printer's solecism, against which one has to be ever on the watch. If the printer had not the contraction &, the word *and* should have been substituted, of course. Similarly, *et* is written for & in the other two places where it occurs. Mook writes *Theoph.* for *Theophr.*, omits the motto, and all after *T. Heath.* He also turns the words *By the* into line with the rest of the title, instead of printing them across. This is a translation of No. 140.

xiv.—1656. Paracelsus of the Supreme Mysteries of Nature.

Described in *Bibliographia Paracelsica*, 1877, No. 5. I have since got another copy which corresponds with the previous one throughout.

Mook gives the date 1655, from the British Museum copy. I have examined the Museum copy (E. 1567 (2)); it is dated 1656, and I have failed to find in the Museum a copy dated 1655. It is not impossible, however, that a copy with that date may exist. See below " Corrections and Additions."

xv.—1656.

PARACELSVS

HIS

DISPENSATORY

AND

CHIRURGERY.

THE

DISPENSATORY

Contains the choifeft of his Phy-
fical Remedies.

And all that can be defired of his

CHIRURGERY,

You have in the Treatifes of *Wounds,*
Vlcers, and *Apofthumes.*

Faithfully Englifhed, by W. D.

LONDON:

Printed by *T. M.* for *Philip Chetwind,* and
are to be fold by Stationers. 1656.

12mo. Title, To the Reader, Table and Contents, pp. [24]. Text, pp. 407 ; last page is blank.

From the copy in the British Museum. E. 1628.

P A R A C E L S U S

OF

The { Chymical Tranfmutation, } of Metals &
{ Genealogy and Generation } Minerals.

Alfo,

Of the Urim and Thummim of the Jews.

WITH

An Appendix, of the Vertues and Ufe of an
excellent Water made by Dr. *Trigge.*
The fecond Part of the *Mumial Treatife.*
Whereunto is added,
Philofophical and Chymical

E X P E R I M E N T S

Of that famous Philofopher

R A Y M U N D   L U L L Y ;

Containing,

The right and due Compofition of both Elixirs.
The admirable and perfect way of making
the great Stone of the Philofophers, as it
was truely taught in *Paris*, and fometimes
practifed in *England*, by the faid *Raymund
Lully*, in the time of King *EDW.* 3.

Tranflated into Englifh by *R. Turner* Φιλομαθής.

London, Printed for *Rich: Moon* at the feven Stars, and
Hen: Fletcher at the three gilt Cups in *Paul's*
Church-yard. 1657.

8vo. Title, Turner to Wm. Bakehouse of Swallowfield,
Turner to the Reader, Verses to Turner, ff. 4. Text:
Metals, pp. 1—45 ; Urim and Thummim, 46—71 ; Trigge's
Essential Water, 72—78 ; Tentzelius, 79—96.

Then, p. [97 :]
Philofophical and Chymical
E X P E R I M E N T S ,
OF The
Famous PHILOSOPHER
R a y m u n d   L u l l y.
Wherein is contained,
The right and true Compofition
OF
Both Elixirs and Univerfal Medicine :
The   admirable   and   perfect   way
of   making   the   great   Stone   of   the
Philofophers,   as   it   was   truely
taught in *Paris*, and fometimes pra-
ctifed in *England* by *Raymund Lully*
in the time of K. *Edward* the third.

Now for the the (*sic*) Benefit of all Lovers of Art
and Knowledge, carefully tranflated into Englifh, out of High-German and Latine, by *W.*
W. Student in the Celeftial Sciences, and
Robert Turner, Φιλομαθής.

LONDON,
Printed by JAMES COTTREL, 1657.

p. [98] blank. Preface to the Reader and the Contents,
pp. [99—102]. Text pp. 103—166.

This was quoted in Part I., 1877, No. 6, but the title was
not given in full. This book, without the title page, was
afterwards associated or issued with the work of John
Heydon, entitled *The Rosie Crucian Crown.* There is a
copy of the *Chymical Transmutation* in the British Museum,
E. 1590 (3).

XVII.—1657. Philosophy Reformed & Improved . . .

This volume contains *The Philosophy to the Athenians*
by Paracelsus, the translator being H. Pinnel. It was

described in Part I. No. 7. I have since got another copy, which contains a portrait of Paracelsus as frontispiece. There is a copy in the British Museum, E. 1589 (1).

XVIII.—1569. . . . Aurora, & Treaſure of the Philosophers, . . . *Bibliographia Paracelsica*, Part II. 1885, No. 108. A copy is in the British Museum, 8907. a.

XIX.—1660.

Paracelſus

HIS

ARCHIDOXIS:

Compriſed in

TEN BOOKS,

Diſcloſing the Genuine way of making *Quinteſſences, Arcanums, Magiſteries, Elixirs,*&c.

Together with his BOOKS

Of RENOVATION *&* RESTAURATION.

Of the TINCTURE *of the Philoſophers.*

Of the MANUAL *of the Philoſophical Medicinal* STONE.

Of the VIRTUE *of the* MEMBERS.

Of the THREE PRINCIPLES.

And Finally his Seven BOOKS,

Of the DEGREES *and* COMPOSITIONS *of* RECEIPTS, *and* NATURAL *Things.*

Faithfully and plainly Engliſhed, and Publiſhed by, *J. H.* Oxon.

London, Printed for *W. S.* and are to be ſold by *Thomas Brewſter* at the *Three Bibles* in *Pauls Church-yard.* 1660.

Small 8vo. A 1—3 ; A 4, containing a Poſtcript to the Reader, wanting ; B—L8, in eights ; A—L8, in eights.

Though this has been already given (*Bibliographia Paracelsica*, 1877, No. 8), I repeat the title-page here, that its form may be compared with that of the issues of 1661 and 1663 which follow.

xx.—1661.

Paracelſus

HIS

ARCHIDOXES:

Compriſed in

TEN BOOKS,

Diſcloſing the Genuine way of making *Quinteſſences, Arcanums, Magiſteries, Elixirs,* &c.

Together with his BOOKS

Of RENOVATION *&* RESTAURATION.

Of the TINCTURE *of the Philosophers.*

Of the MANUAL *of the Philoſophical Medicinal* STONE.

Of the VIRTUES *of the* MEMBERS.

Of the THREE PRINCIPLES.

And Finally his Seven BOOKS,

Of the DEGREES *and* COMPOSITIONS *of* RECEIPTS, *and* NATURAL *Things.*

Faithfully and plainly Engliſhed, and Publiſhed by *J. H.* Oxon.

London, Printed for *W. S.* and are to be ſold by *Samuel Thomſon* at the Biſhops Head in *Pauls* Church-Yard, 1661.

Small 8vo. Title, The Epistle to the Reader, signed ͵. H. ; A Postscript to the Reader (about Basil Valentin's *Chariot of Antimony* and translation of Paracelsus' *Paramirum*, which is described as nearly ready) ; Errata, in all pp. [8]. Text : pp. 158. Contents [2]. A Book of Renovation and Restauration, &c., pp. 171. Contents [1].

This, a nice large copy, is in the British Museum, E. 2268. On comparison it proves to be the book of the previous year, with a new title-page. The latter is printed on whiter paper, the size in this copy is smaller than the other leaves, and it is pasted to the second leaf, so that it is a substitute for the first one, which has been cancelled. The only other difference I have observed is that in the errata at the very end, p. 171, all after "put (,)" which occurs in the 1660 copy, is omitted in this. But the errata remain, of course, in this second issue, as they were.

XXI.—1663.

Paracelſus

HIS

A R C H I D O X I S,

Or, CHIEF TEACHINGS;

Compriſed in

TEN BOOKS,

Diſcloſing the Genuine Way of making *Quinteſſences, Arcanums, Magiſteries, Elixirs,* &c.

Together with his BOOKS

Of RENOVATION *&* RESTAURATION.

Of the TINCTURE *of the Philoſophers.*

Of the MANUAL *of the Philoſophical Medicinal* STONE.

Of the VIRTUES *of the* MEMBERS.

Of the THREE PRINCIPLES.

And Finally his Seven BOOKS,

Of the DEGREES *and* COMPOSITIONS *of* RECEIPTS, *and* NATURAL *Things.*

Engliſhed, by *J. H.* Oxon.

London, Printed for *Lodowick Lloyd,* and are to be ſold at his Shop at the *Castle* in *Cornhil,* 1663.

Small 8vo. Title, Epistle and Postscript to the Reader and Errata, pp. 8; Text of the Archidoxis, pp. 158; Contents [2]. Book of Renovation, &c., pp. 1-90. Book of Degrees, pp. 91-171. Contents [1].

In my first description (*Bibliographia Paracelsica,* 1877, No. 8) of the 1660 edition of this book I mentioned that Mook (No. 222) had quoted that of 1661, and that there was possibly a third edition of 1663. The present volume is a copy of this last issue, which, like that of 1661, consists merely of certain copies of the 1660 edition with a new title-page. This edition is omitted by Mook and I do not know where another copy, besides that which has been now described, is to be found.

XXII.—1674. A New Light of Alchymy: . . . also Nine Books of theNature of Things, written by Paracelsus, . . . translated . . . by J. F.

This is an 8vo reprint of the 1650 edition of the same collection. The description is given in Part I. 1877, No. 10.

XXIII.—1697. Arcana philosophia. . . . Likewife Four . . . Treatifes . . . by . . . Dr. Aurelius Philipus Theophraftus Paracelfus, of Hoheneim. Publifh'd by John Headrich.

Quoted first from the Bodleian Catalogue (*Bibliographia Paracelsica*, 1877, No. 41), afterwards described from an actual copy (Part II. 1885, No. 114).

XXIV.—s. a. Philosophical and Chymical Treatise of Fire and Salt.

This book is ascribed to Paracelsus by Will. Cooper, but I have not had the fortune to meet with a copy. There is another work with a similar title by Blaise de Vigenere, London, 1649, small 4°, but whether they are different or not I am unable to say.

III

THE FIRST CATALOGUES OF PARACELSUS' WORKS.

§ 5. I have thought it worth while to reprint certain lists which if not the earliest are certainly among the earliest bibliographic summaries of Paracelsus' works. They are taken from the *Compendium* of Leo Suavius, about which I have already had to say so much. In the Paris edition, 1567, they will be found on pp. 15, 84-87, and 159, and in the Basel reprint of 1568, on pp. 13, 71-74 and 155. So far as I know they have not been quoted before in any English work on Paracelsus, and though they are mentioned by Mook he has not given reprints of them. Nor do I know any work in which they appear except the present one, and as it is among the rarest of Paracelsian books, it will certainly never become a common book of reference. Whether the present reprint be of any use or not, there will be, at any rate, some interest in seeing what works were ascribed to Paracelsus, within twenty-five years of his death.

§ 6. In his preface or introduction Leo Suavius gives first a brief biographical sketch of Paracelsus, discussing his birth-place, name, ability as a chemist, and quoting the letter from Erasmus. He next speaks of his writings to the following effect.

[p. 15]. Addam fuperioribus quæ fumma
cum diligentia reperi.
Petrus haffardus in præfatione libri Chirurgiæ maioris
attribuit illi libros in Philofophia 136. in medicina 70. in
Theologia, Iuftitia, Politicis & magia complures. Quorum
plerofque iam Adamo à Bodenftein debemus, alios à Ioan.
Sculteto Montano propediem fperamus. Libri quidem illi
Chirurgiæ maioris anno præterito in manus meas inciderant
Germanica lingua nõ à Paracelfo fcripti, è quibus magnã
iam partem vertendam ab hominibus linguæ peritis
curaueram. Adiiciam Aureolum ipfum dici prænomine in
libro de Tartaro quem ego habui cum eius expofitionibus è
viua voce exceptis. Nuper prorfus alius [p. 16] editus eft
ex tertia autoris recognitione cũ defẽfionibus VII. aduerfus
medicos. Petrus quidem Haffardus Philippi etiam nomen
illi addit. Charta de noua methodo medendi mihi eadem
videtur cũ eo libello, quem Ioannes Vvierus lib. de Præ-
ftigiis Dẹmonũ damnat, fub titulo libri Paragrammon, iure
quodam vel inuidia medicæ profefsionis, quãquidem Paracelfus inuento principiorum nouorum conatus eft funditus
euertere : vnde magnas fibi à medicis fuæ regionis ætatifq;
cõtentiones excitauit, quos pafsim in omnibus libris fuis
vehemẽti ftylo perftringit. Sed præcipuè teftimonio eft
libellus VII. defenfionum, à quo refpõfum aduerfus
Vvierum petere licebit. In libro Labyrinthi latino eius
effigies expreffa An. ætatis 45. ftaturam oftendit proceram,
faciem grauem, cum fronte ampla, fincipite caluo, mediocri
capillo : circum quam erat infcriptio ei familiaris, quámq;
frequenter folebat vfurpare.
Alterius non fit qui fuus effe potest.
In lib. de Tartaro germanico, & allis quibufdam, eius
hoc epitaphium reperitur.
[After quoting the Epitaph, Leo Suavius adds, p. 17 :]
In tractatu philofophiæ illius ad Atheniẽfes (quiquidem
plenus eft myfteriorum magnorum, primorum, vltimorum,
melofiniæ (verbotenus) pyromantiæ, necromantiæ, chiro-
mantiæ, &c. titulus eft Philofophia Theoph. Bombaft ab
Hohẽhein Sueui Arpinæ germani eremi ad Athenienfes.

There are some interesting and even important notices in this extract. Pierre Hassard translated the *Chirurgia Magna* into French, of which Mook knew only the edition of 1568 (No. 69). But the allusion to it here confirms the existence of an earlier edition. Two such are mentioned: one by Borellius, dated 1566, quoted by Mook, p. 48, e); the second by Haller, de Vigiliis and Adelung, dated 1567, quoted by Mook, p. 51, c). Considering the dates it is probably the earlier one to which Leo Suavius here refers. The book *de Tartaro* may be Mook's No. 32 or 36 (my own list, No. 51), 1563, while the edition with the *Defensiones VII.* is undoubtedly that published in 1566, Mook, No. 49. The *Liber Paragrammon* is, I suppose, the *Paragranum* of 1565, Mook, No. 46.

The *Labyrinthus* with the portrait is the edition of 1553, Mook, No. 18. This seems to be the earliest likeness of Paracelsus, and, judging by the description, it is the one of which a copy is given in the present work of Leo Suavius, p. 81. It was often reproduced afterwards.

The last book mentioned is No. 52 in my list, or No. 39 in Mook's.

This is the passage of Leo Suavius which, apparently quoted by Marx, has led to Mook's difficulties and criticism, and has induced me to consider them at length. Knowing Marx's reference only from Mook's quotation, I do not feel absolutely certain that Marx after all may not have meant to refer to this passage, but as he speaks specifically of Leo Suavius' *Catalogus*, I still hold to the opinion I have already expressed that Marx meant the Catalogue on p. 85, of which a copy is next given.

53

§ 7.

[p. 84.]   V A L E N T I N V S   D E   R E T I I S
DE OPERIBVS PARACELSI
ad Lectorem.

THEOPHRASTVS Paracelſus ex nobili proſapia ſuedigena,
apud Eremitas Heluetiæ natus, ab Athenienſibus Paracelſus
magnus vocatus 230. in Philoſophia conſcripſit libros, 40. in
medica ſcientia edidit, 12. de repub. 7. in mathematicis, & tria
opera ſimul in vnum compoſuit librum, qui Theophraſtia nun-
cupatur, 66. autem libros de occultis & abſtruſis condidit.
Primum opus de archidoxis dictum, in quo declarat extractiones
& ſeparationes virtutũ ab inualido, Secundum Paraſarchum dictum,
in quo de ſummo bono tractat in æternitate, tertiũ Carboantes
dictum, in quo trãſmutationes declarat in forma & eſſe. Scripſit
Gellius Zemeus de hoc Theophraſto Germano Philoſopho ad
Paſſephallum Ceueum. Apud Germanos nũc vir adoleſcens exiſtit,
cui parem orbis non fert, qui adeò excellenter in Philoſophia,
Medicina & Mathematicis, atque de repub. & iuſtitia ſcripſit, quod
credo aut mira influentia in eo ſit natalis, aut maior ſpirituſſancti
gratia, aut immẽſa demonum [p. 85] exiſtentia. Nam inhumanum
hæc eſt perſcrutari, quod ipse vilipẽdit : ſaltem doctiorem me legiſſe
memor non ſum. Quare tu, Lector, ſyncero animo Theophraſti
ſcripta excipe, nec noua hæc antiquis meritò præferre vereare.
Vale.

PH. THEOPHRASTI
PARACELSI BOMBAST
operum quæ ad noſtram no-
titiam peruenerunt
CATALOGVS.
Libri quatuor de vita longa.
Liber de ſanitate & ægritudine.
Liber de duplici Anatomia.
Libri vii. de gradib⁹ & cõpoſitionibus, &c.
Liber de magia.
Libri tres de morbo gallico germanici ob-
ſcurè ſcripti

Liber de podagra.

    Libri germanici de duplici medicina.

Liber chirurgiæ maioris.

    Liber chirurgiæ minoris.

Libri germanici de impoſturis chirurgorū

Labyrinthus medicorum errantium.

[p. 86.]   Liber de tartaro, duplici editione ab autore recognitus, cum defenſionibus vii.

    Archidoxa Parrhiſia, alias paragrapha.

Liber de humana generatione.

    Prognoſticon xxiiii. annorum.

Libellus de Cometa viſo in Heluetia

    anno. 1531.

Liber de peſte.

    Charta edita Basileæ. anno. 1527.

de noua methodo medendi.

    Liber de aqua realgaris & mercurii.

Theologica opera nondum publicata.

    ad abbatem D. Galli interquae:

Diarium ſupra reuelationem D. Ioannis

    Opus Paramyrum.

Herbarius.

    Tractatus philoſophiæ ad Athenienses.

Liber ii. de cauſa & origine morborū.

    Item de morbis inuiſibilibus.

Plures tractatus de morbo Caduco,

    de Cholica, de Rabie, de Hydropiſi, &c.

· Libri de Thermis.

    Liber de modo pharmacandi.

SVMMATIM.

    In philoſophia libri. 230.

In Medicina lib. 46.

    De Republica lib. 12.

In Mathematicis lib. 7.

[p. 87.]   Theophraſtia, volumen continens opera 3. diuiſa in 66. libros. de rebus abſtruſis

55

Opus 1 Archidoxa
Opus 2. Parafarchus.
Opus 3. Carboantes.
L E O   S V A V I V S
IN CATALOGVM
operum Paracelfi.

N E fit fupra fidem tot effe libros à Paracelfo confcriptos, vir
doctifsimus (fecūdū Terentianū) vndecūq; Varro vt à
fuis Romanis extra inuidiæ aleà eruditifsimus togatorū appellatus,
fcripfit (tefte D. Auguftino de ciuitate Dei) quadringētos nonaginta
libros neglecto cultu verborū : quos Cicero in Academicis paucis
perftrinxit. C. Plinius fecūdus, tefte Plinio nepote fcripfit de
iaculatione equeftri lib. i. de vita Pomponii fecūdi lib. ii. Bellorum
Germaniæ. xx. Studiofos. iii. in. vi. volumina ob amplitudinem
diuifos. Dubii fermonis viii. hiftoriarum à fine Aufidii Bafsi lib.
xxxi. Naturæ hiftoriarum lib. xxxvii. opus diffufum multiplex
& tam varium quàm ipfa natura.

I. G. P.

NATURA DVCE

COMITE INDVSTRIA.

§ 8. The following supplemental list, which is printed
immediately after Suavius' dedication to Capella, dated
1567, on p. 159, may be regarded as giving indirect support
to the correctness of the date of that dedication. For it
makes it probable that the list on p. 85 was printed off
before the present titles were obtained, else they would
have been incorporated with the others. Not being so,
there may be thus indicated a break in the printing of the
book between the conclusion of the *De Vita Longa* on p.
152, and the dedication aforesaid on p. 153, represented by
the dates of the two epistles (see above § 2, No. 126),
during which time the new titles may have come to
Suavius' knowledge. These fragments of evidence all tend
towards confirming 1567, and not 1566, as the date of the
Paris edition.

LEO SVAVIVS I. G. P.
LECTORI.

A Llati funt ad me nudiuftertius, lector, libri nonnulli Th. Paracelfi quos vobis, vt in præfatione Compendii quem plurimos,
vifum eft hîc quoque recenfere.

Philofophiæ magnæ tractatus multi,
videlicet.

De vera influentia rerum.
De inuentione artium.
De tempore laboris & requiei.
De vtraque fortuna.
De fanguine vltra mortem.
De lunaticis.
De generatione ftultorum.
De Nymphis, pygmæis, Salamandris.
De animalibus ex Sodomia natis.
Opus Aftronomiæ mundi.
De Metheoris.　　Liber 4. Paramyri.
De matrice.　　Paragranum.

Item volumen aliud, continens plures tractatus.

De Phyfionomia.
De Therebintina.
De vtroque Helleboro.
De cafu matricis.
De ligno Gaiaco.
Commentarii in aliquot Aphorifmos Hip-
pocratis.

§ 9. When collating the Basel reprint of 1568 Mook
(No. 62) takes the occasion of making remarks upon these
extracts. The summary of Valentinus de Retiis he calls
"ein sehr interessantes Aktenstück," a very interesting
document. But when he comes to the catalogues he says
of the first that it is "fast ganz werthlos wegen blosser
Titelangabe," and of the second list: "ebenfalls ohne
genauere Angabe." As a statement of fact it may be, to
some extent at least, true ; but as a criticism I think that

it is strained. Meagre though it be, the list is not absolutely worthless, because most, if not all, of the works could be identified, though obviously not the editions, seeing that no dates are given. It seems unfair, therefore, to appraise a mere outline-list like the present, without any pretensions either to fulness or completeness, by a scientific bibliographical standard, which has been reached only after three centuries of development and of systematic book study. The method of describing books now was not known, nor perhaps was it required at the end of the sixteenth century. Leo Suavius' short commentary Mook calls a vindication of Paracelsus' fecundity in book making by the example of others who have been equally prolific.

IV.

CORRECTIONS AND ADDITIONS.

§ 10. Fully aware of the difficulty of achieving absolute accuracy in bibliographical work, I have kept watch on the descriptions I have already given and have endeavoured to detect errors or flaws in them, which might have escaped my notice when they were printed. Comparison with other copies than those originally used have enabled me to confirm, sometimes to correct and amplify the descriptions already given, and here and there I have detected a misprint. The results I have hitherto arrived at in this connection are contained in the following paragraphs, and to avoid confusion I have entered the remarks under the running number of the book-title and the year, so that reference to the original entry can be made at once.

§ 11 :—

5.—1656. Of the Supreme Mysteries of Nature.
London, 1656.
Small 8vo, pp. [20], 158, [4, 2].

Another copy of this treatise which I have seen corresponds in every way with that already described. The only difference is that the present copy has the leaf M 4, containing a list of books printed by Nath. Brooke, which is wanting in the other copy. Re-examination of the British Museum copy of this book gives a probable explanation of the date 1655 assigned to it by Mook. For on the title-page of it, the last figure of the date 1656, as printed, has a pen stroke drawn through it, and written beside it in ink, in a contemporary hand, is the date: "December 5, 1655." These alterations apparently mean that although the book is dated 1656, it was in reality published before the end of 1655 ; in other words, that the custom of post-dating a book printed towards the end of a year is an old one. Seeing this correction Mook may have adopted it as giving the true date, but, if so, he should have added what I have now stated.

Against this explanation, however, is the fact that a similar alteration appears in the Museum copy of *Three exact pieces of . . . Phioravant*, on the title-page of which there is written, apparently in the same hand: "Octob. 1st 1651," with a pen-stroke drawn through the last figure of the printed date 1652. Mook, however, has not taken any notice of this alteration, but gives the date as 1652 (No. 214). But from what we know now of Mook's way of working, it is quite possible that he may have examined the one volume, and never have thought of looking at the other, so that he would miss the written date in it altogether.

From these dates, however, being altered in manuscript, the conclusion seems to be almost inevitable, that there are no editions of these two books having respectively the dates 1655 and 1651 *printed* on the title-page.

49.—1536. Prognosticatio.

The copy of this tract from which I took the description given in *Bibliographia Paracelsica*, Part II., 1885, No. 49, wanted the last leaf, containing verses and the colophon, so that I was unable to say whether Mook had reproduced them accurately or not. I have since got another perfect copy which corresponds exactly with the description already given. The last leaf contains the following :

M. Tatii Ad Germaniam
Exhortatio.

Cæfareæ, Regiæq̃; Rho. Maieft. laus.

Si fapis, en Gallos fugies Germania, & Anglos
Nec tecum Venetos fœdus inire fines.
Ecce Philippæa defcendit origine proles,
Ac mundi iufto uindicat enfe nephas.
Hæc fternat Celtas, Venetos, fundetq̃; Brytannos,
Quifquis en in talem mouerit arma ducem.
Teq̃; etiam iniufti priuans Diademate regni,
Ad ueram coget Turca uenire fidem.
Vnanimi fenfuq̃; coli, ftudioq̃; perenni
Inftituet fummi numina trina Dei.
Quum ter quinq; ierint à Chrifto fæcula nato.
Et bis ter fenus, cum tribus, annus erit.
Hæc mihi cœlefti fuperûm regnator Olympo
Per fua prædici Iuppiter aftra iubet.

Excufum Auguftæ Vindelicorum, per Henricum Steyner, xxvi. Augufti,
An. M.D.xxxvi.

In the seventh verse Mook reads *enam* for *etiam*, but otherwise his copy agrees with the above. He has however made one or two typographical alterations.

60.—1568. Compendivm.
Basileae, M.D. LXVIII.
8vo, pp. 334; supplementary matter, ff. [32].

This is identical with the copy already described, but it is larger and finer.

62.—[1568.] Philosophiæ Magnae Avreoli Philippi Theo· phrasti Paracelsi ... Collectanea quædam: ...
Basileae, Apvd Petrvm Pernam.
8vo, Preliminary matter, ff. [7] (f. 8, blank, is wanting). Text, pp. 248. Index, ff. [3, 1 blank].

This is identical with the described copy.

63.—1570. Etliche Tractetlein zur Archidoxa gehörig.
    München, M.D.LXX.
    4°. Signatures, A—I iij. I iv. wanting.
This is identical with No. 63.

64.—1570. Archidoxa.
    München, M.D.LXX.
    4°. Signatures, ⚓, *, A--Z, a—g, all in fours.
This is identical with No. 64.

70.—1577. Avrora Thesavrvsqve Philosophorvm.
    Basileae, 1577.
    Small 8vo, pp. 191.
    The collation of this work formerly given was taken from
    what I should have seen was an imperfect copy, as it
    contained only the *Aurora*, and not the other tracts
    enumerated in the title. The collation of this complete
    copy is as follows: Title and Epistle, pp. [1—]7 ; *Aurora*
    8—63 [64 blank]; *Monarchia Triadis, in Unitate*, 65—127
    [128 blank]; *Anatomia Corporum adhuc viventium*, 129—
    191, with woodcuts.

76-85.—1589-90. Under these numbers I gave in Part II. 1885,
    a description of Huser's collected edition of Paracelsus'
    works in ten volumes. I have since got another copy,
    which, besides being perfect, exhibits certain variations
    that are notable, and gives me the opportunity of making
    one or two emendations in the former account.
    76.—Volume I. This agrees exactly with the description.
    77.—Volume II. The previous copy wanted the last
        leaf, containing the portrait. The present one has
        this leaf, DDd 4. On the recto is the portrait; on
        the verso is the printer's device, but smaller and
        less elaborate than in vol. I.
    78.—Volume III. This agrees exactly with the
        description.
    79.—Volume IV. In the description I have already
        given of this volume, the following correction should
        be made in line 3 : for " Ende des Vierdten," read

"Ende dess Vierdten." This correction being made, the second copy agrees exactly with the description.

80.—Volume V. In the account of this volume it should have been specified that sheet O5) (pp. 289-296) contains five leaves instead of four, an extra leaf with signature O5)ij, but not paged, being inserted between pp. 290-291; and also, that in the Appendix, pp. 177-178 are printed on a folding leaf, which is not included in the signatures. With the original description as well as with these additions the second copy agrees exactly.

81.—Volume VI. This agrees with the description.

82.—Volume VII. The second copy differs from the description by the following version of line 20 of the title: auch der selben Bereitbungen (*sic*), betreffentd (*sic*) die Artzeney, beschrien (*sic*) werden. The signatures of the last leaf, which contains the Index, are different. In the first copy they run : kk7), L7)ij, ll7)iij, where the L and ll are misprints for kk. In the second copy they run : L7), L7)ij, ll7)iij, all of which are misprints for kk. I infer from the preceding that some copies were printed off before the mistakes above quoted were noticed, that the press was afterwards corrected and other copies then printed.

83.—Volume VIII. In the former description, for : "*Index*...Separatim...Habebitvr," read "*Index*... *Separatim...Habebitvr.*" The second copy agrees with the description so far as it goes, but it has besides an Appendix, pp. 365-428, which is wanting in the other. The second copy contains also the portrait, of which the other has been deprived.

84.—Volume IX. The first copy has 6 preliminary pages only, but when complete it should have other two with the contents of the first volume of the "Philosophia." The second copy has these pages, and the two copies agree in all other respects except in the date. In the previous description I specially directed attention to the fact that the volume was dated 1591, although volumes VIII. and X. were both dated 1590. The second copy, however, is dated 1590.

This peculiarity has been alluded to by Drs. Schubert and Sudhoff,* in connection with a dispute between two German historians, Dr. Rohlfs and Dr. Proksch, one of whom asserts that the date is 1590, the other that the date is 1591. They show by comparison of copies contained in several libraries (to which may now be added the present copy) that both dates are found, and not only so, but that volume X. has sometimes the date 1590, like both of my copies, sometimes 1591. So that both these historians are right in what they affirm, and are wrong in what they deny, and their dispute is a further striking illustration of the danger of over-confident opinion and assertion in biblio-graphical questions.

85.—Volume X. The second copy corresponds with the description, so far as that goes. A folding table, however, at p. 68, should have been men-tioned. It is contained in both copies. At the end of the Appendix to this volume, the second copy has one leaf, not paged, containing a *Frag-mentvm Astronomicvm et Magicvm*, supplemental to p. 491 of volume X. This leaf has been removed from the other copy.

86.—1596. A hundred and foureteene Experiments and Cures. London, 1596.
Small 4to. Preliminary matter, ff. [8]; Text, pp. 82.

Of this collection I have recently inspected other two copies, both of which agree with that described under No. 86.

---

* *Paracelsus-Forschungen*, 1887, Heft I. p. 82. For a short reference to this work see below, § 12.

94.—1608. Rosarivm Novvm Olympicvm et Benedictvm.
In the title of the second part of this work, line 5, for *geschen* read *gesehen.*

105.—1652. Three Exact Pieces of Leonard Phioravant, Knight,...

London, 1652.

Small 4to.

A second copy agrees throughout with No. 105. See also above, No. 5 in the present section.

107.—1658. Opera Omnia.

In my notice of what Mook says on this, the Geneva edition of the works, I omitted to notice a very curious, almost ludicrous mistake that Mook has run into. He describes the portrait prefixed to the first volume, in the following terms : " Es ist dieses allerdings ein Bild, das den übrigen ihn repräsentirenden auch nicht im entferntesten ähnlich sieht: Weniges kurzes Haar, ein etwas verwahrloster Bart um Kinn und Lippen schmücken ein ausserordentlich abgemagertes ausgeprägtes Gesicht. Die Rechte hält einen undefinirbaren Gegenstand." I agree with Mook in saying that it is not the least like the ordinary portraits ; I think he rather exaggerates the haggardness of the face ; but the funny thing is that Mook did not perceive that the undefined object in Paracelsus' right hand is merely the arm of the chair he is sitting upon! Mook seems to have been so bent on finding mysteries that he could not decipher what the artist had tried to depict.

109.—1659. In the second line of the title as I have given it : De Genealogia Mineralium en Paracelso, the word "en" is a misprint for "ex."

119.—1771. Chymischer Psalter.
Berlin, bey dem Antiquarius Johann Friedrich Vieweg.
Small 8vo. Pp. [16] 36.

This is identical with the copy already described.

§ 12. In modification of what has been said above (No. 128, and elsewhere) about Mook's use of the British Museum, I am glad to be able to refer to the *Paracelsus-Forschungen* of Drs. Eduard Schubert and Karl Sudhoff, printed at Frankfurt, 1887-89. Two parts are already published, for copies of which I am indebted to the kindness and courtesy of the authors. The first part is a defence of Mook against the criticism of Dr. Rohlfs; the second contains MS. documents illustrative of Paracelsus' biography.

The first part bears directly on Mook's character as a bibliographer, a subject which has been specially considered by me, hitherto. The authors do not conceal or palliate any of Mook's faults, but they show conclusively that Rohlfs' criticism is not justified either in tone or in matters of fact. With their vindication of Mook from such criticism I thoroughly agree. Mook *had* all kinds of shortcomings, as I have myself demonstrated, but it would be unjust to deny him the credit of having drawn up the fullest and, with all its defects, the most correct catalogue of Paracelsus' works which has as yet appeared, and that too from actual personal inspection of the books. There can be no question about this.

But they have also shown that Mook was very negligent, and that he overlooked in the libraries he visited books and editions which with more attentive examination of the catalogues he could not have missed. This he did, for example, conspicuously in the Frankfurt town library, where are *two* copies of a collected German edition of Paracelsus' works, printed at Frankfurt, by Wechel's heirs, 1603, in ten volumes, quarto, which he never saw. So heedlessly has Mook allowed these books to escape him that the authors (p. 89) call it one of the most striking proofs of Mook's " oft kopflosen Oberflächlichkeit."

This, therefore, is the explanation of his having missed so much in the British Museum ; he does not seem to have had the capacity to make sure that he had examined everything. It is not that he never was in the Museum, as I have been led to think, and even to say more than once, but he simply did not exhaust the material that was available for his purpose. At first I was at a loss to comprehend how he could have visited the Museum, gone over the catalogues, and yet either not observe or not examine English and other editions which are in it, and of which he has taken no notice, as for instance, the very edition of Leo Suavius' *Compendium*, Paris, 1567, for a copy of which he had been on the outlook; but the explanation has become obvious from what is said by the authors I am speaking of.

Further insight into Mook's life and training, character and work may be got incidentally from the *Paracelsus-Forschungen*, and as a result I have been led to modify my views regarding the cause of Mook's errors and omissions as I have already stated in § 1 of the present part.

I hope hereafter to give a more detailed notice of these valuable contributions to Paracelsian literature.

BIBLIOGRAPHIA PARACELSICA.

CONTRIBUTIONS

TOWARDS

A KNOWLEDGE

OF

PARACELSUS

AND

HIS WRITINGS.

PART IV.

BY

JOHN FERGUSON, LL.D., F.R.S.E., F.S.A.

PRIVATELY PRINTED.

GLASGOW:
𝔓rinted at the 𝔘nibersity 𝔓ress
BY ROBERT MACLEHOSE, 153 WEST NILE STREET.
1892

100 Copies printed.

COPIES of Paracelsus' works are not, so far as my experience goes, becoming any commoner than they were. Without delaying, therefore, for the problematical acquisition of more of them, I have found it desirable to print the description of the few which I have examined or become possessed of since 1890. I am quite aware that it would have been easy to have swelled the present list by enumerating the copies of Paracelsus' works in the British Museum. I prefer, however, that the account of the Museum collection, which I have kept constantly in view as forming a substantive part of this investigation, should be contained by itself in one of the numbers of the series, which I hope will appear before long.

I have taken advantage of this opportunity to correct some previous errors and misprints, and to supplement one or two descriptions.

JOHN FERGUSON.

THE UNIVERSITY,
GLASGOW, *January* 23d, 1892.

PARACELSIAN BIBLIOGRAPHY

Continued.

§ 1. In the present, as in the preceding parts, the running number is continued for the purpose of reference, and the books are arranged according to their dates. The title-pages are given in full, then the collations, and lastly a comparison of Mook's versions with the copy I have had before me.

§ 2. :—

147.—1575. [THEOPHRASTI PARACELSI LIBER *De Narcoticis ægritudinibus, vt funt Pestis, Pleurefis & Prunella.*]

This is contained, pp. 83-112, (Sig. f2 *recto* to g8 *verso*) in thé book : De Secretis | Antimonii | Liber vnus | Alexandri | A Svch-|ten veræ philofophiæ ac me-|dicinæ Doctoris. | Editus Germanicè quidem anno 1570 : nunc au-|tem in Latinum tranflatus fermonem | per | M. Georgivm For-|bergium Mysium. | Cui additus [*sic*] est Geor. Phaedronis | Medici Aqvila Coelestis, | fiue correcta Hydrargyri præ-|cipitatio. | Basileae | Per Petrvm Pernam. | Anno 1575. | This is a small 8° volume, paged continuously from the title to the end, pp. 112.

Mook (No. 113) in his transcription of the title has omitted all from " Georgivm For-" to " est " inclusive, misled by the occurrence twice of the name Georgius, and oblivious of the havoc introduced into the concords in making *per* be followed by the genitive and leaving *Aquila* without any connection. It reads very funnily in Mook's version.

The above copy is in the University Library, Cambridge.

148.—1582. Avreoli Theophrasti Paracelsi Archidoxorum, Seu de Secretis Naturæ myfteriis, libri decem. *Quibus nunc accefferunt Libri duo, vnus de* Mercvriis Metallorvm, *alter de* Qvinta Essentia. Manvalia *item duo, quorum prius Chemicorum verus thefaurus, pofterius præftantium Medicorum experientiis refertum est: ex ipfius Paracelfi autographo.* Cum Indice Rerum & verborum ditifsimo. *Cum gratia & priuilegio Cæf. Maiest.*

Basileae, Per Petrvm Pernam. M.D.LXXXII

Small 8°. Title, Preface, Index, Vocabulary, pp. [24]. Text, pp. 415, including: Archidoxa, pp. 1-173; De Mercuriis Metallorum, 173-180; De Quinta Essentia, 181-199 [200 blank]; Manuale I. 201-376; Manuale II. 377-415.

Mook (No. 137) quotes this title correctly, but misprints *Paraceli* for *Paracelsi* in the first line, and omits the privilege clause and the date.

149 —1596. Theophrastisch Vade Mecvm. . Das ist: ... Durch Iohannem Hippodamum, Cherufcum. ...

Zu Magdeburgk bey Johan Francken, Anno 1596.

Cvm Gratia et Privilegio, &c.

4°. Title, Preface, Contents, A—B, in fours, or pp. [16]. Text, A—Gg, in fours, or pp. 278, numbered. The pagination, however, is very irregular, and the correct number of pages is 240. Index, Hh—Ii4 *recto;* Errata, Ii4 *verso* to Kk2 *recto.* Title red and black.

The title of this edition corresponds with that of the edition of 1597, which I have already quoted (*Bibliographia Paracelsica*, 1885, Part II., No. 87), the main difference being the date. There is no mention by Mook of any edition earlier than the two of 1597, and I have not seen the present referred to at all.

150—1603. *Nobilis, Clarissimi Ac probatiſsimi Philoſophi & Medici, Dn. Avreoli Philippi* Theoph. Bombast Ab Hohenheim, Dictl Paracelsi, Bertheonea Sive Chirvrgia Minor.

Cum tractatibus eiuſdem
{
De Apoſtematibus, Syronibus & Nodis.
De Cutis apertionibus.
De Vulnerum & Vlcerum curis.
De Vermibus, Serpentibus, ac Maculis a natiuitate ortis.
}

Cum Jndice rerum vbiuis memoratu dignarum.
Prostat In Nobilis Francofurti Paltheniano. *1603.*

4°. Title, 1 leaf. Paracelsus' Preface, dated Basel, nones of June, 1527, 1 leaf. Text, pp. 327. Index rerum to the Bertheonea, Ff2 *verso* to Gg4 *recto*.

Mook (No. 173) transcribes this correctly, except that he omits all the punctuation down to *Apostematibus*, and modernizes the spelling.

This volume forms a separate part of the Palthenian edition, of which the first five volumes were published in this same year (*Bibliographia Paracelsica*, 1885, Part II., No. 93), and the remaining six in 1605, as given in No. 153 below. Mook quotes the following prefixed (?) to the title of the copy he examined: "Prodeunt Opera Theophrasti Latina, quorum cum Chirurgia minore Partes Duodecim. In Nobili Francofurto, E Collegio Musarum Palthenianio (*sic*) iisdem vertentibus et omnia curantibus." He accounts for vols. I.–V. and this, which he calls vol. XII., appearing in 1603, and VI.–XI. in 1605 by saying that the *Chirurgia Minor* appeared independently, and was afterwards included in the complete edition with the added note. A difficulty in the way of accepting Mook's explanation is that in addition to the signature B, the first page of the sheet has also " Pars v." Is this merely a printer's error, or was this volume originally intended to be an appendix to volume v. and was afterwards printed without a number or other distinctive mark? (See Corrections and Additions, p. 23.)

The above is bound up along with No. 153.

151.—1605. Chirurgische Bücher vnd Schrifften, defs Edelen, Hochgelehrten vnnd Bewehrten Philosophi vnd Medici, Philippi Theophrasti Bombast, von Hohenheim, Paracelsi genandt: Jetzt auffs New aufs den Originalen, vnd Theophrasti eygenen Handtschrifften, so viel derselben zubekomen gewesen, auffs trewlichst vnd vleissigest wider an tag geben : Auch vm̃ mehrer richtigkeit vnd Ordnung willen, allen Leib vnd Wundärtzten, wie auch Manniglichen, zu hohem Nutz vñ Verstandt, in vier vnderschiedliche Theil, deren Begriff vnd Ordnung nach den Vorreden zufinden, verfasset : Sambt einem Appendice etlicher nutzlicher Tractat, vnd volkomenen Registren. Durch, Johannem Huserum Brisgoium, Churfürstlichen Cölnischen Raht vnd Medicum.

Strafsburg, In verlegung Latzari Zetzners, Buchhändlers. Anno M.DC.V.

Folio. Title):(1 ; Portrait):(2 ; Huser's dedication to Ernst, Archbishop of Cologne, dated : Gross Glogaw, Dec. 1, 1604,):(3 r; Paracelsus to Thalhauser, dated : Augspurg, July 23, 1536,):(3 v; Thalhauser to Paracelsus, dated : Augspurg, July 24, 1536,):(4 ; Paracelsus to King Ferdinand, Münchraht, May 7, 1536,):(5 ; Paracelsus' preface):(6 ; Contents of the Chirurgical works):(7-8 r; verso blank. Text : A to L in sixes, M-N in fours ; O to Z in sixes, Aa to Dd in sixes, Ee 8; Ff to Vv in sixes, Xx 8; Yy-Zz in sixes, Aaa to Ooo·in sixes, Ppp 4; Qqq to Zzz in sixes, Aaaa 6, Bbbb 8.

The book is divided into four parts; Introductory matter 8 ff; Part I., pp. 1-148; Title of Part II. on O i *recto;* *verso,* Contents; Text pp. 149-329. Then a blank page, and the title to Part III. on Ff 1 *recto; verso,* Contents, p. 330; Text, pp. 331-523. Then a blank page, and the title to Part IV. on Yy 1 *recto; verso,* Contents, pp. [524]-526; Text, pp. 527-680; Alphabetical Index to the four parts Mmm 3 *recto* to Ppp 4 *recto,* verso is blank. Title page to the Appendix (see next number, 152) Qqq 1 *recto,* on the verso the Contents and Huser's note to the reader; Text pp. 115. Index pp. [6], the last page is blank.

The title is printed in red and black, inside the same woodcut border as in the other works.

This copy wants the leaf):(2, which contains the portrait.

Mook (No. 176) omits the comma after *Medici,* writes *Handschrifften, soviel, zu bekommen,* inserts *vnd* before *auffs,* and omits all from *Auch vm̄* to *Registren,* substituting *etc.* He omits the comma after *Brisgoium,* writes *Churfurstlich,* omits the comma after *Strassburg,* writes *Latzeri,* and drops the date.

152.—1605. Chirurgischer. Bücher vnd schrifften defs Edelen, Hochgelehrten vnnd Bewehrten Philosophi vnd Medici, Philippi Theophrasti Bombast von Hohenheim, genant Paracelsi, Appendix Darinnen etliche Alchymistische vnd Artzneyische Tractátlein, deren eins Theils zuvor nie in Truck aufsgangen ; gantz nutzlich zu lesen. Allen der Theophrastischen waren Philosophey vnd Künsten, Liebhabern, zu gutem zusamen geordnet, Durch Johannem Huserum, Brisgoium, Churfurstlichen Colnischen Rath vnd Medicum.

Strafsburg, In verlegung Lazari Zetzners Buchhandlers. Anno M.DC.V.

Folio. Title, *verso* Contents and Huser to the Reader, sig. Qqq1 ; Text, Qqqii to Bbbb v *recto;* Index, Bbbb v *verso* to Bbbb viij *recto, verso* blank. All are in sixes, except Bbbb in 8. Text is paged 1-115. The index occupies 6 pages. Of this *Appendix* Mook (No. 177) gives merely a skeleton title.

Though, for convenience of reference to Mook's list, this *Appendix* is entered here as a separate book, it is in reality an integral part of the Chirurgical works, as is shown by the signatures running on continuously. See the preceding No. 151. These two numbers complete the first folio collected edition of Paracelsus' works, the previous parts of which have been already described under date 1603 in *Bibliographia Paracelsica*, Part II., 1885, Nos. 91, 92. For the second folio edition of 1616-18, see below, Nos. 154-156.

153.—1605. *Nobilis, Clarissimi Ac probatiffimi Philosophi & Medici, Dn. Avreoli Philippi* Theophrasti Bombast, Ab Hohenheim, Dicti Paracelsi, Operum Medico-Chimicorum Sive Paradoxorvm, Tomus Genuinus . . . Recenter Latine factus, & in vfum Affeclarum Nouæ & Veteris Philofophiæ foras datus,

A Collegio Mufarum Palthenianarum in Nobili Franco-furto. *Anno M.DC.V.*

VI. Tomus Genuinus Sextus, *E Chymicis Primus, Continens, Proceffus & præparationes Spagyricas rerum naturalium ad vfum Medicinæ : multaque alia de Tinctura Phyficorum, & cœlo Philofophorum : de Cœmentis item & gradationibus.*

4°. Title, Contents, Portrait, 2 leaves. Text, pp. 324.

VII. Tomus Genuinus Septimus, *E Chimicis Secundus, Continens, vires efficacias, & proprietates Rerum Naturalium, & earum quoad Medicinam, præparationes : Cum multis Alchimicam fcientiam fecretis fpectantibus.*

4°. Title, Contents, Portrait, 2 leaves. Text, pp. 211.

VIII. Tomus Genuinus Octauus, *E Philofophicis vero*

Primus, continens Philofophiam de Generationibus & fructibus quatuor Elementorum,

4°. Title, Contents, Portrait, 2 leaves. Text, pp. 299.

IX. Tomus Genuinus Nonus, *E Philofophicis vero Secundus, continens Arcana Naturalia & Supernaturalia, eorumq; cauffas, origines, fubftantias & proprietates,*

4°. Title, Contents, Portrait, 2 leaves. Text, pp. 239.

X. Tomus Genuinus Decimus, *E Philofophicis vero Tertius, continens Philofophiam Sagaeem* [sic] *& Aftronomiam Magnam,*

4°. Title, Contents, Portrait, 2 leaves. Text, pp. 364.

XI. Tomus Genuinus Vndecimus, *E Philofophicis vero Quartus, continens Aftronomiam Magnam cum Artibus incertis, tranfmutationibus Metallorum, Magicis aduerfus morbos figuris, & planetarum figillis.*

4°. Title, 1 leaf. Text, pp. 160. "Artificiofus Index in libros sex pofteriores medico-chymicos Paracelfi," sigs. A—D4, E2. F1 *verso.* Then, sig. F2 *recto :* Prodevnt Opera Theophrafti Latina, quorum cum Chirurgia minore Partes Duodecim, In Nobili Francofvrto, *E Collegio Mufarum Paltheniano, iifdem vertentibus & omnia curantibus.*

Mook's copies (No. 178) of these titles have not been so much altered as those of vols. I.–V. Apart from his common changes of letters and punctuation, there are the following errors and misprints : T. VII. *Alchymicam,* for *Alchimicam.* T. IX. *et* omitted before *Supernaturalia.* T. XI. *cum* omitted before *Artibus.* In T VIII.–IX. *vero* is omitted. For the twelfth volume, nominally, of this edition, containing the *Chirurgia Minor,* see above, No. 150. The copy from which the preceding has been taken is contained in the library of St. John's College, Cambridge.

154.—1616. Aureoli Philippi Theophrasti Bombasts von Hohenheim Paracelsi, defs Edlen, Hochgelehrten, Fürtrefflichsten,
Weitberümbtesten Philofophi vnd Medici Opera Bücher
vnd Schrifften, so viel deren zur Hand gebracht: vnd vor
wenig Jahren, mit vnd aufs jhren glaubwürdigen eygener
Handgeschriebenen Originalien collacioniert, vergliechen,
verbessert: Vnd durch Joannen Huserum Brisgoium in
zehen vnderschiedliche Theil, in Truck gegeben.   Jetzt
von newem mit fleifs vberfehen, auch mit etlichen bifshero
vnbekandten Tractaten gemehrt, vnd vmb mehrer Bequem-
lichkeit willen, in zwen vnderschiedliche Tomos vnnd Theil
gebracht, deren Begriff vnd Ordnung, nach der Vorrede zu
finden, sampt beyder Theilen fleifsigen vnd vollkommenen
Registern.
   Strafsburg, In verlegung Lazari Zetzners Seligen Erben.
Anno M.DC.XVI.
   Folio in sixes.   Title, 1 leaf; Huser's dedication to
Ernest, Archbishop of Cologne, dated Glogau, January 3,
1589, 1 leaf; Huser's address to the reader, and Linck's
verses to the Archbishop, 1 leaf; Contents of the first
volume, 3 leaves. This first sheet has the signature *.
Text, sigs. a—z, A—Z, Aa—Zz; AA—ZZ, AAa—BBb
vi *recto* (or pp. 1127); Alphabetical Index, BBb vi *verso*
to FFf viii *verso*, all in sixes, except FFf in eight.
   Title printed in red and black, inside an elaborate woodcut border, as in the edition of 1603 (*Bibliographia Paracelsica*, Part II. 1885, No. 91).

Mook (No. 191) merely quotes the first words as far as
" Hochgelehrten," and adds that this is a reprint with
altered orthography of the edition of 1603, Mook's No. 170,
Bibliographia Paracelsica, Part II. 1885, No. 91.

155.—1616. Aureoli Philippi Theophrasti Bombasts von Hohenheim Paracelsi, defs Edlen, hochgelehrten fürtreffenlichsten
weitberuhmbtesten Philofophi vnd Medici Opera Bücher
vnnd Schrifften, so viel deren zur Hand gebracht: vnd vor
wenig Jahren, mit vnd aufs ihren glaubwürdigen eygner

Handgeschriebenen Originalien collationiert, verglichen, vnd verbessert, &c. Ander Theyl. Darinnen die Magischen vnd Astrologischen Bücher, sampt ihren Anhängen vnd Stücken, auch von dem Philosophischen Stein handlende Tractatus, begriffen, &c. Fornen mit einem kurtzen Begriff vnd Ordnung dieses Theyls Bücher, vnd derselben Innhalt: Hinden aber mit einem durchaufs vollkommenen Register vermehret.

Strafsburg, In verlegung Lazari Zetzners Seeligen Erben. *Anno Domini* M.DC.XVI.

Folio in sixes. Title and Contents, pp. [8]; Text, sigs. a—z, A—Z, Aa—Mm 4, or pp. 691 ; Index, Mm 4 *v* —Nn 4 *r*, verso blank; or, pp. [12, 1 blank].

The title page is in black and has no ornamental border.

Mook, No. 192. See the preceding note. *Bibliographia Paracelsica*, Part II. 1885, No. 92.

156.—1618. Chirurgische Bücher vnd Schrifften, defs Edelen, Hochgelehrten vnnd Bewehrten Philosophi vnd Medici, Philippi Theophrasti Bombast, von Hohenheim, Paracelsi genandt: Jetzt auffs New aufs den Originalen, vnd Theophrasti eygenen Handtschrifften, so viel derselben zubekomen gewesen, auffs trewlichst vnd vleissigest wider an tag geben: Auch vm̃ mehrer richtigkeit vnd Ordnung willen, allen Leib vnd Wundärtzten, wie auch Männiglichen, zu hohem Nutz vnd Verstandt, in vier vnderschiedliche Theil, deren Begriff vnd Ordnung nach den Vorreden zufinden, verfasset: Sambt einem Appendice etlicher nutzlichen Tractat, vnd volkomenen Register. Durch, Iohannem Hvservm Brisgoivm, Churfürstlichen Cölnischen Raht vnd Medicum.

Strafsburg, In verlegung Lazari Zetzners, S. Erben. Anno M.DC XIIX.

Folio. Title, Portrait, Huser's dedication to Ernst, Archbishop of Cologne, Paracelsus to Dr. Wolffgang Thalhauser, dated 1536, Thalhauser's reply, Paracelsus to King Ferdinand of Hungary, Paracelsus' preface, contents, verses to Huser by Johannes Politus Leodiensis, sig.):(in six.

Signatures A—L in sixes, M 4, N 4; O—Z in sixes, Aa—Dd in sixes, Ee 8; Ff—Vv in sixes, Xx 8; Yy—Zz in sixes, Aaa—Yyy in sixes, Zzz 4, Aaaa 4, Bbbb 6, of which the last is blank, or, Text, pp. 795; Index, pp. [39, 2 blank].

This volume is divided into 4 parts with separate titles to the second, third, and fourth parts. Although these titles are not included in the pagination, the signatures run on, these titles falling respectively on O 1, Ff 1, and Yy 1. Besides pp. 525-26 are numbered twice. The full pagination therefore is 803.

The main title is in black and red and is surrounded by the woodcut border as in No. 154. This volume of the Chirurgical works forms an integral portion of the 1616 edition, for it is quite uniform with it, and in the copy I have before me it is bound along with the second volume. The *Appendix* has no separate title-page, and the pagination is continuous.

Mook, No. 193. See above Nos. 151, 152.

157.—1619. *Liber Sermonvm* in Antichristos et Psevdoprophetas Veteris & Noui Teftamenti. Das ist: Ein Büchlein wider die Antichristen, Falsche Propheten vnnd Lehrer so wohl altes, als newes Testaments, Philippi Thcophrafti Paracelfi, ab Hohenheim. *Scriptus ab ipfo Salifburgi*, Anno 1540.

Franckfurt am Mayn bey Lucas Jennis zufinden. *Anno* 1619.

Small 4°. Sigs. a-m, in fours, or pp. 96.

In Mook's transcription (No. 197) there is *et* for &, *vnd* for *vnnd, sowohl* in one word, *anno* for *Anno*, and the date is omitted.

158.—1619. Aufslegung oder Bericht Theophrasti Paracelsi Vber die Wort: Svrsvm Corda: Das ist: Wie man sein Hertz alle zeit zu Gott erheben soll.

Franckfurt bey Lucas Jennis zu finden. Anno 1619.

Small 4°. pp. 21 [3 blank] or sigs. A-C in fours, the last leaf being blank. The device is Elias and the mocking children and the bears.

Mook (No. 198) gives the title correctly, but omits the date.

159 —1740. Num. XCI.

II. Th. XVI. Buch 22 cap. § 1-9.

Philippi Theophrafti Paracelfi Tractatus de Cœno Domini, in quo oftenditur, quod fanguis & caro Chrifti fit in pane & vino : & quomodo id fidelibus fit intelligendum.

In Gottfried Arnold's Unpartheyische Kirchen- und Ketzer-Historien vom Anfang des Neuen Testaments biss auf das Jahr Christi 1688. Neue Auflage. Schaffhausen, Emanuel u. Benedict Hurter, 1740, folio. Tom I. p. 1500.

160.—1740. Theophrasti Paracelsi Secretum Magicum *and* Tetragrammaton. *Ibid.* p. 1511.

161.—1740. Von der Magia.

From the *Aurora Philosophorum* and the *Philosophia Occulta.*

Ibid. p. 1525.

Mook, Nos. 233, 234, 235.

CORRECTIONS AND ADDITIONS.

§ 3. In the previous parts I have observed some errors which require correction. There may be others which I have not yet detected.

Part II. p. 39, line 6, for " ^{PP}. 1 44," read " ^{PP}. 1-44."

Part III. p. 9, line 14, for "herkommem" read "her-kommen."

Part III. p. 11, No. 126.—[1567.] Since my last notice of Leo Suavius' (Jacques Gohory) edition of the *De Vita longa*, I have got another copy of that very rare book. As far as the contents go the two copies are identical, but the third epistle (to Sangelasius), which, in No. 126, is placed at the end, is, in this second copy, inserted in the middle of the first sheet, just after the first epistle (to Renatus Perotus). Does this shifting of the third epistle signify that it was printed independently after the book was complete, and placed wherever the owner or binder thought most suitable ? *

The question that is still unanswered, and presents some difficulty, refers to the exact date of the edition. The

---

* In the Basil edition of 1568, however, it is printed after the commentary and before the index as an integral part of the book.

work itself is not dated, but it contains two epistles dated respectively August 1566, and July 1567, and the third epistle above mentioned of January 1567 (i.e. 1568). That the date cannot be 1566 I have already shown, but whether it is 1567, or really 1568, depends upon whether Gohory's third epistle did or did not belong to the book when it appeared originally. As my two copies each contain the third epistle, I suppose they are to be considered as published subsequent to January 1567 (1568). The British Museum copy wants this epistle, and the latest date it contains is July 1567. Was a portion of the edition actually issued without the third epistle, and is the Museum copy one of that portion ; or, was the whole edition held back till the third epistle was ready, and does the Museum copy happen to be merely one which was overlooked when the epistle was added ? When this same question as to copies with and without the third epistle was under consideration before (No. 126), the answer was given in explanation—rather too strongly, perhaps—that there must have been two issues. The possibility now stated had not suggested itself to me, and there may be other alternatives still. ˙ This, however, makes the wished-for decision all the more difficult to be arrived at, for, so far as I know at present, there are no facts bearing upon it.

On the same occasion (No. 126) I omitted to state that in these three epistles Gohory had made dedication of his book to three different persons.

In the first epistle to Renatus Perotus, he confides his four books of Scholia on the *De Vita longa* to him in terms most friendly and flattering, and thereafter gives expression to his admiration of Paracelsus. This epistle is dated

" VIII. Idus Sext." 1566,* and at that time the book was obviously complete. What may be called the first division of the book contains the prefatory matter, Gohory's compendium of Paracelsus' philosophy and medicine, and the text of the *De Vita longa* in four books. Then follow Gohory's Scholia thereon.

Prefixed to the Scholia is Gohory's second epistle, dated July 1st, 1567, addressed to Joannes Capella, the King's physician, and he begins by asking to whom could he more appropriately dedicate his clever new book, clever as being by Paracelsus, new as containing his own commentary. After which he indulges in laudation of Capella's ability, and tries to combat the prejudice which Capella entertained against Paracelsus, and to convert him to a belief in the German reformer. It does not seem to have troubled Gohory in the smallest degree that he had already dedicated this same book in an equally cordial manner to a different person eleven months earlier.

These two epistles form part of the book as it left the press, and they will be found necessarily in the same place in every copy. The third epistle, however, as it is printed on a separate sheet, with a separate signature, may be found in any part of the volume. It is, however, quite uniform as regards type, form and paper with the rest of the book, and must have been printed practically at the same time. Once more in this epistle Gohory dedicates the book to Sangelasius, partly because he considered himself under an obligation to do something of the kind on account of the good will Sangelasius had shown him, partly

---

* By this I suppose Leo Suavius means the 5th of August. If so he might have called it by its special name of Nones.

because on account of Sangelasius' own distinguished merits anyone would justly desire to dedicate his work to him as to a most appreciative judge. He then adds that concealing himself under the name of Leo Suavius, like Teucer under the sevenfold shield, he will have no fear of the stings of censure or rather of sophistical attacks in a new and difficult subject, if only Sangelasius will play the part to him of Telamonian Ajax. This would seem to imply that the book had excited or that Gohory feared that it would excite hostile criticism, as indeed it was bound to do, and that he hoped by the influence of Sangelasius to avert it and the trouble of meeting it as far as possible. This letter is dated January 1st, 1567, that is 1568. Possibly, therefore, this epistle did not form part of the original book, which indeed is quite complete without it. It may have been that after a number of copies had been issued, and the critics were becoming troublesome, he added this epistle.* In that case the book must have been in circulation before January 1567 (1568).

In connection with the first and second epistles, some questions arise. As the second epistle is dated eleven months after the first we may enquire if the volume was printed as a whole, or if the first division of the volume was printed, say in 1566 ; if some delay thereupon took place, and the printing was not proceeded with till the following year, and if Gohory then found it convenient to

---

* In the Basil edition he is attacked vigorously, after the unmealy-mouthed manner of the time, both by Gerard Dorn and by Peter Perna, the printer of the book. But as Perna's letter is dated Basil, Ides of February (13th), 1568, a whole year after the letter to Sangelasius, it could not have been these criticisms that prompted him to write that letter.

prefix a new epistle to the Scholia themselves. If all that were not so, and the whole volume were printed in 1567 consecutively without any delay, it is noteworthy that Gohory should have retained at the very beginning a dedication that was eleven months old, and that had been followed by another to a different person.

The book therefore contains certain anomalies difficult to reconcile, and presents certain alternatives between which it is difficult to decide. In any case the conclusion seems to be that the book must have appeared subsequent to July 1567, and prior to the date of the Basil reprint (No. 60, Mook No. 62), the earliest possible date of which is February 13th, 1568 (1569).

Part III. p. 28. Between No. 143, 1653, and No. 144, 1663, fall to be inserted the English translation of the *Dispensatory*, 1656, and that of the *Archidoxis*, 1661. These are described under Nos. XV. and XX. of the English list, but they ought to have appeared in the general enumeration as well.

Part III. p. 33, No. III.—1580. The first part of the *Bibliographia Paracelsica* (1877, No. 12) contained a notice of an imperfect copy of the *Key of Philosophie*, which I inferred was of the edition of 1580. Subsequently, under No. III. of the list of English editions contained in Part III., I quoted Herbert's account of the 1580 edition, and as my imperfect copy corresponded so far exactly with that account, I considered my inference as to its date to have been confirmed. I have recently acquired another copy of the 1580 edition, which, while supplying the portions the other copy lacks, shows by their identity otherwise that the two belong to the same edition. I give now a description of the book, which can be substituted for that of Herbert, as it exhibits the arrangement of the title-pages and supplies a more detailed collation. Herbert's transcript is almost perfect, but he omits the duplication of "ex" in the fourth line of the title ; writes "mineralles" without the capital; "Englifh" for "Englifhe"; "fhop" for "Shop"; "Ende" for "ende." In the note at the very end of the book Herbert writes "profite & com-moditie" for "profite and commoditie." In my original quotation of the title of the second part of the *Key* (*Biblio-graphia Paracelsica* 1877, No. 12, p. 29) "*preparyng*" ought to have been printed "*pre*parying", as it stands in the original, and as is given in the transcript below.

III.—1580.　　　The firft part of the Key
of Philofophie.
Wherein　is　contained　mofte　ex-
excellent (*sic*) fecretes of Phificke and
Philofophie, deuided into
twoo Bookes.
In the firfte is fhewed the true and perfect
order to diftill, or drawe forthe the Oiles,
of all maner of Gummes, Spices,
Seedes, Rootes, and Herbes,
with their perfect tafte,
fmell, & vertues.
In the feconde is fhewed the true and perfect
order to prepare, calcine, fublime, and diffolue
all maner of Mineralles, and how ye fhall
drawe forthe their Oiles and Saltes, whiche
are mofte wonderfull in their operations, for
the health of mannes bodie. Firft written in
the Germaine tongue by the mofte learned
Theophraftus Parafelfus (*sic*), and now publifhed in the Englifhe tongue

by Ihon Hefter practitio-
ner in the Arte of
diftillation.
1580.

AT LONDON.

Printed by Richard Day, to be fold at the
long Shop at the Weft ende of Paules.
Small 8°. *j Title; The Epistle dedicatorie, "To the
righte reuerende | Father in God, and his fingular | good
Lord Jhon Watfon, by the | grace of God Bifhop of Win-
chester, and | Prelate of the right honourable order of | the
Garter. j. H. wifheth healthe | and peace, and long life|
in Jefus Chrift. | , *ij to *v *verso;* To the Reader, *vj
recto to *viij *recto.* The *verso* is blank. The text of
Part I. begins on Aj *recto* and ends on Dv *recto.* On the
verso is a note to the effect that the ' Oyles' can be had
from Ihon Hester.

Dvj *recto* contains the title to the second part as follows:
THE KEY OF
Philofophie.
The feconde parte.
Containyng the orderyng & pre-
paryng of all Metalles, Mine-
ralles, Alumes, Salts, and fuch like.
For Medicines both inwardly,
and outwardly, and for di-
uers other vfes.
¶ At London printed
by Richard Daie.
Cum Priuilegio.

On Dvj *verso* begins the address to the Reader which
ends Ej *recto.* Text of part II. begins on Ej *verso* and
ends Gvij *verso.* On Gviij *recto* is the following note:
Well-beloued Reader, I would | here have fet forth diuers
and | fondry other fecretes, but that | tyme would not fuffer
me, the | whiche I meane God willing | hereafter to fette
forthe to thy | great profite and commoditie. | The *verso*
is blank.

The book is printed in black letter, except portions of the titles, the dedication and prefaces to the reader, the running title at the top of the page, the contents of the different sections, the note at the end of Part I., and incidental words and sentences, which are in roman or italic letters. There is no pagination. The signatures are * in eight, A to G in eights, or 64 leaves in all.

Part III. p. 42, l. 8, for "additions" read "Additions."

Part III. p. 46, No. XVIII., for the date "1569" read "1659."

Part III. p. 46, No. XIX., Archidoxis. In line 13 of the title, for VIRTUE read VIRTUES.

Part IV. p. 7, No. 150. I have queried what Mook says about the note prefixed to the title page of the *Chirurgia Minor*, because there is no such note in the copy I have seen, and because the note does appear on the last leaf of the eleventh volume of the collected works. See No. 153, Tomus XI. note. It seems, therefore, either as if he had made a mistake as to the proper position of the leaf, or as if he had been misled by its having been possibly transposed so as to appear to belong to the *Chirurgia Minor*. In his transcription of the note Mook has given *Paltheniano* instead of *Paltheniano*.

BIBLIOGRAPHIA PARACELSICA.

PART V.

AN

ALPHABETICAL CATALOGUE

OF THE DIFFERENT EDITIONS OF
THE WORKS OF

PARACELSUS.

BY

JOHN FERGUSON, LL.D., F.R.S.E., F.S.A.

PRIVATELY PRINTED.

GLASGOW:
Printed at the University Press
BY ROBERT MACLEHOSE, 153 WEST NILE STREET.
1893.

150 Copies printed.

THE original draft of the present catalogue was meant to be included in *Bibliographia Paracelsica*, Part II., printed in 1885. It was at first a meagre list, devoid of cross references, a bare counterpart of Mook's catalogue and quite useless apart from it. It has been extended, and I hope improved, by constant criticism and revision, until it has got into its present shape. It is not the final form of a catalogue of the kind, but it may serve till it is superseded by one better and completer.

JOHN FERGUSON.

THE UNIVERSITY,
GLASGOW, *February* 10*th*, 1893.

§ 1. The following catalogue aims at exhibiting in alphabetical order the different editions of Paracelsus' works as enumerated in the chronological lists by Mook and by myself, and it attempts to supply a desideratum which I mentioned in 1877. After describing the general characters of Mook's Catalogue, I said (*Bibliographia Paracelsica*, 1877, p. 12): " It would have increased the " value and facilitated the use of this Catalogue, had " there been an alphabetical list of the separate treatises, " with references to the editions published in different " years. This list might have been made quite short ; " but it would have been very handy to enable one to " ascertain what editions and how many there are of any " particular treatise." There is this drawback to the chronological order, that while all the works which appeared in any one year can be ascertained, there are no means of finding out in what years any one work was printed, without going through every year separately. When the sentence above quoted was written I was not fully aware how indispensable such a list was ; but a few years later when I had entered more minutely into Paracelsian literature, and my acquaintance with the editions had extended, I found the hunting through successive yearly lists for the different editions of a book so irksome, that I resolved to take the trouble once for all, and compile for my own use an alphabetical catalogue of Paracelsus' works, with the different editions of each arranged as far as possible in chronological order. It is this which I have ventured now to print.

§ 2. The list was begun on no defined plan except that of including all the works jointly and severally which I knew, a task which seemed simple enough. As I proceeded, however, I encountered certain peculiarities in the books which forced me to modify the method I was pursuing, and to elaborate the details to a greater extent than I could have supposed necessary, if the list were really to be of use. I discovered that a distinction must be made between authenticated and unauthenticated editions, and between treatises printed by themselves and in collections along with others, that, while the alphabetical arrangement by the first principal word of the title must be followed generally, treatises more familiarly known by a prominent word or phrase in the title than by its first word, might be difficult to find, if such word or phrase also were not given an independent place in the catalogue.

§ 3. All this necessitated cross references of various kinds, and I have not stinted them. Copious as they are, however, I am not sure that even more might not have been inserted with advantage. The consideration that has influenced me in this matter has been that Paracelsus students would prefer finding a title referred to in several places, or under different headings, to considering under what word a particular work was likely to be placed, and perhaps missing it after all. By the cross references I have tried to bring not only the varying titles of one and the same book together, but also different books on cognate subjects, so that to the student these cross references to some small extent discharge the functions of a subject catalogue as well.

§ 4. It will be objected that the strict alphabetical order has not been always observed. That is correct; but in those cases I have thought it more important to enumerate the successive editions by their dates, than to arrange them alphabetically merely to suit perhaps some arbitrary variation in the spelling, or modification of the title, which would certainly have had the effect of separating related books or editions from one another with hardly any compensation in increased ease of reference. While, therefore, the general arrangement is alphabetical by the first main word of the title, I have not hesitated under particular titles to depart from this, and adopt a chronological order for the sake of exhibiting successive editions. By this plan, too, it is made possible to form some notion of the importance or popularity of a work by observing the number of editions of it. I do not think that in any case the alphabetical dislocation is such that it will cause greater inconvenience than what would result from having to consult a number of cross references.

§ 5. It may be as well to explain the details of the catalogue.

1°. The first column, headed "No.", refers to the running numbers under which Mook has given the title and description of the books. As in all these cases Mook saw actual copies in the libraries he mentions, the books exist, and are authenticated by him.

2°. The second column, headed "Page," refers to the page, and, when the number is followed by a letter, to the note on the page, in which Mook quotes editions he had not himself seen and the existence of which, therefore, he could not guarantee, but which he had found mentioned by other writers, such as Adelung, Spachius, Gesner, etc., and gives on their authority. Every book, therefore, in the following list, opposite such a figure alone, must be regarded in the meantime as doubtful; some may exist; others almost certainly do not.

3°. The third column, headed "Bibl. Para.", contains the running numbers of my own lists. The numbers contained in the different parts are as follows:—

Part I.	1877.	Nos. 1-48.
Part II.	1885.	Nos. 49-121.
Part III.	1890.	Nos. 122-146.
Part IV.	1892.	Nos. 147-161.
Part V.	1893.	No. 162. [See below, § 9.]

When Part I. was printed, I had seen only Nos. 1-11, and Nos. 12-48 were quoted from other writers, especially Graesse.* These, therefore, must be considered as unauthenticated, except in so far as copies of some of them have come into my hands and have been described in my subsequent lists; but of Nos. 1-11 and Nos. 49-162 the descriptions have been taken from actual copies.

4°. The fourth column contains the titles of the books and tracts, and these have been made as brief as possible, consistent with their identification. In these transcripts no regular attempt has been made to preserve the peculiarities of spelling, punctuation, and typography of the original, but whenever I have been in doubt about Mook's titles and have not been able to check them by reference to the books themselves, I have reproduced his version unchanged. Some of his titles seem to me to be inaccurate, but it is possible that they stand in the original as he gives them; anyhow I have refrained from altering them. A small Roman numeral in column 3, or prefixed to a title in column 4, refers to the list of English translations contained in *Bibliographia Paracelsica*, 1890, Part III., § 4.

5°. The fifth column contains the place of printing or publication. The names are spelt as they occur in the books or in Mook's transcriptions as the case may be, and hence such

* I can see now that the quoted works (Nos. 12-48) should not have been included in my running numbers, but I did not anticipate in 1877 the continuance of this investigation to which I seem committed.

variations as Strasburg and Strassburg, Nürnberg and Nurmberg, and so on. When no place is entered opposite a full title it means that it is not known. When the name is within parentheses it means that, though the name does not appear in the book, it is known or it is almost certain that the book was printed at the place indicated. When the name is followed by a query it signifies that it is not certain that the book was printed at the place named.

6°. The same rules apply to the date column.

7°. The last column gives the size and requires no remark.

§ 6. Three forms of cross reference have been employed :—

1°. From a leading word or phrase to the actual title—*e.gr.*, from "Pfeffers" to "Bad (vonn dem) Pfeffers"; or from "Experiments and Cures" to "Hundred (a) and fourtene Experiments and Cures." In this case the title referred to is preceded by the word *See*, and there is neither running number, place, date, nor size inserted. In one or two cases the phrase *See under* has been employed, when a title has been put out of its alphabetical position, so as to connect it with related treatises.

2°. From the title of a tract in one language to the same tract in another, so as to bring them together. In this case the cross reference is preceded usually by the words *See also*. This phrase is likewise employed to refer to tracts on cognate subjects.

3°. From the title of a tract to that of the collection which contains it. In this case the number in column 1 or 3 is preceded by the word *in*, which denotes that the corresponding treatise will be found in the book, the title of which in small type, also preceded by the word *In*, is placed immediately below, and the place, date, and size are usually added. Sometimes, when there are several editions of the book or collection referred to, these are not repeated, but one entry only is given—*e.gr.*, "Three (of the) Principles," "*In* Archidoxis." The practice, however, has not been quite uniform in this respect, for sometimes all the editions have been (unnecessarily) repeated—*e.gr.*,

"Natürlichen (von) Dingen" is entered four times when one entry and the cross reference would have been sufficient.

§ 7. I have little doubt that, notwithstanding my efforts to be accurate, misprints, slips in figures, omission of cross references, possibly even of titles, and other defects will be met with. I hope that none of these will be misleading or will form a drawback to the use of the list.

I am aware also that the list is very far from complete, and does not represent all Paracelsus' works that are known. Mook describes 248 editions which he saw, besides those he quoted from other writers, which were doubtful to him. Drs. Schubert and Sudhoff, however, say * that they have seen 118 editions not quoted by Mook, including many against the existence of which he has argued; that they possess 201 editions; that they have examined 349 editions; and they calculate that altogether the number of the editions of Paracelsus' works may amount to about 450, or fully 200 more than Mook described.†

No account of these editions is given anywhere, so far as I know. One can only hope that a fuller bibliography than any that has yet appeared will be published some day. When that comes it will be time to draw up a new alphabetical list which will embrace the additional titles as well as those now given.

§ 8. Originally I had the intention of giving cross references to the collected works. The compilation of these would have added much to the extent of my labour, it would have increased the complexity of the list, and as it would have involved the use of a larger collection of Paracelsus' works than can be commanded even in the British Museum, it would have postponed

---

* *Paracelsus-Forschungen*, Frankfurt, 1887, Erstes Heft, p. 14.

† Some of these may be in the British Museum, but I have not yet examined that collection.

indefinitely the printing of this Part. Besides, though such an addition might be useful for critical or editorial purposes, it would not be so specially for bibliography. If such an index were to be made it would be simplest to confine it to a comparison of the editions of the collected works with each other in an appendix devoted to that purpose alone.

§ 9. Since finishing Part IV. a year ago, I have been able to add only one new title to my list, that of the *Metamorphosis* of 1574. It is as follows :—

162.—1574. (1584.) Metamorphosis Theophrasti Paracelsi, Dessen werck seinen meister loben wirt. Was nun darin tractirt wirt, wirt volgends blat nach der prefation anzeigen. Durch D. Adamen von Bodenstein mit besten fleifs, sich zu commendieren dem hochwürdigen seinem Gn. Fürsten vnd herrn, herrn Melchior, Bischoff zu Basel, in druck gegeben. M. D. LXX iiij. Ανέχου καὶ ἀπέχου.

Small 8vo. Signatures:):(in eight (?), a to x in eights, or ff. [6] 166. Title, Bodenstein's preface or letter to Melchior, Bishop of Basel, dated : Basel, August, 16th, 1574, and Innhalt, ff. [6]. Text, ff. 1—166. The last two leaves of):(and of x are wanting in this copy. There is no place or printer's name. It is not such a striking book as the 1572 edition described under No. 133.

Mook (No. 105) omits the sentence *Was nun … anzeigen*, the commas after *Melchior* and *Basel*, and the date. Comparing the above with Mook's description, there seems to be no preliminary matter except Bodenstein's preface or letter, so that the two wanting leaves,):(7 and 8 are probably blank. On further comparison, however, it appears that the rest of the book does not tally with Mook's account of the 1574 edition. The latter is only partially paged, and has the imprint of Samuel Apiarius for Peter Perna, whereas the above copy is foliated all through and has no imprint, but corresponds with Mook's description of the 1584 edition. The present, therefore, is a copy made up of the later issue of the text, with an earlier title page and preface prefixed. This combination however has been made long ago, not much later than 1584, I should suppose, from the appearance of the book. It would be curious to know if any other similarly made up copies exist.

The present copy (really one of the 1584 edition) contains the following :—

1. Von natürlichen dingen, ff. 1-88. There are nominally 10 books, but book 8 is omitted, book 9 is entitled De cimentis, and book 10, De gradationibus. Mook points out that this version differs materially from that given by Huser. Mook, however, has omitted the interesting entry on f. 88 *verso:* " Das elfft Buch. De proiectionibus. Hic deficiebat manus Theophrasti, &c.," which occurs also in the 1572 edition.
2. Manual...vom stein der Weisen, ff. 89-108.
3. Alchymia...vom einfachen fewr, ff. 108-129. The second book is entitled : von den tincturen.
4. De Tinctura Phisica, ff. 129-142.
5. Paracelsisch Büchlein belangend lapidem, ff. 143-148, followed by the words : Finis libri Metamorphoseos Paracelsicæ. Then comes Bodenstein's Preface to the Bürgermeister and Rath of Basel, dated December 2nd, 1571, ff. 148 *verso-150.*
6. Liber primus de viribus spiritualium, ff. 151-156. Liber secundus de viribus membrorum interiorum, ff. 156-160. Liber tertius de confortatione membrorum, ff. 160-166.

   Of these tracts Mook says that Nos. 2 and 5 agree with Huser's version, Nos. 4 and 6 differ considerably from his, and No. 3 is wanting in the collected editions.

   The 1572 edition of the *Metamorphosis* contains only the first three tracts mentioned above.

§ 10. Here follows the alphabetical catalogue.

13

B

14

NO.	PAGE.	BIBL. PARA.				
in 34			Apostematibus (von), ulceribus, sironibus vnd nodis, waarhaffter...bericht,	... (Basel)	(1563)	8°
		in 19	— — — — — — ...		1565	8°
	69a)		— — — — -- — ...		1574	2°
			In Ersten (von) dreyen Principiis.			
in 247	62b)	in 129	Apostematibus (de), Syronibus et Nodis, ...	Basilea (*c.* 1568-70)		8°
in 102			— — — — — — ...	Argentorat.	1573	2°
		in 69	— — — — — — ...		1573	2°
in 173		in 150	— — — — — — ...	Francofurt.	1603	4°
			In Bertheonea.			
in 244			Apostematibus (de) Syronibus et Nodis, ...	Basilea		8°
	56c)		— — — — — ...	Basilea	1569	
	56c)		— — — — — ...	Colonia	1569	8°
			In Chirurgia Vulnerum.			
in 204			Apostemes (des) syrons ou noeuds. *In* Petite (la) Chirurgie.	Paris	1623	8°
		41 and 114	XXIII. Arcana Philosophia ... Likewise Four...Treatises, *viz.* the I. of Fevers, the II. of the Jaundies, the III. of Madness, and the IV. of Diarrhæas, Lientries, &c., by...Paracelsus, ...	London	1697	8°
236			Arcanum Arcanorum, seu Magisterium Philosophorum. Geheimnüss aller seiner Geheimnüsse, ...	Franckfurt	1746	8°
			See also Geheimniss.			

ARCHIDOXA.

73	34	Archidoxae Libri X., ...	Cracovia	(1569)	4°
74		Archidoxorum de Secretis Naturae mysteriis libri decem, ...	Basilea	1570	8°

This edition contains also :
De Tinctura Physicorum.
De Praeparationibus.
De Vexationibus Alchimistarum.
De Cementis Metallorum, et
De Gradationibus eorundem.

| 80 | | Archidoxa, von heymlichkeyten der Natur zehen Bücher, ... | Strassburg | 1570 | 8° |

Contains also :
De Tinctura Physicorum.
De Occulta Philosophia.

| 82 | | Archidoxa ex Theophrastia, ... | München | 1570 | 4° |

Contains also :
Die Bucher Praeparationum.
De Tinctura Physicorum.
De Renovatione et Restauratione vitae.
De Vita longa, alle teutsch.

| 85 | 64 | Archidoxa zwölff Bucher, ... | München | 1570 | 4° |

Contains also :
De Antimonio.
De Tinctura Physicorum.
De Renovatione et Restauratione vitae.
De longa Vita.

NO.	PAGE.	BIBL. PARA.			
84			Archidoxorum Theophrastiae Pars Prima Libri Novem, De Misteriis Naturae, Còlln		1570 4°

Archidoxorum Theophrastiae Pars Prima
Libri Novem, De Misteriis Naturae,   Còlln   1570 4°
Contains also :
De Renovatione et Restauratione.
De Vita longa.
De Mineralibus.
De Sale.
De Vitriolo.
De Arsenico.
De Sulphure.

242
Archidoxorum Theophrastiae pars prima,   4°
Novem Libri De Mysteriis Naturae.
Contains also :
2 Bücher Praeparationum.
De Tinctura Physicorum.
De Renovatione et Restauratione.
De longa Vita.

87
Archidoxorum X. Bücher, ... Basel   1570 4°
[The preface : de Mysterio Microcosmi, is
reckoned as Book I.]

99
Archidoxorum X. Bücher, ... (Basel)   1572 4°
Besides Book I. de Mysterio Microcosmi,
this edition contains :
De Tempore.
De Imaginibus.
De Speculi Constellatione.
De Compositione Metallorum.
De Sigillis Planetarum.

109   134
Archidoxa zehen Bücher,...   ...   ... Strassburg   1574 8°
Contains also :
De Tinctura Physicorum.
Tesaurus Tesaurorum.
Manuale.
Occulta Philosophia.

78b)
Archidoxa oder zwölf Bucher darin alle
Geheimnisse der Natur eroffnet werden, Basel   1579 8°

137   148
Archidoxorum seu de Secretis Naturae
mysteriis, libri decem, ... Basilea   1582 8°
Contains also :
De Mercuriis Metallorum.
De Quinta Essentia.
Manualia duo.

89
Archidoxa, ... Basel   1592 8°

206
Clavis, oder, das zehende Buch der Archi-
doxen, ... Magdeburg   1624 4°

8
XIX. Archidoxis : Comprised in Ten
Books, ... London   1660 8°

222
XX. Archidoxes : Comprised in Ten
Books, ... London   1661 8°

144
XXI. Archidoxis, or, Chief Teachings :
Comprised in Ten Books,   ... London   1663 8°

NO.	PAGE.	BIBL PARA.			
			The English editions contain also : Of Renovation and Restauration. Of the Tincture of the Philosophers. Of the Manual of the Philosophical Medicinal Stone. Of the Virtues of the Members. Of the three principles. Of the Degrees and Compositions of Receipts, and Natural Things.		
		in 112	Archidoxen (Das zehende Buch der).		
			In Lapis Vegetabilis, ...	Strassburg	1681 8°
in 227		in 145	Haupt-Schlüssel der Paracelsischen Arcanen, oder das zehende Buch der Archidoxen.		•
			In Kleine Hand- und Denck-Bibel, ...	Franckf. u Leipz.	1684 12°
in 231		in 146	*In* — — — — ..	Muhlhausen	1736 8°
			See Abregé de la Doctrine de Paracelse et de ses Archidoxes. *See* Commentaria in Archidoxorum Libros X. *See* Etliche Tractetlein zur Archidoxa gehorig. *See* Tractatlein zu dem Archidoxis gehorig.		
in 84			Arsenico (de).		
			In Archidoxorum Theophrastiae pars prima, ..	Cöln	1570 4°
		51d)	Artzneybuchlein vom Franzosen-Holz, ...	Cöln	1567 4°
			See also Holtzbuchlein. *See also* Holtz (vom) Guaiaco. *See also* Ligno (de) Guaiaco.		
		73b)	Astrologiae Fragmenta.		
			In Meteoris (de), ...	Basilea	1575 8°
56		56	Astronomica et Astrologica Opuscula, ...	Cöln	1567 4°
		22	— — — — — ...	Ulm	1567
in 72		35	Astronomica et Astrologica Fragmenta.		
			In Praesagiis (de).	Basilea	1569 8°
in 243			Astronomica et Astrologica Fragmenta. ...	Basilea	8°
		35	— — — — — ...	Basilea	1569 8°
		62a)	— — — — — ...	Basilea	1570
			In Meteoris (de)		
91		66	Astronomia Magna : oder die gantze Philosophia sagax der grossen und kleinen Welt, ...	Franckfurt	1571 2°
			See Philosophia sagax.		
			Astronomiae Magnae Compendium.		
			See Compendium Astronomiae Magnae.		
240		2	Aurei Velleris oder der Guldin Schatz und Kunstkammer Tractatus II., ...	Rorschach	1598-99 4°.
		88	Aureum Vellus, oder Guldin Schatz und Kunstkammer, ...	Rorschach	1599 8°
			See also Eroffnete Geheimnisse des Steins der Weisen. *See* Tincturen (von).		
		73c)	Aurora Philosophorum, ...	Basilea	1575 8°
125		70	Aurora Thesaurusque Philosophorum, ...	Basilea	1577 8°
			[*See* Bibliographia Paracelsica, Part III., Corrections and Additions.] *Contains also :* Anatomia Viva.		

NO.	PAGE.	BIBL. PARA.			
	113	108	XVIII. Aurora and Treasure of the Philosophers, ... _See also_ Auszug aus der Aurora.	London	1659 12°
141			Auroram (in) Philosophorum, Thesaurum Mineralem Oeconomiam, Commentaria, cum quibusdam Argumentis, ...	Francofurt.	1583 8°
145			— — — — — ...	Francofurt.	1584 8°
			Ausslegung des Commeten. _See_ Wunderbarlichen (von den) .. Zeychen, _See also_ Usslegung des Commeten.		
70			Ausslegung der Figuren, so zu Nürnberg gefunden seind worden, ...		1569 8°
97		in 101	— — — — — ...		1572 8°
			_In_ Reformir-spiegel des weltlichen Bapsts, .. _See also_ Erklärung der magischen Figuren. _See also_ Explication der magischen Figuren. _See also_ Expositio vera... Imaginum. _See also_ Joyfull newes. _See also_ Theophrastus Paracelsus als Bekämpfer des Pabstthums.		1620 4°
			Ausslegung etlicher seiner Wórter. _See_ Onomasticon.		
198		158	Ausslegung oder Bericht... uber die Wort: Sursum Corda, ...	Franckfurt	1619 4°
in 199			— — — — — _In_ Drey vnderscheydene Tractätlein, ...	Franckfurt	1619 4°
	104c)		Auslegung uber die Epistel Juda, ... _See also_ Commentatio.		1618 4°
235		161	Auszug aus der Aurora Philosophorum uber die Magia, und aus der Philosophia Occulta. In Arnold's _Kirchen- und Ketzer-Historien_, II. XVI. 22, § 1., ... _See also_ Aurora. _See also_ Philosophia Occulta.	Schaffhausen	1740 2°
in 40		in 124	Ausszug der Karntischen Chronick. _In_ Drey Bücher..., ... _See_ Kärnthen.	Cöln	1564 4°
8			Bad (vonn dem) Pfeffers in Oberschwytz gelegen, ...		(1535) 4°
	26		— — — — — ...		1534 4°
	26		— — — — — ...		1536 (?)
94		67	Bad (von dem) Pfeffers. Gelegen in ober Schweitz, ...	Strassburg	1571 8°
in 121			Bad (vom) zu Pfeffers. _In_ Schreiben von warmen oder Wildbäderen, ..	Basel	1576 8°
			Bad Pfeffers. _See_ Vrsprung (vom) und herkommen des Bads Pfeffers. _See_ Kurtze und eygentliche Beschreibung vom Ursprung, ... dess .. Bads Pfeffers		
	90b)		Bade (von dem) Pfeffers, ...	Basel	1594 4°
30			Baderbüchlein. Sechs köstliche Tractat,...	Mülhausen	1562 4°

NO.	PAGE.	BIBL. PARA.				
in 32			Baderbüchlein.			
			In Schreiben von Tartarischen Kranckheiten,	(Basel)	(1563)	8°
	41	—	*In* Tartarischen (von) Krankheiten, ...	Strassburg	1563	
53			Badenfart Büchlein. Sechs kostliche Trac- tat, ...	Franckfurt	1566	8°
			[2d Edition of No. 30 Baderbuchlein.]			
58		58	Bergsucht (von der) oder Bergkranckheiten drey Bucher, inn dreyzehen Tractat verfast vnnd beschriben worden, ...	Dilingen	1567	4°
	80a)		Bericht von der Pest, ...	Strasburg	1583	8°
			See also Pestis.			
			BERTHEONEA.			
	41		Bertheoneae III. Bücher... welche... auch die kleine Chirurgie genannt werden,		1563	
	41		— — — — — ...	Ingolstadt	1563	4°
247		129	Chirurgia minor, quam alias Bertheoneam intitulavit [A. P. T. Par.]	Basilea (*c.* 1568-70)		8°
			Contains also :			
			De Apostematibus, Syronibus et Nodis.			
			De Cutis Apertionibus.			
			De Vulnerum et ulcerum curis.			
			De Vermibus, serpentibus, &c. ac maculis à nativitate ortis.			
	62b)		— — — — — ...	Basilea	1570	
			[This, which is probably identical with the pre- ceding, is quoted by Mook from Gesner.]			
102			— — — — — ...	Argentorat.	1573	2°
		69	— — — — — ...		1573	2°
173		150	Bertheonea sive Chirurgia minor cum tractatibus ejusdem [Paracelsi], ...	Francofurt.	1603	4°
204			Petite (la) Chirurgie autrement ditte la Bertheonee. Plus les traittez	Paris	1623	8°
			[All the editions contain the additional tracts.] *See also* Chirurgia parva, die kleine Chirurgie, die kleine Wundartzney, *and* la petite Chirurgie.			
in 79		in 132	Beschreibung etlicher Kreutter, ...	Strassburg	1570	8°
in 139			— — — — ...	Strassburg	1582	8°
in 153			— — — — ...	Strassburg	1587	8°
	90		— — — — ...	Strassburg	1597	
			In Ettliche Tractatus.			
116			Brevis Carinthiae Ducatus ut Nobilis. ita etiam Antiquis. Descriptio, ...	Argentorat.	1575	8°
			See also Ausszug der Karntischen Chronik. *See also* Kurze Chronik von Karnthen.			
50		125	Buch (das) Meteororum. Item Liber Quartus Paramiri de Matrice	Cöln	1566	4°
			See also Meteoris (de).			
46			Buch (das) Paragranum... Darinn die vier Columnae,... auff welche Theophrasti Medicin fundirt ist, tractirt werden, ...	Franckfurt	1565	8°

NO.	PAGE.	BIBL. PARA.			
		29	Buch (das) Paragranum darin die Philosophie, Astronomie, Alchemie und Virtus, auf welche Theophr. Medizin fundirt ist, tractirt werden ; item von Aderlassens... rechtem Gebrauch, ... Basel	1586	8°
87		29	Buch (das) Paragraphorum (*sic for* Paragranum) von den vier Columnen der Medicin, ... Basel	1589	4°
			Buch (das) Paramirum. *See* Paramirum.		
			Buch (das) vom Tartaro. *See under* Tartarus.		
in 82			Bücher Praeparationum. *In* Archidoxa ex Theophrastia, ... München *See also under* Praeparatio.	1570	4°
154	76		Bücher und Schrifften I., ... Basel	1589	4°
155	77		— — II., ... Basel	1589	4°
156	78		— — III., ... Basel	1589	4°
157	79		— — IV., ... Basel	1589	4°
158	80		— ' — V., ... Basel	1589	4°
159	81		— — VI., ... Basel	1590	4°
160	82		— — VII., ... Basel	1590	4°
161	83		— — VIII., ... Basel	1590	4°
162	84		— — IX., ... Basel	1590·1*	4°
163	85		— — X., ... Basel	1590·1*	4°
			See Chirurgischer Bücher... Erster Theil, *under* CHIRURGIA, ... Basel	1591	4°
			See also Opera, Bücher und Schrifften, .. Strassburg	1603	2°
			— — — ..	1616	
			See Chirurgische Bücher, ... Strassburg	1605	2°
			— — — ..	1618	
			See Opera Medico-Chimica sive Paradoxa, .. Francofurtum	1603	2°
			— — — ..	1605	
			See Opera Omnia, ... Geneva	1658	4°
88			Büchlein von der Tinctura Physica, ... Basel *See also* Tinctura.	1570	4°
in 55			Caduco (de) Matricis. *In* Medici Libelli, ... Cöln	1567	4°
			Carinthiae Descriptio. *See* Brevis Carinthiae... Descriptio. *See also* Kurze Chronik von Kärnthen. *See also* Ausszug der Kärntischen Chronik.		
in 44			Causa (de) et Origine Morborum, ... Coln	1565	8°
in 54			— — — — ... ... Cöln *In* Libri Duo.	1566	4°
			Causis (de), signis & curationibus morborum ex Tartaro, libri quinque. *See* Libri quinque de Causis.		
in 74			Cementis (de) metallorum, et de Gradationibus eorundem. *In* Archidoxorum... libri decem, ... Basilea	1570	8°

* For the differences in date of these volumes, see *Bibliographia Paracelsica*, Part III., 1890 § 11. Corrections and Additions.

NO.	PAGE.	BIBL. PARA.				
in 89		in 65	Cementis (de).			
			In Spiritibus (de) Planetarum, ...	Basilea	1571	4°
138	80a)		Centum quindecim Curationes experiment-aque, ...		1582	8°
			See also Hundert und vierzehen Experimenta. *See also* Hundred and fourteen experiments and cures.			
	23		Charta, ...	Basilea	1527	
			See Programma *and* Intimatio.			
			CHIRURGIA.			
	24		Grosse (die) Wundarznei, der erste Theil,	Ulm	1530	
11			Grossenn (der) Wundarzney, das erst Buch,	Augspurg	1536	2°
12			— — das ander Buch,	Augspurg	1536	2°
	31a)		— — das dritte Buch,	Augspurg	1536	
	31a)		— — das erste Buch,	Ulm	1536	2°
13			— — das erst Buch,	Augspurg	1537	2°
	32		— — das 1, 2, 3 Buch,		1537	
	34b)		Grosse (die) Wundarzney, ...	Strasburg	1549	8°
27			Grossen (der) Wundartzney erster Theil,	Franckfurt	1562	4°
	40c)		Grosse (die) Wundarzney lateinisch,	Frankfurt	1562	4°
	40c)		Chirurgia Magna germanice, ...	Francofurt.	1562	4°
	41		Grosse (die) Wundarzney, ...	Strasburg	1563	4°
in 38			— —	Strassburg	1564	2°
in 51			—	Strassburg	1566	2°
	48a)	20	—	Franckfurt	1566	2°
in 93			— —	Collen	1571	2°
in 136			— —	Basel	1581	2°
			See Opus Chyrurgicum, *for the preceding five.*			
	84a)		Grosse (die) Wundarzney, ...	Basel	1586	8°
in 113			Von dem rechten Drittentheil der grossen Wundartzney.			
			In Kleine Wundartzney, ...	Basel	1579	8°
	48e)		Chirurgia Major gallice, ...	Antverpia	1566	8°
	51c)		Grande (la) Chirurgie, ...	Anvers	1567	8°
69			Grande (la), vraye, et parfaicte Chirurgie,	Anvers	1568	8°
165			Grande (la) Chirurgie, 1re Edition, ...	Lyon	1593	4°
174			— — 2de Edition, ...	Lyon	1603	4°
186		95	— — 3me Edition, ...	Montbeliart	1608	8°
101		68	Chirurgia Magna, ...	Argentorat.	1573	2°
			Chirurgia Minor.			
			See Bertheonea.			
	114		Chirurgia parva de cura vulnerum, ...		1673	8°
			Chirurgie (la petite).			
			See Petite (la) Chirurgie.			
			Chirurgy (die kleine).			
			See Kleine (die) Chirurgy.			
			See also Kleine (die) Wundartzney.			

NO.	PAGE.	BIBL. PARA.			
	56c)		Chirurgia vulnerum, cum recentium tum veterum occultorum et manifestorum vulnerum : Cui libri duo, prior de Contracturis, de Apostematibus Syronibus et Nodis alter, accessere, ... Basilea	1569	
	56c)		— — — — — ... Colonia	1569	8°
244			— — — — — ... Basilea		8°
167			Chirurgia Vulnerum : das ist, von Heylung der Wunden, ... Schlesswig	1595	8°
149			Chirurgia. Warhafftige Beschreibunge der Wundartzney, ... Basel	1585	2°
152			— — — — — ... Basel	1586	2°
			[Mook refers to *Opus Chyrurgicum*, Nos. 38 and 51.]		
164			Chirurgischer Bücher vnnd Schrifften, erster Theil, ... Basel	1591	4°
176		151	Chirurgische Bücher und Schrifften, ... Strassburg	1605	2°
177		152	Chirurgischer Bücher und Schrifften... .. Appendix, ... Strassburg	1605	2°

The Appendix contains :

1. Zwey Manualia Theophrasti : Ein Alchimisch vnd ein Artzneiisch.
2. Anatomia corporum ad huc viventium oder de destillandis Urinis.
3. Alchimia oder de Spiritibus Metallorum : in drey Bücher abgetheilt.
4. Aurora Philosophorum.
5. De Quinta Essentia.
6. De Mercuriis Metallorum.
7. Ein kurtzes Büchlein De Lapide, genannt Paracelsica.
8. De Secretis Creationis.

NO.	PAGE.	BIBL. PARA.			
193		156	Chirurgische Bücher und Schrifften, ... Strassburg	1618	2°
			Chirurgische Bücher.		
			See Drey Chirurgische Bücher.		
			Chirurgery.		
			See Dispensatory and Chirurgery.		
			Chronik von Kärnthen.		
			See Kurze Chronik.		
			See Kärnthen.		
		in 3	X. Chymicall Dictionary, explaining hard places and words met withall in the writings of Paracelsus.		
			In A New Light of Alchymie, edited by J. F(rench), ... London	1650	4°
		in 10	XXII. — — — —		
			In A New Light of Alchymy, by J. F., .. London	1674	8°
			See also Dictionarium.		
			See also Erklärung ettlicher Worter.		
			See also Lexicon.		
			See also Onomasticon.		
220		6	XVI. Chymical (of the) Transmutation, Genealogy and Generation of Metals and Minerals, ... London	1657	8°

NO.	PAGE.	BIBL. PARA.				
	65b)		Chymischer Psalter, ...	Berlin	1572	12°
	80b)		Chymischer Psalter, ins latein. übersetzt, ...		1582	8°
238		119	Chymischer Psalter, ...	Berlin	1771	8°
		120	— —	Berlin	1791	8°
	119		— —	Amsterdam	1771	

See Psalterium.

101a)	in 97	Clavis operum Paracelsi.

In *Solis e Puteo emergentis ... libri tres,* by Johann Rhenanus. Adelung, from whom Mook quotes it, gives the title "*Clavis et manuductio in proprios libros,*" .. .. Francofurtum 1613 4°

206		Clavis, oder, das zehende Buch der Archi-doxen. wie auch... Manualis Auss-legung, ... Magdeburg 1624 4°

	113	Coelum Philosophorum oder Liber Vexa-tionum, erklart von J. R. Glauber (*Opera Chymica*), ... Frankfurt 1658 4°

	in 11	— — — — — *In* Hermetische (der) Nordstern, ... Frankfurt 1771 8°

See also Pyrophilia.

Coena (de) Domini Tractatus.
See Tractatus de Coena Domini.

Collectanea quaedam Philosophiae Magnae.
See Philosophiae Magnae... Collectanea.

144		75	Commentaria in Archidoxorum libros X.,... Francofurt. 1584 8°

Contains also :
Compendium Astronomiae magnae.

Commentaria in Auroram Philosophorum.
See Auroram (in) Philosophorum... Comment-aria.

Commentarii tres, de summis Naturae mysteriis.
See Summis (de) Naturae mysteriis Commentarii.

in 199		Commentatio uber die Epistolam Judae.

In Drey underscheydene Tractatlein, ... Franckfurt 1619 8°
See Auslegung uber die Epistel Juda.

Commeten.
See Usslegung des Commeten.
See Wunderbarlichen (von den).. Zeychen.

in 144		in 75	Compendium Astronomiae Magnae.

In Commentaria in Archidoxorum libros X.,.. Francofurtum 1584 8°

	48c)	55	Compendium Philosophiae et Medicinae utriusque universae ;... De Vita longa,	Parisii	1566 (?) 8°
	51a)	23	— — — — — ...	Parisii	1567
		126	— — — — — ...	Parisii	1567 8°
62		60	— — — — — ...	Basilea	1568 8°
	55e)		— — — — — ...	Franckfurt	1568

Contains also:
Scholia in libros IIII. de Vita longa.
See Vita (de) longa.

in 99		Compositione (de) Metallorum.

In Archidoxorum X. Bücher, ... 1572

NO.	PAGE.	BIBL. PARA.				
134		71	Congeries Paracelsicae Chemiae de Trans-mutationibus Metallorum,... Accessit Genealogia Mineralium atque metal-lorum omnium, ...	... Francofurt.	1581	8°
	90		— — — — —	... Ursellae	1602	8°
	98		— — — — —	... Argentorat.	1613	8°
	109		— — — — —	... Argentorat.	1659	8°
			These three are in *Theatrum Chemicum.*			
	115		— — — — —			
			In Manget's *Bibliotheca Chemica,* ..	.. Geneva	1702	2°
in 122			Consilia Theophrasti Paracelsi,			
			In Peste (de), ...	.. Strassburg	1576	8°
in 66		in 128	Contracturarum origines et curae.			
			In Pyrophilia Vexationumque liber. ..	.. Basilea	1568	8°
in 90			Contracturen (von den) vnd iren glidern.			
			In Schoner (ein) Tractat...	.. Strassburg	1571	8°
	56c)		Contracturis (de), ...	... Basilea	1569	
	56c)		— —	... Colonia	1569	8°
in 244			— —	... Basilea		8°
			In Chirurgia Vulnerum. *See* Lame (von)... *in* Ersten (von) dreyen principiis.			
	78e)		Cura (de) Morbi Gallici, ...	... Argentorat.	1579	8°
	78e)		— — Germanice,	... Strassburg	1579	8°
			See also Morbo (de) Gallico.			
	41		Cura (de) pestis, ...	... Ingolstadt	1563	
			See also Pestis.			
in 135			Curae Medicae.			
			In Fasciculus, ...	.. Francofurtum	1581	4°
			Curationes experimentaque.			
			See Centum quindecim curationes.			
			Cure of Wounds and Diseases.			
			See Magical (the)... Cure of wounds.			
			Curis (de) Vulnerum (et) ulcerum.			
			See Vulnerum (de)... Curis.			
in 247	62b)	in 129	Cutis (de) apertionibus, ...	... Basilea	(1568-70)	8°
in 102			—	... Argentorat.	1573	2°
		in 69	— —		1573	2°
in 173		in 150	— —	... Francofurt.	1603	4°
			In Bertheonea. *See also* Oeffnung (von) der Haut. *See also* Petite (la) Chirurgie:			
150		136	Cyclopaedia Paracelsica Christiana, ...		1585	4°
	54c)	24	Declaration zu bereiten Hellebori in sein Arcanum, ...	... Basel	1568	8°
in 49			Defensiones septem.			
			In Libri duo, ...	.. Argentoratum	1566	8°
	48d)		— —	... Argentorat.	1566	4°
			Defensiones septem adversus aemulos suos.			
			See Septem Defensiones *in* Libri duo, .. .	Col. Agrippina	1573	8°
			Defensiones (Siben) oder Schirmreden.			
			See Siben Defensiones *in* Labyrinthus, ..	.. Basel	1574	8°

NO.	PAGE.	BIBL. PARA.			
			Degrees (of the) and Compositions of Receipts, Seven books. *In* Archidoxis. *See* Gradibus (de).		
	36a)		Descriptio Laudani, quo usus est in deploratis morbis, ...	Basilea	1560 8°
			Dictionarium. *See under* Fasciculus.		
142		26	Dictionarium, continens obscuriorum vocabulorum, quibus in suis Scriptis passim utitur, definitiones, ...	Francofurt.	1583 8°
146			— — — — — ...	Francofurt.	1584 8°
			Dictionary. *See* Chymicall Dictionary. *See* Erklarung ettlicher wörter, *See also* Lexicon. *See also* Onomasticon.		
219			xv. Dispensatory and Chirurgery, ...	London	1656 12°
	34f)		Drey andere Bucher der Wundarzney, 1. Von Wunden. 2. Von offenen Schäden.		
			3. Von Franzosen.	Frankfurt	1549 8°
	45b)		— — — — — ...	Frankfurt	1565 8°
			See also Drei Bücher von Wunden.		
	76d)		— — — — — ...	Strassburg	1577 8°
			See also Ofenen (von den) Schäden...		
212			Drey ausserlesene Tractat von der Pest. I. A. T. Paracelsi cum Commentariis Jobi Kornthaueri, ...	Franckfurt	1640 4°
			See also Pestis.		
	35		Drey Bucher Theophrasti etc., die Verantwortung etc., von dem Irrgang und Labyrinth der Aerzte, und vom Uisprung und Herkommen der tartarischen Krankheiten etc., ...	Nürnberg	1553 4°
			See also Labyrinthus Medicorum Errantium.		
40		124	Drey Bucher. I. Die verantwortung vber etzlich verunglimpfung seiner missgunner. II. Von dem Irrgang und Labyrinth der Artzten. III. Von dem ursprung und herkommen der Tartarischen kranckheiten, nach dem alten namen vom Stein, Sandt oder Griess, auch heilung derselbigen. Ein warhaffter kurtzer ausszug der Karntischen Chronick, ...	Cöln	1564 4°
	87		Drey Bucher an die Stande von Kärnthen, Apologie, Labyrinthus * medicorum errantium, und das Buch vom Tartaro d. i. von Sand und Stein, nebst einer kurzen Chronik von Kärnthen,... ...		1589
			Drey Bücher von der Bergsucht. *See* Bergsucht.		

NO.	PAGE.	BIBL. PARA.	
34			Ersten (von) dreyen principiis, was jre formen und wirckung. Item zwen tractat von láme... auch LXIII. Capitul von apostematibus, ulceribus, sironibus, und nodis, ... (Basel) (1563) 8°
	41		— — — — — ... Strassburg 1563
		19	— — — — — ... 1565 8°
	69a)		— — — — — ... 1574 2° *See also* Tribus (de) Principiis.
27			Erster Theil der grossen Wundartzney, ... Franckfurt 1562 4° *See also* Grosse (die) Wundartzney.
in 122			Etliche Consilia. *In* Peste (de), ... Strassburg 1576 8°
41		53	Etliche Tractaten. Vom Podagra. Vom Schlag. Von der Fallender sucht. Von der Daubsucht. Vom Kaltenwehe. Von der Colica. Von dem Bauchreissen. Von der Wassersucht. Vom Schwinen oder Aridura. Vom Schwinen oder Schwindsücht Hectica. Von Farbsuchten. Von Würmen. Vom Stullauff, ... Cöln 1564 4°
60		59	Etliche Tractaten zum ander Mal in Truck aussgangen, ... Cöln 1567 4°
79		132	Ettliche Tractatus. I. Von naturlichen dingen. II. Beschreibung etlicher Kreütter. III. Von Metallen. IIII. Von Mineralen. V. Von edlen Gesteinen ... ... Strassburg 1570 8° Etliche Tractat.
139			I. Von natürlichen dingen, *etc., as above,* Strassburg 1582 8°
153			— — — — — ... Strassburg 1587 8°
	90		— — — — — ... Strassburg 1597
83		63	Etliche Tractetlein zur Archidoxa gehorig. 1. Von dem Magneten. 2. De occulta Philosophia, darinnen tractirt wird De Consecrationibus, De Coniurationibus, De Caracteribus. Von allerley erscheinungen im schlaff. Von den jrrdischen Geistern oder Schrotlein. Von der Imagination. Von der verborgnen Schätzen. Wie der mensch vom Teuffel besessen wird. Wie man den bosen Geist von den besessenen leuten ausstreiben sol. Von dem Vngewitter.

NO.	PAGE.	BIBL. PARA.			

3. Die recht weiss zu administrirn die Medicin.

4. Von vilerley gifftigen Thiern, wie man jhnen das gifft nemen, und tödten sol, ... München 1570 4°
See also Tractätlein zu dem Archidoxis gehörig.

13 v. Excellent (an) Treatise teaching howe to cure the French-Pockes, ... London 1590 4°
See also Frantzosen (von den).
See also Morbo (de) Gallico.

Experimenta.
See Hundert und vierzehen Experimenta.

Experiments and Cures.
See Hundred (a) and fourteene Experiments and Cures.

in 55 Explicatio aliquot Aphorismorum Hippocratis.
In Medici Libelli, ... Cöln 1567

54b) Explicatio aliquot Aphorismorum Hippocratis : item tres utiles tractatus de occulta vi et operatione Corallorum, Hyperici et Persicariae. in deutscher Sprache, ... Augusta 1568 8°
See also Aphorismorum... Hippocratis genuinus sensus.
See also Afforismi.

in 101 Explication der magischen Figuren über das Bapstumb.
In Joannes de Hyperiis' *Reformir-Spiegel des weltlichen Bapsts*, ... 1620

78 131 Expositio vera harum imaginum olim Nurembergae repertarum ex fundatissimo verae Magiae Vaticinio deducta, ... 1570 8°
See also Ausslegung der Figuren.

in 90 Eygenschafften (von) eines... Wundtartzets.
In Schöner (ein) Tractat, ... Strassburg 1571 4°
See also Proprietatibus (de) perfecti Chirurgi.

190 Fasciculus ofte Lust-Hof der Chimescher Medicijnen,... Mitzgaders eenen Dictionarium dienende tot vertalingh aller onduytsche woorden die Paracelsus in syne Schriften is gebruyckende, ... Utrecht 1614 8°

135 I Fasciculus Paracelsicae Medicinae Veteris et non Novae,... In quo de Vita Morte et Resuscitatione rerum, de tuenda et conservanda sanitate,... de præparationibus medicamentorum.... Item, de generatione homunculi pygmei,... Cum Elucidationibus .. obscurorum quorumcunque locorum atque dictionum, ... Francofurt. 1581 4°
See also Dictionarium.

175 Fonderia (la)... Nella quale si contiene tutta l'arte spagirica di Teofrasto Paracelso, et sue medicine, ... Fiorenza 1604 8°

NO.	PAGE.	BIBL. PARA.				
in 89		in 65	Gradationibus (de) Liber I.			
			In Spiritibus (de) Planetarum, ... Basilea		1571	4°
26			Gradibus (de), de compositionibus et dosibus receptorum ac naturalium Libri septem, *See* Septem libri de Gradibus,... *See* Libri Septem de Gradibus.	Mylœcium	1562	4°
in 182			Gradibus (von den) vnnd Compositionibus der Recepten.			
			In Zween unterschiedene Tractat, ... Strassburg *See also* Degrees and Compositions of Receipts, *in* Archidoxis.		1608	8°
	51c)		Grande (la) Chirurgie, ... Anvers		1567	8°
69			Grande (la) vraye et parfaicte Chirurgie, ... Anvers		1568	8°
165			Grande (la) Chirurgie 1ʳᵉ Edition, ... Lyon		1593	4°
174			— — 2ᵈᵉ Edition, ... ·... Lyon		1603	4°
186	95		— — 3ᵐᵉ Edition, ... Montbeliart [*This third edition contains* Un discours de la goutte *and* Traittez de la preparation des medicamens.]		1608	8°
			Griess (vom) Sand unnd stein. *See* Schreiben von Tartarischen Kranckheiten. *See* Labyrinthus und Irrgang. *See* Tartarischen (von) Krankheiten.			
	24		Grosse (die) Wundarzney, der erste Theil, Ulm		1530	
11			Grossenn (der) Wundarzney, das erst Buch, Augspurg		1536	2°
12			— — das ander Buch, Augspurg		1536	2°
	31a)		Grossen (der) Wundarzney, das dritte Buch, Augspurg		1536	
	31a)		— — das erste Buch, Ulm		1536	2°
13			— — das erst Buch, Augspurg		1537	2°
	32		— — das 1, 2, 3 Buch,		1537	
	34b)		Grosse (die) Wundarzney, ... Strasburg		1549	8°
			Grossen (der) Wundartzney erster Theil. *See* Erster Theil der grossen Wundartzney.			
	40c)		Grosse (die) Wundarzney lateinisch uber- setzt, ... Frankfurt		1562	4°
	41		Grosse (die) Wundarzney, ... Strasburg		1563	4°
in 133			Grossen (der) Wundartzney, von dem rech- ten Drittentheil.			
			In Kleine Wundartzney .. .. Basel		1579	8°
	84a)		Grosse (die) Wundarzney, ... Basel *See also* Chirurgia.		1586	8°
			Guajaco, de ligno. *See* Ligno (de) Guajaco. *See also* Artzneybüchlein vom Franzosenholz. *See also* Holtzbüchlein. *See also* Holtz (vom) Guaiaco.			
			Hand- und Denck-Bibel. *See* Kleine Hand- und Denck-Bibel.			

NO.	PAGE.	BIBL. PARA.				
in 182			Harns (von dess) und Puls Urtheil. *In* Zween unterschiedene Tractat, ... *See also* Urinarum (de) ac Pulsuum judiciis.	Strassburg	1608	8°
			Haupt-Schlüssel der Paracelsischen Arcanen, oder das zehende Buch der Archidoxen. *See under* Archidoxa.			
			Heimlichkeiten (von) der Schöpffung aller Dingen. *See* Secretis (de) Creationis.			
			Heymelijcheden (van de) der Scheppinge aller Dinge, ... Grässe *Bibliotheca Magica*, p. 47.	Leyden	1619	8°
		11	Hermetische (der) Nord-Stern,... nebst... sechs Tractatlein Philippi... Theophrasti Bombast ab Hochenheim.			
			I. Psalterium Chymicum seu Manuale Paracelsi. II. De Tinctura Physica. III. Apocalipsis Hermetis. IV. Thesaurus Thesaurorum Alchimist-arum. V. Coelum Philosophorum. VI. Secretum Magicum, ...	Franckfurt	1771	8°
in 81			Heylung (von) der Wunden. *In* Trei Tractat, ...	Strassburg	1570	8°
in 90			— — *In* Schöner (ein) Tractat, ... *See also* Vulnerum (de)... Curis.	Strassburg	1571	8°
			Hippocratis Aphorismi. *See* Aforismi. *See* Aphorismorum... sensus. *See* Explicatio aliquot aphorismorum Hippocratis.			
42		54	Holtzbüchlein ... darinnen grüdtlich der recht nutz... des Frantzosen holtzes,... würt angezaigt. Item, ein nutzlicher Tractat von dem Vitriol, vnd seiner tugendt, ...	Strassburg	1564	8°
in 45			Holtzbüchlin (das). *In* Drey Bücher, ...	Strassburg	1565	8°
3			Holtz (vom) Guaiaco, ... *See also* Artzneybüchlein vom Franzosen-Holz. *See also* Ligno (de) Guaiaco *in* Medici Libelli.	Nurmberg	1529	4°
180			Hundert und vierzehen Experimenta und allerhand treffliche und bewehrte stuck der Artzeney, ...	Strassburg	1606	8°
		42	IV. Hundred (a) and fourtene experiments and cures,...	(1584)		8°
		86	VII. — — — — — ...	London	1596	4°
in 214		in 105	XII. — — — — — — *In* Three exact pieces, ... *See* Centum quindecim curationes experiment-aque.	London	1652	4°

NO.	PAGE.	BIBL. PARA.				
133			Kleine Wundartzney, drey Bücher begreiffendt... auch zwey Fragment, das ein von dem rechten Drittentheil der grossen Wundartzney, das Ander von den fünff Bucher de vita longa, ...	... Basel	1579	8°
181			Kleine Wund-Artzney, ... *See also* Chirurgia Minor.	Strassburg	1608	8°
200			Krancke (das) romische Reich, ...		1620	4°
			Kranckheyten (von den) so die vernunfft berauben, ... *See* Schreyben von den Kranckheyten.			
120			Kranckheiten (von den), so den Menschen der Vernunfft naturlich berauben, sampt jren Curen, ...	Strassburg	1576	8°
		27	— — — — — ... *See also* Aegritudinibus (de) amentium. *See also* Morborum (de) qui hominem ratione destituunt, cura.	Basel	1576	4°
			Kreutter (von). *In* Ettliche Tractatus.			
196			Kurtze und eygentliche Beschreibung vom Ursprung, Natur, Qualitet und Würckung, dess Weitberumbten Heylsamen, und Warmen Bads Pfeffers in Obern Schweytz,... gelegen, ... *See also* Bad Pfeffers.	Embs	1619	4°
	87		Kurze Chronik von Karnthen. *In* Drey Bucher an die Stande von Kärnthen, *See also* Brevis Carinthiae.. descriptio.		1589	
187			Kurtzer... Tractat vom Podagra, ... *Spurious*, Mook.	Mäintz	1611	4°
18			Labyrinthus Medicorum Errantium, ...	Noriberga	1553	4°
37			Labyrinthus ofte Doolhof vom de dwalende Mediciins,...	Antwerpen	1563	8°
			Labyrinth der Artzten, *See* Irrgang (von dem) vnd Labyrinth der Artzten, *in* Drey Bucher.			
106			Labyrinthus und Irrgang der vermeinten Artzet. Item, Siben Defensiones oder Schirmreden, Item, von vrsprung vnd vrsachen des griess, sands, vnd steins,... kurtzer begriff, ...	Basel	1574	8°
	87		Labyrinthus medicorum errantium. *In* Drey Bucher an die Stande von Kärnthen,		1589	
	90a)		Labyrinthus medicorum errantium, ...	Hanau	1594	8°
169		138	Labyrinthus Medicorum errantium :... accessit Dialogus, De Crisi et Catacrisi Mali cuiusdam Medici, ...	Hanovia	1599	8°
			Läme (von) sampt gründlicher gewisser jrer cur. *In* Ersten (von) dreyen Principiis. *See also* Contracturis (De).			

NO	PAGE.	BIBL. PARA.				
			Langen (von dem) Leben. *See* Fünff Bücher von dem langen leben. *See also* Vita (de) longa.			
	65d)		Lapide (de) Philosophorum germanice, ...	Antwerp	1572	
	65f)		— — Drey Tractat,	Strassburg	1572	
		112	Lapis Vegetabilis,... sambt dem zehenden Buch der Archidoxen, ...	Strassburg	1681	8°
		4	Lexicon Chymicum, ...	London	1652-3	8°
		106	— — — ... ... *See also* Dictionarium. *See also* Erklärung ettlicher wörter. *See also* Onomasticon.	London	1660	8°
63		61	Libellus de Vrinarum ac pulsuum iudicijs, tum de Physionomia... accessit de Morborum Physionomia Fragmentum, ... *See also* Urinarum (de)..judiciis..Libellus. *See also* Harns (von dess) und Puls Urtheil *in* Zween unterschiedene Tractat.	Argentina	1568	8°
25			Liber de duplici Anatomia, ... *See also* Septem Libri de Gradibus.	(Basilea)	(1561)	8°
113		147	Liber de Narcoticis aegritudinibus, ut sunt Pestis, Pleuresis et Prunella, ...	Basilea	1575	8°
76			Liber Paramirum, in quo universalis Theorica Physices et Chirurgiae origines et causae morborum traduntur,... accesserunt... libri, De Modo Pharmacandi ; De Xenodochio ; De Thermis, ... *See also* Paramirum.	Basilea	1570	8°
197		157	Liber Sermonum in Antichristos... Das ist : Ein Buchlein wider die Antichristen,...	Franckfurt	1619	4°
in 111			Liber Vexationum. *In* Schreiben von tribus Principiis aller Generaten, Basel *See also* Pyrophilia.		1574	8°
	88		Liber Vexationum erklärt vom J. R. Glauber. *See* Coelum Philosophorum. *See also* Vexationibus (de).			
44			Libri X. de mysteriis microcosmi, ...	Basilea	1590	4°
			Libri duo. De Causa et Origine Morborum. Das ist : von vrsachen vnd herkomen der Kranckheiten. De Morbis Invisibilibus. Das ist : von den vnsichtbaren Kranckheiten, ...	Cöln	1565	8°
54			— — — — — ...	Cöln	1566	4°
49			Libri duo. I. Defensiones Septem. II. De Tartaro, siue morbis Tartareis, ...	Argentorat.	1566	8°
103			— — — — — ...	Col. Agrippina	1573	8°

NO.	PAGE.	BIBL. PARA.				
112			Libri XIIII. Paragraphorum, ...	... Argentorat.	1575	8°
			Contains das Programm der Vorlesungen.			
	73a)		— — — — —	... Basilea	1575	8°
	77b)		— — — — —	... Argentorat.	1578	8°
	84b)		— — — (übersetzt),	... Basel	1586	8°
			See also Les XIV. Livres des Paragraphes.			
			See also Paragrapha.			
22			Libri Quatuor de Vita longa, ...	... Basilea	1560	8°
	50		— —	...	1560	8°
			See Vita (de) longa.			
140			Libri Quinque de Vita longa, brevi et sana. Deque triplici corpore, ...	... Francofurt.	1583	8°
248			Libri quinque de Vita longa, ...	... Basilea		8°
			See Vita (de) longa.			
36		51	Libri quinque de causis, signis & curationibus morborum ex Tartaro utilissimi,	... Basilea	1563	8°
			See also Tartarus.			
	39b)		Libri septem de gradibus et compositionibus receptorum ac naturalium ins deutsche übersetzt, ...	... Basel	1562	8°
	100		Libri septem de gradibus ac compositionibus receptorum ac naturalium cum libro de pulsibus, ...	... Nürnberg	1608	8°
			See also Gradibus (de).			
			See also Septem libri.			
in 55			Ligno (de) Guaiaco.			
			In Medici Libelli, ... Cöln		1567	4
			See also Artzneybuchlein vom Franzosenholz.			
			See also Holtzbüchlein.			
			See also Holtz (vom) Guaiaco.			
			Longa (de) Vita.			
			See Vita (de) longa.			
			Maculis (de) a nativitate ortis.			
			In Bertheonea.			
in 216		in 5	Magical (the) ... cure of wounds.			
			In Supreme (of the) Mysteries of Nature, .. London		1656	8°
223		110.	Magnalia Medico-Chymica, ... Nürnberg		1676	8°
in 83		in 63	Magneten (von dem), unnd seiner wunderbarlichen tugend.			
			In Etliche Tractetlein zur Archidoxa gehörig, .. München		1570	4°
	65g)		Manuale de lapide medicinali de tinctura planetarum, ... Antwerpia		1572	8°
in 109		in 134	Manuale.			
			In Archidoxa.. Zehen Bücher, ... Strassburg		1574	8°
		in 8	Manual of the Philosophical Medicinal Stone, ... London		1660	8°
in 222		in xx.	— — — — — ... London		1661	8°
		in 144	— — — — — ... London		1663	8°
			In Archidoxis.			

NO.	PAGE.	BIBL. PARA.			
	62a)		Meteoris (de), item de matrice, et de tribus principiis libri 2. Quibus Astronomica et Astrologica fragmenta quaedam accesserunt, ...	Basilea	(1570)
	62a)		— — — — — ...	Coln	1570 8°
	73b)		Meteoris (de), de matrice: de tribus-principiis lib. 2 cum quibusdam Astrologiae fragmentis, ...	Basilea	1575 8°
	77a)		Methodus Pharmacandi was ein Artzt am Menschen zu curiren hat, ... *See also* Modus Pharmacandi.	Strassburg	1578 4°
			Mineralen (von). *In* Ettliche Tractatus.		
in 84			Mineralibus (de), Ein Tractat. *In* Archidoxorum Theophrastiae Pars Prima, ..	Cölln	1570 4°
	110b)		XI. — — Eine Englische Ubersetzung,	London	1650 4°
			Mineralium Genealogia. *See* Genealogia Mineralium *in* Congeries Paracelsicae Chemiae.		
in 76			Modo (de) Pharmacandi. *In* Liber Paramirum, ...	Basilea	1570 8°
129			— — , deutsch, ...	Strassburg	1578 8°
31			Modus Pharmacandi. In dene beschrieben vnd gelehrt wirt was der Artzt in dem Menschen zu purgieren hat, ... *See also* Pharmacandi Modus. *See also* Methodus Pharmacandi.	Cöllenn	1562 4°
			Morbi Gallici, (de cura). *See* Cura (de) Morbi Gallici.		
in 44			Morbis (de) invisibilibus, das ist : von den vnsichtbaren Kranckheiten. *In* Libri Duo,..	Cöln	1565 8°
in 54			— — — — ... *In* Libri Duo,..	Cöln	1566 ‹
in 49			Morbis (de) Tartareis. *In* Libri Duo,..	Argentoratum	1566 8°
in 103			Morbis (de) Tartareis. *In* Libri Duo,.. .. .. *See also* Tartarus.	Col. Agrippina	1573 8°
131			Morbo (de) Gallico. Warhaffte Cur der Frantzosen, ... *See* Drey chirurgische Bucher. *See* Excellent (an) Treatise. *See* Frantzosen (von den).	Strassburg	1578 8°
in 66		in 128	Morborum capitalium quatuor Epilepsiae, Podagrae Paralysis et Hydropisis Curae. *In* Pyrophilia Vexationumque Liber, ...	Basilea	1568 8°
in 63		in 61	Morborum (de) Physionomia Fragmentum. *In* Libellus...de Vrinarum...iudicijs... ..	Argentina	1568 8°
	74a)		Morborum (de) qui hominem ratione destituunt cura, ... *See also* Kranckheiten (von den).	Argentorat.	1576 8°

D

NO.	PAGE.	BIBL. PARA.				
178		153	Operum... VI.-XI., ... Francofurt.		1605	4°
38			Opus Chyrurgicum, warhaffte vnnd vollkomne Wundartznei, ... Strassburg		1564	2°
51			Opus Chyrurgicum vollkommne Wundartz-ney, ... Strassburg		1566	2°
	48a)	20	— — —, germanice, ... Francofurt.		1566	2°
93			— — — — — ... Collen *See* Wund und Artzney Buch.		1571	2°
136			Opus Chyrurgicum. Warhaffte vnd Volkhommene der waren von Got beschaffenen Medicin, ... Basel		1581	2°
			Opus Paramirum, *See* Paramirum.			
	84	37 &72 30 & 137	Pandora, das ist, die Edleste Gab Gottes,... Basel		1582	8°
			Pandora, ... Basel		1588	8°
		116	Pandora explicata, ... Franckfurt		1706	8°
		96	Pandora Magnalium Naturalium Aurea et Benedicta, ... Strassburg Contains *Apocalypsis Hermetis*, translated by Paracelsus, and *Tinctura Physicorum Paracelsica.*		1608	8°
185			Paradisus Aureolus Hermeticus, ... Francofurt.		1608	4°
			Paradoxa. *See* Opera Medico-Chemica.			
			Paragranum. *See* Buch (das) Paragranum.			
	87		Paragraphorum (das Buch) von den vier Columnen der Medicin, ... [Paragraphorum here is a misprint for Paragranum.]		1589	
			PARAGRAPHA.			
92			Dreyzehen Bücher Paragraphorum, ... Basel		1571	4°
112			Libri XIIII. Paragraphorum, ... Argentorat. Contains das Programm der Vorlesungen.		1575	8°
	73a)		Quatuordecim libri Paragraphorum, ... Basilea		1575	8°
	77b)		Libri Paragraphorum XIV., ... Argentorat.		1578	8°
	84b)		Ubersetzung der 14 Bücher der Paragraphen, ... Basel		1586	8°
211		141	Les XIV. Livres des Paragraphes, ... Paris		1631	4°
			PARAMIRUM.			
28			Das Buch Paramirum, ... Mühlhausen		1562	4°
	39		— —-		1562	2°
47			— — ... ... Franckfurt		1565	8°
	45a)		Opus Paramirum, ... Coln		1565	4°
	48b)		Opus Paramirum, ... Coln		1566	4°

NO.	PAGE.	BIBL. PARA.			
in 50		in 125	Liber quartus Paramiri de Matrice. *In* Buch (das) Meteororum.	Cöln	1566 4°
76			Liber Paramirum... Accesserunt huic et hi... libri. De modo Pharmacandi. De Xenodochio. De Thermis, ...	Basilea	1570 8°
118			Volumen Medicinae Paramirum... De medica industria, Von des Artzt geschicklichkeit, ...	Strassburg	1575 8°

PESTILENTZ.

NO.	PAGE.	BIBL. PARA.			
20		123	Fur Pestilentz. Ain seer nützlicher vnnd bewerter Tractat, ...	Saltzburg	1554 4°
24			Von der Pestilentz, ...	Straubing	1561 4°
35			Von der Pestilentz, ...	Straubing	1563 4°
43			Zwey Bücher von der Pestilentz vnd ihren zufallen, ...	Strassburg	(1564) 8°
115			Vom Ursprung der Pestilentz vnd ihren zufallenden Krankheiten, ...	Basel	1575 8°

PESTIS.

NO.	PAGE.	BIBL. PARA.			
		41	De cura pestis, ...	Ingolstadt	1563
in 55			{ De Peste Commentarius, } { Fragmentum aliud de Peste. } *In* Medici Libelli, ...	Cöln	1567 4°
86			De la Peste, ...	Anvers	1570 8°
122			De Peste, an die Statt Stertzingen geschrieben. Item Etliche Consilia Theophrasti Paracelsi,... ... ... [Mook compares *Vom Urspung des Pestilentz,* No. 115.]	Strassburg	1576 8°
		80a)	Bericht von der Pest, ...	Strasburg	1583 8°
189			De Peste, so er an die Statt Störtzingen geschrieben, ...	Oppenheim	1613 4°
203			— — — — — ...	Franckfurt	1622 4°
212			Von der Pest, ... *See* Drey ausserlesene Tractat. *See also* Liber de Narcoticis Aegritudinibus.	Franckfurt	1640 4°
204			Petite (la) Chirurgie autrement ditte la Bertheonee. Plus les traittez.. des Apostemes syrons ou noeuds, des ouuertures du cuir &c., ... *See also* Bertheonea. *See also* Apostematibus (de). *See also* Cutis (de) Apertionibus.	Paris	1623 8°

Pfeffers.
See Bad (vonn dem) Pfeffers.

Pharmacandi methodus.
See Methodus Pharmacandi.

NO.	PAGE.	BIBL. PARA.				
130			Pharmacandi modus. Was der Artzt in dem Menschen zu purgieren habe : vnnd was fur schaden auss missverstand des purgirens entspringen, ... *See also* Modus Pharmacandi. *See also* Modo (de) Pharmacandi.		1578	8°
39		52	Philosophiae ad Athenienses drey Bücher. Von vrsachen und Cur Epilepsiae, das ist, des Hinfallenden siechtagen,... Item, vom vrsprvng, Cur oder heilung der contracten glidern, ...	Cöln	1564	4°
			Philosophiae ad Athenienses, vier Bücher. *See* Vier Bucher Philosophiae ad Athenienses.			
		in 7	XVII. Philosophy to the Athenians. *In* Philosophy Reformed and Improved, by H. Pinnel.	London	1657	8°
195			Philosophia de Limbo .. .. *See also* Philosophia Paracelsica.	Magdeburg	1618	4°
59			Philosophiae magnae... Tractatus aliquot, *Contains* (*all in German*) : 1. De vera influentia rerum. 2. De inventione artium. 3. De sensu et instrumentis. 4. De tempore laboris et requiei. 5. De bona et mala fortuna. 6. De utraque fortuna. 7. De sanguine ultra Mortem. 8. De obsessis a malis Spiritibus. 9. De somniis et Erynnibus in somno et annexis. 10. De animabus Hominum post mortem apparentibus. 11. De lunaticis. 12. De generatione Stultorum. 13. De Homunculis. 14. De Nymphis, Silvanis &c. 15. De Imaginatione. 16. De Maleficio et eorum operibus. 17. De Animalibus ex Sodomia natis.	Coln	1567	4°
		21	— — — — — ...	Ulm	1567	4°
	56b)		Philosophiae magnae collectanea, ...	Basilea	1569	
	56b)		— — —	Colonia	1569	8°
245		62	— — — ... ... [The Contents of this last are the same as in No. 59. Compare the Contents given by Leo Suavius, *Bibliographia Paracelsica*, Part III. p. 56.]	Basilea		8°
194		99	Philosophia mystica,... ... ... *Contains* : De Poenitentiis. Astronomia Olympi novi.	Newstadt	1618	4°

NO.	PAGE.	BIBL. PARA.				
			Theologia Cabalistica de perfecto homine in Christo Jesu, et contra. Commentarius in Danielem Prophetam *ascribed to Paracelsus.*			
	83		Philosophia occulta latine, ...	Basilea	1584	8°
	117a)		Philosophia occulta deutsch, ...		1686	8°
235		161	Philosophia occulta, Auszug. *In* Arnold's *Kirchen- und Ketzer-Historien,* .. *See* Occulta (de) Philosophia.	Schaffhausen	1740	2°
213			Philosophia Paracelsica : das ist ausfuhrlicher Unterricht ; vom Limbo, ... *See* Philosophia de Limbo.	Franckfurt	1644	4°
	33		Philosophia sagax, ...	Wien	1537	2°
	74b)		Philosophiae sagacis von der grossen und kleinen Welt II. Bücher oder Astronomia magna, ... *See* Astronomia Magna.	Francofurt.	1576	4°
		18	XXIV. Philosophical and Chymical Treatise of Fire and Salt, ...			8°
in 63		in 61	Physionomia (de). *In* Libellus de Vrinarum... iudicijs.	Argentina	1568	8°
in 64		in 127	Physionomia. *In* Urinarum (de)... judiciis... libellus. ..	Colonia	1568	4°
in 55			Physionomia morborum. *In* Medici Libelli.	Cöln	1567	4°
in 63		in 61	— — Fragmentum. *In* Libellus de Vrinarum... judiciis. ..	Argentina	1568	8°
			Podagra (vom). *See* Kurtzer... Tractat vom Podagra.			
1			Practica, gemacht auff Europen, anzufahen in dem nechst kunfftigen dreyssigsten jar, Biss auff dz Vier vnd dreyssigst nachuolgend, ...	Augspurg	1529	4°
2			Practica gemacht auff Europen, ...	Nürmberg	1529	4°
7			Practica Teutsch auff das MDXXXV. Jar,	(Augspurg)	1535	4°
	26		Practica deutsch auf das Jahr 1535, ...		1595	4°
14			Practica Teutsch auffs MDXXXVII. Jar, ..	(Augspurg)	(1537)	4°
			PRAEPARATIO.			
	54c)	24 } 36 }	Praeparatione (de) Ellebori germanice,	Basilea	1568	8°
67			Praeparationum Libri duo, ...		(1568)	8°
			Praparationum Schreiben. *See* Schreiben praparationum.			
71		130	Praeparationibus (de), Libri duo, ... *See also* Zwey Bücher Praeparationum.	Cracovia	1569	4°
	56a)		Praeparationibus (de) mineralium libri II.,	Basilea	1569	8°
	114		— — — — — ...	Basilea	1669	
in 74			Praeparationibus (de). *In* Archidoxorum... libri decem, ...	Basilea	1570	8°

NO.	PAGE.	BIBL. PARA.			
90			Schoner (ein) Tractat... von Eygenschafften eines vollkomnen Wundartzets,.. ... Strassburg		1571	8°
			Contains :			
			2. Von offnung der Haut.			
			3. Von heylung der Wunden.			
			4. Von Wurmen, secunda editio.			
			5. Von den contracturen vnd iren glidern, tertia editio.			
			See also Trei Tractat.			
128	76a)		Schreiben von den Frantzosen in IX. Bucher verfasset, ... Basel		1577	8°
			See also Frantzosen (von den).			
57		57	Schreyben von den kranckheyten so die vernunfft berauben als da sein S. Veyts Thantz Hinfallender siechtage, Melancholia vnd Vnsinnigkeit, &c. Sampt ihrn warhaften curen, ...		1567	4°
			See also Kranckheiten (von den), so den Menschen der Vernunfft natürlich berauben.			
	55f)		Schreiben Praparationum, ... Basel		1568	8°
110			Schreiben Preparationum oder von zubereitung etlicher Dingen notwendig... zu wüssen den Medicis, ...		1574 (?)	8°
			See also Praeparatio.			
32			Schreiben von Tartarischen kranckheiten nach den alten nammen, Vom griess sand vnnd Stein. Sampt dem Baderbuchlin, ... (Basel)		(1563)	8°
	41		Schreiben von Tartarischen Kranckheiten, Frankfurt		1563	8°
	51b)		— — — — — ... Basel		1567	4°
	54d)		— — — — — ... Strasburg		1568	8°
			See also Tartarus.			
111			Schreiben von tribus Principiis aller generaten. Item Liber vexationum. Item... Thesaurus Alchimistarum, ... Basel		1574	8°
			See also Tribus (de) Principiis.			
121			Schreiben von warmen oder Wildbaderen, Basel		1576	8°
			See also Baderbuchlein.			
			See also Badenfart Büchlein.			
			Schrifften.			
			See Bücher und Schrifften.			
			See Opera, Bucher und Schrifften.			
201			Sechs Prognostica, ...		1620	4°
202			—		1621	4°
			[No. IV. by Paracelsus.]			
			See also Prognosticatio.			
	69b)	135	Sechste (das) Buch in der artznei. Von den Tartarischen oder Stein Kranckheiten... zwei Tractat, ... Basel		1574	8°

NO.	PAGE.	BIBL. PARA.				
188			Secreet (dat) der Philosophien, inhoudende hoemen alle aertsche Dingen, gelijck als Alluyn, Solfer, Coperoot ende diergelijcken bereyden sal ende gebruycken. Ende ook hoemen alle Olien wt den Metallen distileren ende maken sal... ...	Leyden	1612	8°
119			Secretis (de) Creationis. Von Heimlichkeiten der Schopffung aller Dingen, ...	Strassburg	1575	8°
in 124			— — Secunda editio. *In* Drey Tractat, ...	Strassburg	1577	8°
	123b)		— —	Strassburg		8°
		142	IX. Secrets (The) of Physick and Philosophy, *See also* Key (The) of Philosophy.	London	1633	12°
230			Secretum Magicum, ... Reprinted in Arnold's *Kirchen- und Ketzer-Historien*, II. 445, ...	Schaffhausen	1729 1740-52	2°
234		160	Secretum Magicum, im auszuge abgedruckt. *In* Arnold's *Kirchen- und Ketzer-Historien*, ..	Schaffhausen	1740-52	2°
		in 11	— — — *In* Hermetische (der) Nordstern,.. .. .. *See also under* Thesaurinella.	Frankfurt	1771	8°
	84c)		Secretum secretorum, ... *See also* Wunder Artzney vnnd verborgine Geheimnisse aller geheimnissen.	Basilea	1586	8°
in 103			Septem Defensiones adversus aemulos suos. *In* Libri duo, ... *See* Defensiones septem.	Col. Agrippina	1573	8°
in 106			Siben Defensiones, oder Schirmreden. *In* Labyrinthus.	Basel	1574	8°
65			Septem libri de Gradibus, de Compositionibus, de Dosibus receptorum ac naturalium : cum scholiis .. quibus 17 capita de Anatomia in fine addita sunt, ... *See also* Libri septem. *See also* Gradibus (de).	Basilea	1568	8°
in 199			Sermones in Antichristum. *In* Drey vnderscheydene Tractätlein, ... *See also* Liber Sermonum.	Franckfurt	1619	4°
			Serpentibus (de). *See* Vermibus (de).			
in 99			Sigillis (de) Planetarum. *In* Archidoxorum... X. Bücher, ...		1572	4°
in 75			Signis (de) Zodiaci et Mysteriis eorum. *In* Summis (de) Naturae Mysteriis, ...	Basilea	1570	8°
in 89		in 65	Signis (de) Zodiaci et ejus mysteriis. *In* Spiritibus (de) Planetarum, ...	Basilea	1571	4°
in 143		in 74	— — — *In* Summis (de) Naturae Mysteriis, ...	Basilea	1584	8°
in 216		in 5	XIV. — — — (English), *In* Supreme (of the) Mysteries of Nature.	London	1656	8°
	101a)	97	Solis e Puteo Emergentis : sive Dissertationes Chymico-technicae Libri tres, ... *Contains* Clavis operum Paracelsi.	Francofurt.	1613	4°

NO.	PAGE.	BIBL. PARA.				
32			Schreiben von Tartarischen Kranckheiten, nach den alten nammen, vom griess sand vnnd stein, sampt dem Baderbüchlin, ...	(Basel)	(1563)	8°
	41		Tartarischen (von) Krankheiten, vom Griess, Sand und Stein. Sampt dem Baderbuchlein, ...	Strassburg	1563	
			Tartarischen (von) Kranckheiten. *See* Schreiben von Tartarischen Krankheiten...			
			Causis (de)... morborum ex Tartaro. *See* Libri quinque de causis...			
in 40		in 124	Ursprung (von dem)... der tartarischen Krankheiten, nach dem alten namen vom Stein, Sandt oder Griess. *In* Drey Bucher, ...	Cöln	1564	4°
in 49			Tartaro (de) sive morbis tartareis. *In* Libri duo, ...	Argentoratum	1566	8°
	51b)		Schreiben von tartarischen Krankheiten,	Basel	1567	4°
	54d)		— . — — ...	Strasburg	1568	8°
77			Tartaro (de) libri septem, ...	Basilea	1570	8°
in 103			Morbis (de) Tartareis. *In* Libri Duo,..	Col. Agrippina	1573	8°
			Tartarischen (von den) Kranckheiten. *See* Sechste (das) Buch in der artznei.			
	73d)		Tartaro (de), ...	Colonia	1575	8°
	87		Buch (das) vom Tartaro, d. i. von Sand und Stein. *In* Drey Bucher an die Stande von Kärnthen.		1589	
in 99			Tempore (de). *In* Archidoxorum... X. Bucher, ...		1572	4°
in 109		in 134	Tesaurus tesaurorum. *In* Archidoxa... Zehen Bücher, ... *See also* Thesaurus.	Strassburg	1574	8°
108			Testamentum, ...	Strassburg	1574	8°
234		160	Tetragrammaton. *In* Arnold's *Kirchen- und Ketzer-Historien*, ..	Schaffhausen	1740	2°
		149	Theophrastisch Vade-Mecum, das ist: etliche sehr nutzliche Tractat, von der warhafftigen bereittung vnd rechten gebrauch der Chymischen Medicamenten,	Magdeburgk	1596	4°
168			— — — — — ...	Eissleben	1597	8°
		87	— — — — — ...	Magdeburgk	1597	4°
		100	Theophrastische Practica, das ist, Auss-erlesene Theophrastiche Medicamenta,		1618	8°
239			Theophrastus Paracelsus als Bekampfer des Pabsthums, ...	Leipzig	1845	8°

See also Ausslegung der Figuren.
See also Joyfull newes.

NO.	PAGE.	BIBL. PARA.				
.	104b)		Theosophisches (ein) Büchlein, von dem wahren uberbliebenen saamen Gottes in uns,... ... ... Neustadt		1618	4°
in 55			Therebinthina (de) et utroque Helleboro. *In* Medici Libelli, ... Cöln		1567	4°
in 76			Thermis (de). *In* Liber Paramirum, ... Basilea		1570	8°
	62e)		Thermis (de) Fabarianis in Helvetia. ... Argentorat.		1570	
184			Thesaurinella Olympica aurea tripartita, ... Franckfort		1608	4°
226		113	— — — — ... Franckfurt *Contains* Secretum Magicum *by* Paracelsus.		1682	8°
in 111			Thesaurus Alchimistarum. *In* Schreiben von tribus Principiis aller Generaten,.. .. .. Basel		1574	8°
		in 11	Thesaurus Thesaurorum Alchimistarum. *In* Hermetische (der) Nord-Stern, ... Frankfurt *See also* Tesaurus.		1771	8°
214		105	XII. Three exact pieces of Leonard Phioravant... whereunto is annexed Paracelsus his one hundred and fourteen Experiments, ... London *See also* One hundred and fourteen Experiments.		1652	4°
			Three (of the) Principles. *See under* Tribus (de) Principiis.			
			Tinctura (von der) Physica, *See* Büchlein von der Tinctura Physica.			
in 89		in 65	Tinctura (de) physica. *In* Spiritibus (de) Planetarum, ... Basilea		1571	4°
		in 11	— — *In* Hermetische (der) Nord-Stern, ... Frankfurt		1771	8°
in 74			Tinctura (de) Physicorum. *In* Archidoxorum... Libri decem, ... Basilea		1570	8°
in 80			— — *In* Archidoxa... Zehen Bücher, ... Strassburg		1570	8°
in 82			— — *In* Archidoxa ex Theophrastia, ... München		1570	4°
in 85		in 64	— — *In* Archidoxa... zwölff Bucher, ... München		1570	4°
in 109		in 134	— — *In* Archidoxa... Zehen Bücher, ... Strassburg		1574	8°
in 242			— — *In* Archidoxorum Theophrastiae pars prima, ..			4°
		in 96	— — *In* Pandora Magnalium Naturalium Aurea et Benedicta,.. .. .. Strassburg		1608	8°
			Tincture (of the) of the Philosophers. *In* Archidoxis.			
224			Tincturen (von), Stein der Weisen und andere Chymische Tractatlein, ... Helmstadt *See also* Aurei Velleris... Tractatus II. *See also* Eroffnete Geheimnisse.		1677	8°
in 205		in 103	Tractaet van de Alchymie. *In* Princelijck Gheschenck, ... Amstelredam		1633	4°

NO.	PAGE.	BIBL. PARA.				
			VITA LONGA.			
22			Libri quatuor de vita longa, ...	... Basilea	1560	8°
		50	— — — — ...	... Basilea	1560	8°
	36b)		De vita longa Libri IV.	... Francofurt.	1560	8°
	37b)		De vita longa libri tres, ...	... Tigurum	1561	
	39a)		De vita longa, ...		1562	
	39a)		— — libri quinque, ...	... Basilea	1562	
	48c)		— — ed. Leo Suavius,...	... Parisii	1566	8°
		55	— — — ...	... Parisii	1566 (?)	8°
	51a)	23 & 126	— — — ...	... Parisii	1567	8°
62	55e)	60	— — — ...	... Basilea	1568	8°
	55e)		— — — ...	... Francofurt.	1568	
in 82			— — — *In* Archidoxa ex Theophrastia, ..	.. München	1570	4°
in 84			— — — *In* Archidoxorum Theophrastiae Pars prima,	Cöln	1570	4°
in 85		in 64	— — — *In* Archidoxa Zwölff Bücher, ...	.. München	1570	4°
107			Fünff Bucher vonn dem langen leben, ...	Strassburg	1574	8°
	78d)		De Vita longa, ...	... Basilea	1579	8°
in 133			— — ... *In* Kleine Wundartzney.	.. Basel	1579	8°
in 140			De Vita longa, brevi et sana. *In* Libri quinque, ...	.. Francofurtum	1583	8°
	80b		De vita longa, ...	... Basilea	1583	8°
in 242			De longa Vita. *In* Archidoxorum Theophrastiae pars prima. Cf. No. 84, Coln 1570.			4°
in 248			Libri V. de Vita longa, incognitarum rerum, et hucusque a nemine tractatarum refertissimi...	... Basilea		8°
in 42		in 54	Vitriol (von dem), und seiner tugendt. *In* Holtzbuchlein, ...	.. Strassburg	1564	8°
in 45			Vitriol (von dem) vnd seinen krankhaiten, *In* Drey Bücher, ...	.. Strassburg	1565	4°
in 84			Vitriolo (de). *In* Archidoxorum Theophrastiae Pars prima, ..	Cölln	1570	
			Volumen Medicinae Paramirum. *See under* Paramirum.			
			Vulnerum (de) et ulcerum curis. *In* Bertheonea. *See also* Heylung (von) der Wunden.			
		32	Wahrhaffte Beschreibung einer Prophecey was es mit dem jetzigen Krieg, fur eine Endschaft gewinnen, ...		1632	4°

E

NO.	PAGE.	BIBL. PARA.			
		33	Zween Tractat von der signatura aller • Erdgewachse, ...	Nürnberg	1647 8ᵘ
182			Zween vnterschiedene Tractat. I. Von dess Harns vnd Puls Urtheil : wie auch von der Physiognomj : so viel einem Artzt von nothen. II. Von den Gradibus vnnd Compositionibus der Recepten vnd Naturlichen Dingen, ...	Strassburg	1608 8ᵘ
			Zwen tractat von lame sampt grundlicher gewisser jrer cur. *In* Ersten (von) dreyen principiis.		
98			Zwen Tractatus. I. De viribus membrorum spiritualium. II. De Electro. Mit erklarung ettlicher worter vnd praeparationum, ... *See also* Dictionarium.	Strassburg	1572 8°
in 242		•	Zwey Bücher Praeparationum. *In* Archidoxorum Theophrastiae pars prima, .. *See also under* Praeparatio.		
43			Zwey Bucher von der Pestilentz vnd jhren zufallen, ... *See also* Pestilentz	Strassburg	(1564) 8°

BIBLIOGRAPHIA PARACELSICA.

PART VI.

PARACELSUS

REVIEWS

BY

JOHN FERGUSON, LL.D., F.R.S.E., F.S.A.

GLASGOW:
Printed at the University Press by
ROBERT MACLEHOSE AND CO.,
1896

150 Copies printed

CONTENTS.

FOR convenience of reference I have brought together in this present part three articles upon Paracelsus. Permission to include the second and third of these has been kindly granted by the editor of the *Academy* and Messrs. A. & C. Black respectively. Except for a few verbal alterations in the first paper, the present are reprints of the articles as they originally appeared without any modification or correction. They must not, therefore, be regarded as containing necessarily my present, and certainly not my final, estimate of the subject of them. One's knowledge is too imperfect at the present moment for the passing of a decisive or even of a fairly accurate judgment upon a man whom it has been the fashion for three hundred and fifty years to malign, and whose works are in so chaotic a condition that one hardly knows what is genuine and what is spurious. Some of his countrymen now realize that the obloquy which has been so long his portion may have been grievously misdirected ; that, at any rate, considering what Paracelsus effected, it would be no more than scientific and reasonable to ascertain by examination and criticism how far the traditional estimate of him can be justified, and to assign him his right place, whatever that may be, on an unprejudiced consideration of his merits—or demerits—alone.

The most recent indication of the revival of interest in Paracelsus is displayed in the work of Aberle upon his portraits, and in the splendid bibliography by Sudhof of the works attributed to him.

The first of the following papers was the result of the perusal of a few easily accessible biographies and notices in dictionaries and journals, and was read to the Dialectic Society in the University of Glasgow on March 7, 1873. It was printed in 1874 in a volume of essays edited by students. My acquaintance at that time with books whether by or about Paracelsus was very limited, and an account of the man and his system was much easier for me to draw up then than it would be now. The article, therefore, represents merely a stage in my own knowledge of the subject and is not an unassailable verdict on Paracelsus himself. Still, even if it be imperfect in some details and inaccurate in others, and therefore amenable to correction and criticism, it was meant, at all events, to present as impartial a view as I could at the time of one of the most conspicuous personalities of the 15th-16th century. In making this reprint I had at first meant to add corrections of certain statements which it contains, but I see so much to alter that I should have to recast the whole paper. I have preferred therefore to leave it as it is, and to let it represent the opinions expressed now more than twenty years ago.

The second article is from the *Academy* for October 20, 1877. The criticism of Mook's work originally intended for that journal having proved too lengthy was put aside, and this summary of it was substituted. But not to lose the labour I had expended on the original review, I went still more minutely into the questions raised, and, when I had used up all my available material, printed the results. It was this extended examination which formed the first part of the present series, and which, having started me in the collecting of the literature, has since led me farther into Paracelsus studies and researches than I ever intended to go. In that first part I thought that all that was requisite on the subject had been said; after twenty years I can realize more correctly how much has still to be done before a critical and just estimate of Paracelsus can be formed.

The third paper was written in 1884, for the last edition of the *Encyclopaedia Britannica*, and was printed in the XVIIIth volume of that work. I have reprinted it without change, not ignorant that it too could be amended.

THE UNIVERSITY,
GLASGOW, May 29th, 1896.

PARACELSUS is a fortunate man; his enemies were his first biographers. By their exertions he has had every one of his faults, every one of his delinquencies, every one of his sins and shortcomings carefully portrayed, minutely, almost lovingly described, unweariedly repeated. While it is no use, therefore, for any subsequent historian to try to make him out worse than he has been already depicted, an opportunity is thereby afforded to those who, whether actuated by charity and wholesome scepticism to believe him not so bad as has been said, or by perversity to think differently from the mass, or by curiosity to examine the statements, the inferences, and the credibility of the authorities, might be inclined to represent him as better. Compared with those who repeat with indifference what is detrimental to Paracelsus, the charitable and doubtful, the perverse and curious are, it is true, in a minority; nor is it difficult to see why. It is, generally speaking, easier to copy what has been said before than to say something new; it is less troublesome to reiterate statements than to examine patiently the grounds on which they rest; brilliant sarcasm and crushing invective, hard names and mockery, come more easily to one's call than cautious, critical judgment and cordial appreciation. To find evidence for the evil in one's neighbour, one has only to question one's own consciousness; but to believe that a man has in him much good as well as evil, one has not unfrequently to go out of one's self for the fact, and convince the reason that it actually exists. So to Paracelsus it has happened, that since his life, like that of others, has two sides, it has been, and will probably continue to be, represented in two ways, according as those who care a single tittle about him are impressed by his faults or his merits. It is not likely that any one at the present day would deliberately write an *éloge* of Paracelsus, without the discovery of facts which would undermine the credibility of the present authorities, and reverse the judgment of the last three and a half centuries. That any such exist there is no reason at present to suppose; and even though there were, Paracelsus does not fill such a place in the interests of to-day as that many would know, much less care, that he was different from what had been generally supposed. In the meantime the incidents as originally narrated must be accepted with the constant reflection that, even when most minute and circumstantial, contemporary information is true to a certain point only; true, perhaps, as to matter of fact, as to the general outline, but not to be depended on either for shading or colour. As has been excellently said by Wilhelm von Humboldt, "no faculty is rarer" (it might be said 'is more rarely exercised') "than the purely descriptive. In every narrative are intercalated everywhere (unconsciously, perhaps) incidental comments, passing judgments are mixed up; and it is almost impossible to resist the tendency of the mind to generalize, to group the facts so as to make an effective story, or a striking picture." Keeping this in remembrance, the cautious reader will accept with due qualification the statements of one or two witnesses only, and particularly when, unfavourable, they come from enemies. Erastus, Conring, Oporinus, and others, who made so fierce an onslaught upon Paracelsus and his system and followers, may be—indeed must be—believed as to certain facts bearing upon his life and manners; but all of them show so much virulence in their several accounts, that one is doubtful about the extent to which they may be trusted.

At this distance of time, when all immediate personal concern in the people and their disputes has disappeared, it is remarkable how, with a slight interpretation, which Paracelsus' contemporaries either could not or would not allow, some of his so-called self-assertion and vulgarity is found to be intelligible and even endurable. By such favourable explanations his more recent biographers have, to a certain extent, modified previous opinion, and given him that position in the history of science to which he seems fairly entitled. Nevertheless, one feels that a critical and impartial life of Paracelsus has still to be written; and after acknowledging what has been already done, and making allowance for the limited interest which the subject presents, one confesses that the surprise expressed by Brucker one hundred and fifty years ago is not without foundation still.

The details of Paracelsus' life are both meagre and disputed.

He tells us himself that his father was one William, of the Swabian family Bombast von Hohenheim, to which belonged George Bombast von Hohenheim, Grand Master of the Order of St. John. His father lived for a time at Maria-Einsiedeln, in the Canton of Schwyz, and it was there that Paracelsus was born in or about the year 1493. Two houses, one of which was demolished even during the present century, formerly claimed the distinction of being the spot where he first saw daylight. There is another account, however, which is put forward in opposition to the preceding, but which is not quite so flattering to Paracelsus. According to this, his father came from Gais, in Appenzell, and his name was not Hohenheim, but Höhener, or Höchener. It is hardly necessary to enter here into the proofs of these accounts. The older writers[1] incline to believe with Erastus that he belonged to the lower strata of society; while more recent and less biassed authorities say that he was certainly a Hohenheim, and that all other accounts are false. Some go the length of exhibiting the arms of the family; but others assert that heralds regard with sinister aspect certainly the shield of Paracelsus' father, and probably his own as well. Respecting his mother, it is only said that she was the superior or superintendent of a lazaretto at Einsiedeln when William von Hohenheim married her.

When Paracelsus was nine years old, his father removed with his family to Villach in Carinthia. There he resided

---

[1] Le Clerc, however, supports the nobler extraction of Paracelsus, and says that Erastus does not seem to have taken the trouble to ascertain the true state of the case. It is singular that, while following Erastus in other matters, it did not occur to him that Erastus might be as inaccurate in them.—*Histoire de la Médécine*, p. 793, Amsterdam, 1723

for thirty years as a physician, dying in 1534. When Paracelsus afterwards wrote a treatise, which he dedicated to the magistracy of the place, he thanked them for the kindness they had shown his father. How he passed those years of youth it is impossible now to say. He was brought up, he says, upon cheese, and milk, and black bread, and he repeats that his youth was spent in "hunger mixed with thirst." His education—such education as could then be got—was not altogether neglected. His father, if we can trust Van Helmont, had a large library, replenished with what kind of books we need hardly ask— scholastic theology and metaphysics, astrology, magic, alchemy, the works of Hippocrates, Galen, and the Arabic physicians—all dusky volumes in manuscript. Into these Paracelsus looked, first induced by his father, and then carried on by his own ambition to excel in the mystery of knowledge. Desultory as he doubtless was, he seems never to have imbibed that implicit faith in any one of his teachers, dead or alive, which would compel him to sub- scribe to any set form of doctrine. He viewed all that he learned as imperfect, as inaccurate, something to be enlarged, something to be amended—and by him. When he left his father's house and went into the world to complete his education, he rushed hither and thither, from school to university, from the lecture on logic to the practical work of the miner, the metallurgist, the concocter of herbs, and drugs, and charms. He gives a list of his masters—Scheyt, of Settgach; Erhart, of Lavant; Trith- emius, of Würzburg; Fugger, of Augsburg, who had rich silver mines. Unfortunately for Paracelsus—if it be he who actually wrote the passage—the dates of the death of some of these men form a difficulty in the way of believing that he ever studied under them. The longer he wandered among the learned of the time, the less satisfying to his wants he found the matter they concerned themselves with, and wished to teach him. He had been too ill grounded in the rudiments of knowledge to profit by any training which they might have given him, and thus driven, he had recourse to whatever persons could display to him positive knowledge, and bring him in contact with existing nature. It was when in this state of desperation that he assumed the garb of the travelling scholastic—a common enough tribe then—

> " Wente wide in this world,
> Wondres to heare,"

and then frequented the company, not only of learned doctors, but of bath-keepers, barbers, old crones, gipsies, and such people. Too much appears to have been made out of this declaration of Paracelsus. He seems only thereby to show that he did not despise knowledge, however humbly accommodated. Although a physician or a student of natural science now would not think of associating with such teachers, in order to study the science upon which medicine rests, it is to be remembered that at the beginning of the sixteenth century these were the people who had more or less empirical knowledge of natural history, and the healing and destroying properties of plants and minerals. The days of witchcraft were not over, when aged women were supposed to have more than earthly power over the forces of nature; the gipsies, the mysterious soothsayers, the mutterers of strange spells in a strange tongue, had just arrived in Europe, from some dim land, where magic was the common gift of all ; they really had some knowledge of what herbs were poisonous, and what healing. The barbers were also surgeons, and the symbol of their ancient union may still be seen at the shop doors of their modern representatives. In our days of accumulated learning, the teachers of a past time are themselves subjected to examination. Even from the gipsies the garb of mystery is almost at last stripped. But when Paracelsus met them in his wanderings over Europe, the very tone of mind which sees nothing as too mean for examination was not yet dreamed of, much less in operation as now.

To a man of Paracelsus' nature, academical distinction could not present great attraction, and it thus remains questionable if he ever graduated at any university. Upon this, as on most other points of his personal history, we are left swimming in a turmoil of contradictions and probabilities. He says in one place, that of the great seminaries he visited he was a distinguished ornament—in others he cries out against the doctors of his time, in his valiant preaching down of shams : " What good does a name do ? —a title, a high school, if we have not high skill to boot ? It is the skill that makes the physician, not the name or the school. What the better are we that we enjoy great deference and live in grand style, if we are lacking in art ? What is there in the high school which is not to be found in the low ? Is a higher wisdom, a higher piety taught yonder ? Ah, very likely. Yonder are enthroned Potentes, in whom is no truth, no wisdom, no pity ; but only falsity, truculence, rascality. But what does it matter to me whether the high schools choose to follow me or not ?

They will be low enough by and by, and I shall do more harm to them after my death than during this my life—now, when they despise me because I stand alone, because I am an upstart, because I am German." It really matters very little, as he himself says, whether he had a degree or not. If he had had it, there was no need for arguing about it; he had only to produce evidence, unless he had some special reason for keeping it concealed. If he had not a degree, he was only in this among the first of those who have studied science without any assistance from high school or university.

If we can trust Paracelsus himself and his disciples, he travelled over a great part of the then known world during some ten years of his life. There is no particular ground for doubting this, unless—as has been argued—his ignorance of geography is a proof that he never was in the countries he mentions. Subsequent investigation, however, has shown that he actually was in certain countries in which it had been asserted that he never was, and his familiarity with certain historical events implies that he was an eye-witness of them. He travelled chiefly in Central Europe, but he resided also in Denmark, and accompanied the army of King Christian II. in the capacity of surgeon. He went to Poland and Russia, thence he was taken—not without compulsion—to Tartary, ingratiated himself apparently with the Khan, who sent him as tutor or companion with his son to Constantinople, where "in the house of the Greek astrologer" he was indoctrinated into the secrets of Hermes Trismegistus, and at last "touched the verity" of the philosopher's stone. He speaks also of a visit paid by him to a Spanish magician at Salamanca or Toledo, who had great power over spiritual existences, and from whom he learned some valuable hints. Much farther was the journey which he took to dispute upon the true theory of medicine with Avicenna, who had been lying in his grave under the palm trees at Hemdan about five hundred years. Such a journey as this must be regarded as one of Paracelsus' richly coloured descriptions of the controversy which he, all his life through, waged with the Avicennists—or it may be a statement by one of his too forward followers.

What adventures he met with upon these journeys there is not probably any means now of knowing. He mixed with all sorts of people, from the lowest to the highest; for if his tastes and habits inclined him to associate with the grosser sort, his skill, or at least his success, made him often consulted by princes and dukes, barons and knights, for diseases which had baffled the physicians of the time. These great people were not very profitable connections. He was not always well used or generously paid. Sometimes he was cheated out of his fee altogether by those he attended or cured. No doubt there is exaggeration on this point; but that vow which Paracelsus solemnly recorded tells too much of a wormwood experience for one to think that his grievances were imaginary. Paracelsus, from his way of life, was not always presentable in good company; he was far from being a courtier, still farther from being a retainer or hanger-on of any man of influence; his free expressions made him enemies, when the least exercise of prudence would have rendered them either friendly to him, or without positive dislike. Thus acting, however, would have changed his whole character,

B

or rather would have indicated a different character from what he had by nature—a nature, the defects of which he aggravated, but never once attempted to remedy. He flung away all books, because he had never been shown their use; he would himself make his own knowledge, his own reasonings, his own philosophical system, himself would ask nature. Rather than waste his time with learning the folly either of the dead or living, "he would be a fool on his own account." He threw away his friends, because he thought that they were not worth distinguishing from his enemies, and the results are seen both in his works and in the accounts of his life.

Having exhausted all that he could learn in other countries, he returned to Germany about 1520, when he was some thirty years of age. His fame went with him. His distant journeys seemed to the stay-at-home people to savour of sorcery and Lapland travel; he had a natural power of describing what he had seen or done, which he did not always sufficiently rule. He had acquired notions about pharmacy and medicine which were strange to the German doctors. He brought with him new substances obtained from the vegetable and mineral worlds; he employed strange words which no one could explain but himself; and as he was very successful in curing so-called incurable diseases, in soothing pain and procuring sleep by minute quantities of his drugs, when the graduated physician failed, it is not to be wondered at that he attracted much attention wherever he went, and that he would be waited upon by numerous and attentive audiences, if he would only condescend to enlighten them. In the year 1526, accordingly, he was appointed physician to the city of Basel, at the urgent recommendation of Oecolampadius; and when he was fairly established, he began to give a course of lectures. As they were delivered in German and not in Latin, there was a rush of students from all parts, and the doctors were full of envy at the success which he achieved. There were other causes, however, of dislike, which caused a rupture between him and his colleagues. They were teaching a well established system in which they had been trained, and on the acquisition of which they had spent years of thought and labour. The magnitude and finish of the whole concealed their imperfections as originators and as teachers; and what they could not have devised for themselves, they found ready to their hand to acquire and dispense. The independence, however, with which Paracelsus had begun mainly from ignorance, and afterwards from habit and dislike, was now ingrained in him, and it was at the commencement of his Basel lectures that he gave the proof that he had broken with tradition, and was now going to point out a road which he had discovered for himself, and which, in his thought, was to lead, not like the other roads to the Rome of cramping authority, but into the infinite freedom of Nature. He burned the works of Avicenna and Galen before his students. Galen's writings had been printed for the first time in 1525, and this act of summary vengeance upon the originator of an erroneous system was in marked contrast with the treatment which the great founder of humoral pathology received from the other lecturers upon medicine. Their aim was to explain the difficulties of the author, and to give a running commentary upon the text. Paracelsus' text and commentary consisted of what he had seen with his own eyes, touched with his own hands, and garnered by the toil of his own mind. There must have been a striking contrast between the lecture rooms. The quiet, listlessly-attentive audiences taking down the remarks of the solemn professors, who, in copious Latin, gave utterance to the formulae of diseases, and the prescriptions which they required. As everyone knows how lavish in uncomplimentary epithets these men were to Paracelsus, it is worth while hearing what he says of them: "Not one of them has ever thoroughly known their art, or experimented in it, or comprehended it; they go round and round about it, like a cat round a dish; they teach what they do not know themselves; their disputations they do not understand . . ." How different in Paracelsus' room! A crowded audience, some believing, some in doubt; in the back-ground those already graduated, who looked with detestation on the man who was laying open their secrets, who was depriving them of their gains, who was not unfrequently exposing their ignorance. The herald of the new system in his rostrum, not over well dressed, nervously active, restless, pouring forth torrents of words —a strange exposition of dimly seen far-off truths grasped after from the vantage ground of some definite knowledge of nature and her ways, of which his contemporaries were profoundly innocent.

There must have been, after all, some merit in his teaching. The students must have felt that they were in contact with a man who had experienced much, and who was speaking accordingly, and who not only could describe but also act. There must have been something more than mere charlatanerie when Ramus wrote of him—

"That he had so penetrated into the inmost secrets of nature, he had explored and tested with such acuteness and skill the powers and properties of metals and roots in healing all kinds of diseases, even the most hopeless, and in the opinion of all men incurable, that medicine seemed to have had no existence until he appeared."

It was not in the human nature of the sixteenth century long to endure such rivalry, and the faculty soon found an opportunity to show of what stuff they were framed. They forbade him to lecture at the university, and his students were refused a degree. There is something very original in the rest of their request, that he should undergo an examination by them because they did not know whether he was a doctor or not ; this, with a man whom they themselves had chosen for his outstanding ability. Not content with angering the doctors, he brought down on himself the wrath of a commercial corporation—the apothecaries. As city physician, he showed the necessity for a regular supervision of the apothecaries, to ascertain that they understood their business, had sufficient apparatus for preparing drugs, and did not overcharge their wares. He wanted also to have a check upon both them and the physicians, in order to make sure that there was no collusion between two professions so closely connected, and so dependent upon each other. He never was on good terms with the apothecaries, as the numerous references to them in his writings show. He says they did not like him, because he not only did not empty their canisters and drawers fast enough, but taught others the same parsimonious doctrine. The result of the controversy is not brought out. Paracelsus appealed to the magistracy, and urged that he had relinquished a very fine practice in order to reside in Basel.

The dispute would doubtless have been smoothed down, had not Paracelsus got into a fresh complication with that canon who promised 100 florins to any one who would cure him, and when by Paracelsus he was made well, paid only for the three pills of laudanum which had been efficacious. Again the magistrates were appealed to, but the decision was against Paracelsus, who, without any consideration for himself "unpacked his heart" with such terrible force that, to avoid being put in prison, he, by the advice of his friends, fled from Basel, and, having nothing else to do, resumed his previous migratory life. He spent about a year in Alsace, and made considerable sums of money by cures effected among the nobility. It was now, however, that the dissipated habits which had been growing on him became too public to be hidden. He spent whole nights over wine with men who were unworthy of him, lavishing the money which he had gained by his talents. Paracelsus' defence, regarded simply as such, does not seem to be quite sufficient—that if he squandered the interest, he had the whole of his capital intact ; that though he had not the shelter of a roof for weeks together, he had still his art and his skill ; and upon that ground he would meet with his opponents. It is no excuse for him that, because he was a very clever practitioner, a reformer of medicine—maybe even a genius, and because he was much persecuted by his con-temporaries, and misunderstood—perhaps wilfully, by them, he should not observe the decencies of society, but waste his strength of body and mind in excesses which only made him more obnoxious to every one, and which have ever since formed one of the gravest accusations against him.

Be this as it may, he wandered about from place to place during the remainder of his life. The dedications of his works indicate his movements, and the tone in which he writes exhibits a settled misery, which is none the less that it was in great part his own fault. He visited Colmar, Arnberg, Esslingen, went to Nürnberg, where he was refused his fees, and where his writings were forbidden to be printed. Then to Munich, and into Switzerland. He tried to settle in Innspruck, but his clothes were so worn out that he was hustled out of the town. At Sterzingen he fell in with two friends, and there wrote his treatise on the Plague, in which he says that he had two great faults which made him enemies wherever he went: "these were his poverty and his piety. The burgomasters could never get over the former; and they at once said he was no doctor. The latter was objected to by the priests, so that between the two he fell into utter disrepute." Under these circumstances he removed to Meran, where he was a little more comfortable. This was about 1535, and the following years were spent in the same way. After residing at Pfeffers, and giving a description of the baths, he went to Augsburg, then to Carinthia, and finally settled, in 1541, at Salzburg, whither he was summoned by Archbishop Ernest. He was now in a fair way of spending his life without those harassing quarrels which he had had for thirty years; but on the 24th September of the same year, 1541, he died. Even to this point the rancour of his enemies pursued him—

his death was the result, they said, of a fit of dissipation which lasted several days, and when he was at last found, it was on the floor of a mean tavern, from which his boon companions had fled. A more authentic account, however, is that he died in the hospital of St. Stephen, in Salzburg. What the cause of his illness was, it is not easy to say. Some of his biographers tell us that the physicians of the town organized a conspiracy, sent a band of their servants to an inn where they knew he was, and either in the brawl which ensued, Paracelsus received his death-blow, or else he was thrown down a steep place, and did not survive the injuries he received. An examination of his skull in the early part of this century showed a flaw, which there is no reason to doubt resulted from some injury when Paracelsus was still alive.[1] He was buried in the churchyard of St. Sebastian; his remains were afterwards removed to another part of the same cemetery, and his monument is still to be seen. A pyramid of white marble, with his likeness sunk into one side, and over it the well-known inscription, in which he is described as the curer of incurable sores.

If the life of Paracelsus is imperfect and obscure, still more obscure is the heritage of writings which his disciples have transmitted to us. The man who for years hardly ever read a book, whose library at his death consisted of half-a-dozen volumes, who wrote and published during his lifetime a few treatises on various parts of medicine, has given his name to a collection of writings which, in some editions, fills three folio volumes, and in another

[1] [28th May, 1896. On the contrary, there is every reason to doubt t.—See Aberle, p. 52.]

ten quartos. All these works were collected and published after his death, and much that is spurious has got inseparably mixed up with what Paracelsus may have thought, written, or dictated to his pupils and immediate followers. When even Oporinus says that words were ascribed to Paracelsus which, in his most fantastic or drunken hours, he never imagined, much less dictated, we may assume that some of these less authentic passages are just what would most likely be quoted to his detriment by those adverse to his innovations.[1] It is indeed singular with what unanimity the same statements are repeated over and over again, every other ten or twenty years, by the author of a new biography, a literary, or scientific dictionary. So that the repetition by some dozen writers of Paracelsus' failings does not substantiate their existence, but only proves that they have all drawn independently from one source, or, as is more likely, that they have drawn from it through each other.

They may, however, be excused. Folio volumes are not attractive reading, and, with the exception of some diligent historians who have consulted the originals, no one now thinks of studying Paracelsus' writings. The doctrines which he tried to enunciate are under no small obligations to those who have systematized what is distinguished for its want of all system—who have arranged

---

[1] A modern biographer of Paracelsus has tried to reduce the list of his authentic works to ten tracts; some of them, like that *Von dem Bad Pfeffers*, consisting of a few pages only. The older critics are willing to admit that the writings are not all genuine; for example, Conring, who made a fierce attack upon Paracelsus, follows Oporinus in this.—*De Hermetica Medicina*, 1648, p. 179.

and co-ordinated thoughts which their author is said to have uttered without premeditation—who have explained away apparent contradictions in his views, of which he was perhaps ignorant himself, by showing that they are only different sides of a deeper principle, which, in view of certain phenomena, the author proclaimed, now in one form, now in another.

Whether or not by these commentaries it is possible to arrive at a complete representation of Paracelsus' system, or whether each commentator does not feel constantly tempted to fill up great gaps in its primitive enunciation from the knowledge of system acquired since then, and acts accordingly, one result is certainly exhibited—the large range which Paracelsus took as the foundation of a scientific medicine, rising from that in his own inverted style to a more òr less pure philosophy. It is this which makes the statement of Paracelsus' philosophy in few words so difficult, because, though technically he was a physician, yet his was far too ambitious and powerful a mind to be contented with such gymnastic as mere medical theory, as now understood, could furnish. Starting from empirical generalizations, he essayed to give a reasoned view of the position of man in the universe, the inter-dependence of all parts of nature upon each other, and, as an immediate consequence, the action of natural forces on both his mind and body. Based to a large extent upon experiment and observation, with experimental deductions justified to a certain point, his theory could not miss clashing with the received views of the time. The physicians, his contemporaries, and the physicians for more than a century and a half later, were so self-bound to authority, that rather than believe Galen their master, or Avicenna, his commentator, mistaken in any fact, important or unimportant, they would affirm that nature had changed, or that themselves had observed amiss.

Paracelsus was incapacitated by nature for such faith as the medical schools required of its graduates. Rather than comply with such a request, he preferred rejecting even the truth which it may have contained, and came out with the startling statement that every country and every age produces its own physician. Just as in nature the poisonous plant and the antidote are often found growing side by side, so the genius of a people produces a physician suited for its own peculiar diseases: Galen for the Pergamenians, Hippocrates for the Greeks, Avicenna for the Arabs, Paracelsus for the Germans. In Paracelsus' view, however, the genius of the people went much farther, demanding a new medical theory, and a new treatment of disease founded upon the new theory and wider experience. With these demands it was Paracelsus' aim to comply, and it is from his multiplicity of aims, and the way he tried to compass them, that he slips through the grasp of the expositor or critic. Fully to estimate his ideas—and however useless they may be, they cannot be ignored—one must be skilled, not only in philosophy and theology, not only in mysticism or magic, or any vagary of the kind in which the human mind indulges, but one must be a physician, a surgeon, a physiologist a pharmacist. Hence the difficulty of meeting with a fair estimate of the man, or of forming one which shall not be tinged with one's favourite hypothesis, or bear signs of the topic in which one feels greatest interest.

The following is a mere gleaming from the mass of literature relating to the different parts of his system, which is contained in the histories of philosophy, medicine, and mysticism. It must not be forgotten, however, that there are those who question the authenticity of some of the theological opinions ascribed to Paracelsus. In fact, if we are to believe Oporinus, who lived with Paracelsus as his secretary, Paracelsus was one of the most irreligious of men. But Oporinus—after long staying with this irreligious person, in the hope of learning some of his methods of cure, some say, even of getting the philosopher's stone—was never gratified, and ultimately left Paracelsus. Thereafter, the character of his quondam master becomes very black, and most of the stories against him have emanated from the irritated amanuensis.

The material universe, and all individual life, existed not at first, but as an unrealized potency of the Archetype or Creator. By the action of the Creator was first produced the chaos, limbus, or substance of which all subsequent existence is but the determination. "This chaos or limbus has no form or properties, it was not real existence, it was rather a shapeless nothing—the mysterium magnum." In it, however, were contained the elements of all things—fixity, solidity, liquidity, volatility, inflammability, and gaseity—principles of which the most perfect embodiments are salt, mercury, and sulphur. The first act was a process of division into the earth and heavens; the elements arranging themselves according to their tenuity. The heavenly fire formed the ether, and afterwards the firmament and stars; of the air were produced spiritual and vague existences; the waters flowed together and became the ocean, and gave deposits of salt, coral, even fishes and sirens; the earthy principle formed the solid parts of the world, and gave rise to all kinds of rocks and stones, plants, animals, gnomes, and giants. As all these objects were produced at the same time, from the same material, and by the same process, they have, of necessity, an inner connection with each other, and a community of qualities; many of these qualities are obvious, but many are discovered only by intense scrutiny, while some are so recondite that they completely baffle man in his attempt to follow them out. Every part of the universe is thus a mirror of every other part. The great world, and all the smaller worlds, are part and parcel of the same Divine Creation, and every future existence is accordingly conditioned by its antecedents. When matter was made into discrete portions, man was constructed. All the qualities of every individual thing were brought together and heaped upon him. In the most multifarious ways he has thus become an embodi- ment of the outer and greater world. The macrocosmus is reflected mediately and immediately in him, the micro- cosmus. Every part of his body is thus connected directly with some planet or star, some herb, or mineral, or metal, and as these are connected with each other, he is in contact with nature several times over. Hence every part of the world re-acts on every other part, and man, especially, is subject both to the terrestrial and to the higher influences.

It is remarkable how near Paracelsus, by mere force of thought, and the dim expressions in his cabalistic sources of knowledge, had approached to what stands out so distinctly in the writings, not only of modern philosophy, but even of science. "There is an intimate union," says Mulder, "between material man and the material world which surrounds him ; all things stand in immediate contact with his body; he could not exist without these things about him."[1] Similarly Schiller—"The great embodiment which we call world, now remains to me remarkable only because it is at hand to denote by symbols the manifold expressions of mind. All within and without me is only a hieroglyph of a power which resembles me. . . . A new experience in this kingdom of truth, gravitation, the discovered circulation of the blood, the nature-system of Linnæus, tell me directly the same as an antique recovered from Herculaneum: both give only a reflection of a spirit, a new acquaintance with an existence like my own. I converse with the Infinite through the instrument of Nature—through universal history. I read the soul of the artist in his Apollo."[2] And so, less loftily perhaps, and in a way a little more exaggerated, the *Autocrat of the Breakfast Table*—"Nothing is clearer than that all things are in all things, and that just according to the intensity and intension of our mental being we shall see the many in the one, and the one in the many. Did Sir Isaac think what he was saying when he made his speech about the ocean—the child and the pebbles, you know? Did he mean to speak slightingly of a pebble? . . . A body which knows all the currents of force that traverse the globe ; which holds by invisible threads to the ring of

---

[1] *Berzelius*, herdacht door G. J. Mulder, 1848.
[2] Schiller's *Philosophische Briefe.*

Saturn and the belt of Orion! A body, from the con-
templation of which an archangel could infer the entire
inorganic universe as the simplest of corollaries!"

Upon all parts of nature, then, man depends for the
maintenance of his body. Besides a body, however, man
also possesses a spirit and a soul. Thus, consisting of
three parts, he is like the rest of the world, an embodiment
of the threefold constitution of all things derived from the
salt, sulphur, and mercury. The distinction between the
soul and the spirit, by Paracelsus, is well marked. The
spirit is that light of nature which guides to all instinctive
acts, all mechanical skill, and which comes from, and is
nourished by, what Paracelsus terms the "Astra"—the
stars. Thus the sun and stars, which are the natural and
sensible projections in the objective universe of certain
ideas of the Iliaster, have a double force. Elementally
and materially, they are in relation with the body which
they foster, warm, and regulate; but as representatives of
the super-sensual light of nature, they act as "Astra" embodied, they operate "siderically," supporting in him all
his perceptive operations. "In addition, however, to the
elemental life of the body and the sidereal of the spirit,
man has also a soul, which comes direct from God, and
is not derived either from the firmament or from the
elements. This soul is the reason, and the higher faculties
in man." The body and spirit may therefore cease, but
not the soul. In the formation, therefore, of an individual
mind, there are many co-operating influences—the inherited
qualities of the parents, and the external power of the
elements, and of the "Astra," so that the character of the
individual is determined by the balance of influence in

favour of one or the other. In man, there is, therefore, a threefold knowledge, the animal, the sidereal—that of the understanding, and the spiritual. The first two are mortal, the third, as directly Divine, is not.

The original matter of all things Paracelsus deduces not from fire, air, earth, and water, but from the salt, sulphur, and mercury which had been advocated in the more concrete conceptions of Basil Valentin and Isaac Hollandus. These primal elements are found in all matter; indeed, they form all matter, and by analysis only these can be got. Without sulphur nothing grows or blossoms; mercury is the cause of fluidity; salt gives firmness and strength. Consequently, they are present in all matter. The principles themselves cannot be isolated; we see them only in their efforts, as in sulphur, which is combustible: mercury, which is volatile; ash, or salt, which is solid and fixed, and ncombustible. The body which contains these, properly mixed, is sound or perfect; if one is in excess, it is sick.

Out of these three elements were developed by the Divine Spirit the four elements—fire, air, earth, and water. But in the world, besides, were required active principles, for which the elements furnish the matter; the active power must be something different. To this power Paracelsus gave the name of "Archæus," the animating principle, so to speak, of the elements; not a spirit, but a working force. Thus, while all things are in and out of the elements, their actions are not due to the elements, but to their hidden powers—a doctrine at which modern chemistry has arrived by a very different road, when it affirms that the character of a compound depends, not merely on what elements, but in what form they are present. Not that it would be correct to view this as an anticipation of the modern deduction from certain experiments, the existence of which in the time of Paracelsus was, so far as we know, impossible—but the analogy shows persistence and revival, ever and anon, of certain ideas relative to the constitution of matter, so that we might venture on a different conclusion, and say that the modern idea may have been based less on the experiments than its author supposed. By this reasoning it was simple to show that the qualities of all matter were but so many expressions of the life it contained. Over each of the elements, whether primal or secondary, there was a force, a spiritual principle, which was setting it ever in motion to fulfil its nature. Every part of nature has, therefore, a life of its own, derived from a spiritual source. The body which exhibits it may be destroyed, but not the spirit itself. When the two separate, the spirit returns to the original chaos or limbus.

It would be absurd to try to identify this with any modern doctrine of physical philosophy; it is rather the ever repeated recoil of the mind upon itself for an explanation of what is driven in upon it by the senses, when it gets back to first principles, to a "universal yea"—and the result of which is expressed in one age by spirit, and stars, and chaos, and Creation, and in another by matter, and gravity, and vortices. Now, as in the time of Aristophanes, Δῖνος βασιλεύει, Whirl reigns, and Zeus is for the moment in disgrace; but in the mind of Paracelsus there was no endowing matter with self-determination; everything worked and moved by its connection with the original Source of Life.

The term quintessence was employed by Paracelsus, not to denote a fifth element, but rather to express the dominating element of a thing; that which gives it its special virtue and character. It especially denoted, therefore, the healing virtue of a mineral or plant.

In this system, as has been already noticed, man occupies an altogether peculiar position. He is emphatically the head of the visible Creation, and in that respect his relations are the most complex. Everything in the great world has its analogue in man, so that to comprehend him we require a knowledge of all things. He consists of two parts—the visible, elementary body, and a sidereal spirit—and in this he agrees with animals. But he has, besides, the immortal part which is directly from God, and through this he is raised to the knowledge of Divine things and love.

This soul is the centre of man, and is located in the heart. Round it is ranged the inferior parts of man—while, in the soul itself, is the very essence of the soul, the *mind* which seems to have almost denoted the *conscience*, the judge of right and wrong.

Now, as can be easily seen, these different parts of man's nature are related to the corresponding parts of the outer world, and they perform different functions. The astral spirit, for example, is nourished from the astral world, and by spiritual influences, and to it belongs natural reason, art, and wisdom. It is of importance therefore for man to keep his nature pure, so that he may draw these influences, and be enabled to commune with the spirits from whom the muddy vesture of decay is so apt to cut him off.

But over all the soul rules, to keep the lower nature right, and to protect the man from the influence of evil spirits, which solicit him to destruction. For man is endowed with free will, and like a king surrounded by councillors, the soul may follow good or bad advice; wherefore, it is endowed with Divine wisdom.

Now, since all parts of man's nature are essential, the body is not to be despised, but only regulated, that it does not go beyond the bounds assigned to it. For when this happens, and the body, and soul, and spirit become divorced, the man falls wholly under evil influences, the earthly elements and the adverse constellations obtain the mastery, and he becomes nothing better than an animal.

From these doctrines Paracelsus advances to the theory of the Fall of Man, and his Regeneration.

The first man before the Fall had no connection with the animals. In this state, however, he was as a child, and was liable to temptation. Hence he fell into sin—lost the Divine Image, and sank into mere naturalness. The animal part, which had before been invisible, now appeared in all its coarseness, and thus man has become, in his body and soul, mortal.

Man, therefore, can be restored only by rehabilitation in the Divine form; and as this belongs to the soul, inasmuch as it forms the centre of it, the new birth of man is the entire reformation of man's nature.

Such is a very rough sketch of the system of things according to Paracelsus. This connection of man with the Universe opens up two questions—the sources of his knowledge, and the maintenance of his life in the highest state of perfection. The former leads to Paracelsus' distinction between reason and faith, the latter to his medical system.

In the first he points out that the three parts of man get this knowledge from three different sources, and by different faculties. Thus, the spirit gets the knowledge of the things of time by reason, while the soul gets the knowledge of Divine things by faith. He therefore objects altogether to the application of the discursive reason to the questions of the soul. Both domains must be kept distinct—they are not contradictory, because both are of . God; but only error can arise by confounding them.

But while man's reason is incompetent to deal with the things of the soul—and one can so far agree with Paracelsus that some conceptions are beyond the reason to explain satisfactorily—Divine wisdom is the condition of a true knowledge of the cosmical—that is, of philosophy. The whole world being a Divine idea, all Nature being but characters of the Divine Scribe, our knowledge of these can come only in and out of Him. Without God, then, man is powerless to do anything of himself, and he can do what he does only in so far as he is enlightened by the Divine Spirit. All truth is thus derived from the theology which is the science of Divine things—it is the corner-stone of philosophy.

Paracelsus thus arrives at the source of Divine illumination, the cabalistic art, which is necessary not only for the philosopher, but also for the physician.

So far from this interfering with man's activity in the

region of knowledge, it should act rather as an incentive to investigate all things, for he is formed to speak of the wonderful things of creation. And here he must use both experience and science. If he will have reliable knowledge, theory and practice must be combined. Separate, they are of no avail, for theory is but speculative practice, and practice but applied theory. An experiment without science has no weight or worth—it is not reliable; but he who has science can trust it, because he knows the reason why things are so. Thus, while founding on experiment, one must rise to causes, and so escape the danger of mere fanciful hypothesis unbased on experiment, or of working upon a pure theory without right observation of Nature.

This is the work of philosophy, which has to investigate all nature; in other words, Nature is concrete or visible philosophy; philosophy is unseen Nature. The knowledge of the great world is the foundation for that of man, and the philosopher has to trace the relations between them—all the heavenly and earthly forces which emanate from natural objects, and work on man.

And now, having investigated the relations of the Universe, and laid his foundations of knowledge in God and the faculties of man, the next and noblest art is to keep man in the highest state of perfection.

The Art of Medicine is thus based, according to Paracelsus: (1) In Theology; (2) In Philosophy; (3) In Astronomy or Meteorology; and (4) In Alchemy—which is the art of so dealing with matter that its properties become, in the first place, perfect, and then of use for healing—a sort of refined or transcendental pharmacy.

For, according to Paracelsus, alchemy, or chemistry, is not the mere art of making, or of perfecting gold, but is the preparation by fire of all natural materials for use. Hence he extends the term chemist to the baker, the cook, the metallurgist—to everyone, in fact, who works transformation of matter by heat.

The medical system of Paracelsus is that by which he is best known. One writer has gone the length of saying, that only the medical parts of his writings, and not the whole even of these, are genuine, and that the portions occupied with religious doctrines are interpolated. This opinion, however, is not that generally held; still, Paracelsus is remembered, not so much for philosophical views, as for the application made of them to the healing art. Into the minutiae of this part of the subject it is impossible to enter. A very brief statement of the main features, and of some of the changes which Paracelsus made, can only be referred to.

He insisted especially upon the study of natural phenomena; the books of the physician, he maintained, were Nature's, not Galen's and Avicenna's. He twitted the physicians of the time with their reluctance to put their hand to the work; and compared them with the iatrochemist who spent days in the preparation of his medicines and in studying the effects of fire upon salts, and minerals, and metals. Guided by his theory of quintessence, or the dominant quality in a thing, he strove to get these qualities, and thus altered to a great extent the form in which medicines were administered. Instead of giving mixtures of a dozen or two different bodies, the effects of which, singly or combined, were hardly known, even empirically, he substituted small doses of the active parts. He taught the preparation and use of compounds of antimony, copper, mercury, and other of the more potent mineral medicines; and of those which had been previously employed he extended the knowledge and value.

In this he was violently opposed both by the physicians and apothecaries. His drugs were despised, he himself was vilified, and the controversy raged in no elegant terms during Paracelsus' lifetime, and for long after. It was under these circumstances that Paracelsus crowed defiance to all the schools of the time. "All of you are after me; I shall be the monarch; mine will be the kingdom." As we have already seen, while Paracelsus merely spoke, his opponents acted; there is no doubt that he was more or less persecuted, and that even by those who might have known better. Many of his special views in connection with medicine have been praised by modern writers,—the doctrine of Tartar, for example, which is that disease which exhibits itself by the formation of various concretions in the body. The Tartar, or Tartarus, is the impure part of a thing, as of water, wine, or food. This poisonous part is always taken in with the food, but the archæus of digestion separates it, and rejects it. If, however, the Tartarus is not so separated, but remains in the body, then disease, and the most terrible burning pains—as of Tartarus itself are the result.

Then, as he seems to have done with his own special ideas, he enlarges their comprehension, and thus Tartar becomes the origin of all disease which is attended with coagulation of the fluids of the body, the rigidity of the solid parts, or the concentration of earthy matter.

He held, also, singular views with regard to the healing of wounds, which he ascribes to an inherent balsam in the different parts of the body, which balsam has to be nourished in the case of a surgical operation. This balsam, or mumia as it was called, has to be kept at a proper temperature, that the flesh may grow again properly.

These topics, as well as his contributions to surgery and so forth, are entirely technical, and are of interest only for the history of medicine.

Apart from the dissipated life, arrogance, and charlatanerie of which Paracelsus has been accused, he has also got the blame of giving an impulse to superstitions of all kinds. His doctrine of the universal life of the world led to that of the existence of beings in fire, air, and water, endowed with life, though not with a soul, but which by marriage with human beings became so endowed. This doctrine survives in many of the most popular legends of the present day, notably in *Undine*, and a couple of hundred years ago was ascribed to that curious and mysterious brotherhood, the Rosicrucians, out of which so much fantastical literature has grown.

He certainly himself believed in, and advocated magic, astrology, talismans, and the crudest forms of uneducated superstition. At the same time, he has been blamed with much, which after all is due to him only remotely: as, for example, the doctrine of signatures—with the fancies of which, as displayed in the writings of Crollius and others it would be unfair to charge him.

When, therefore, we seek to form an estimate of

Paracelsus' character and work—when we compare him with some of his contemporaries—with Agricola and Palissy on the one hand, or on the other with Luther, as has been done by one of his countrymen—we find the task by no means a simple one. If one praises Paracelsus for anything, one is obnoxious to the accusation of theosophist, or cabalist, or mystic; and yet historical fairness will not suffer us to ignore the enormous influence he has exercised. It is not possible to point to any great discovery of facts that he made. His knowledge, indeed, even for his time, was vague, inaccurate, and imperfect. Agricola, his contemporary, wrote a book on mining and metallurgy, which is valuable for its facts, even at the present day. Palissy, his contemporary, not only discovered the pottery which bears his name, and which is so beautifully designed, and glazed, and coloured, but he was one of the most original of men, with the coolest judgment, the clearest observation, the most rational in his deductions from observed facts; yet Agricola and Palissy, for all the influence they exerted on their own or any subsequent age, might never have lived. But we cannot say the same of Paracelsus. He no sooner appeared than he influenced men. He broke through the traditions which had fettered all physicians as hopelessly as the Church had fettered mankind. Prior to Luther were many attempts at Church reform. Before Paracelsus, so far as one knows, there were none in medicine; and this impulse, as has been already said, did not die out after Paracelsus' death. His doctrines were taken up and advocated by many men, by Van Helmont, Quercetanus, Thurneysser, Libavius, and others. And though in a hundred, or a hundred and fifty, years later, the Paracelsian elements were attacked and controverted, men never returned to the Galenic medicine. Paracelsus had conquered. *His was the kingdom.*

In glancing over his writings, one is struck especially with one thing—the entire originality of the whole. There are no quotations from other writers, more especially from the classics. He had evidently thought out his own system, and, right or wrong, he stands or falls by it. His works have all the marks of a powerfully originative mind ; in one sense they are worthy of that nature for which Paracelsus in his philosophy gave up no little. They are wide, many-sided ; they seem indifferent whether they are accepted or rejected.

But, however cosmogonic in its range, it was faulty in its foundations and superstructure. The facts and theories of metaphysics and morals he started from, not as already proved, but because they were to him self-evident, and to question them would have been almost impious.

The physical part of his cosmogony is evidently based on the Scriptural account of the Creation, but interwoven with such an amount of physical facts as had been attained by theorizing up to his time, filtered, besides, through mystical theology and cabalism. It may be viewed, therefore, as an attempt to state his observations on the world in such a way as, not perhaps to explain the origin of all things, but to place them in such lights that, by reflection from them, places dark and sombre in life and action may be illumined and made available for future progress, and utilized in the form of a more perfect medicine.

Taken thus, while remembering that what is called scientific training was unknown, and that it was Paracelsus' aim to awaken men to the necessity of such a thing— and, while admitting all his faults, both as a man, and as a physician and philosopher, Paracelsus cannot be said to have lived in vain; and in the tumultuous up-turning of the sixteenth century, he stands out at once a representative of the great spirit of reformation, and the inheritor of all the weakness of the period which ended in him.

II.

Theophrastus Paracelsus. Eine. kritische Studie von Friedrich Mook. (Würzburg: Staudinger, 1876.)

WHY is it that historians cannot decide, or at least have not decided, whether Paracelsus was a quack or a genius? To this question Dr. Mook, after an introductory display of the diversity of opinions, answers: "On account of the state of his writings." It is obvious that, if any of the numerous works passing under his name be not genuine, their contents, whatever be their character, should form no part of a systematic exposition of the ideas of Paracelsus. In his attempt to solve the problem of Paracelsus' real character, Mook accordingly finds himself face to face with a prior question: What did Paracelsus write? To decide this important preliminary, three things, according to Mook, are required: (1) the marks or tests of authenticity; (2) an enumeration of the works ascribed to Paracelsus, or published under his name; (3) the application of the tests to the works. And in accordance herewith Mook's "Study" is divided into three sections.

In the first he considers briefly the tests by which a work may be recognized as of Paracelsian authorship, and of these he enumerates five: (1) Original MSS. are genuine. (2) Works published by Paracelsus himself during his lifetime are genuine. (3) A comparison of these two tests with Huser's edition must decide whether Huser's edition is to be trusted. (4) If Huser is thus found trustworthy, the works said by Huser to have been taken from a MS. of Paracelsus must be held genuine. (5) Works bearing in form and contents indubitable marks of Paracelsus' authorship must be considered genuine. These criteria are doubtless sufficient; they would certainly require tact and care in their application.

The second section is occupied with a chronological bibliography of Paracelsus' writings. It contains 276 titles—248 of printed works, and 28 of manuscripts. The bibliography begins in 1529, in which year was printed at Augsburg a quarto pamphlet entitled *Practica D. Theophrasti Paracelsi*, and goes down to 1845, which saw the publication at Leipzig of a version of the Nürnberg "Figures." To obtain these titles Mook has rummaged European libraries during twelve years for copies of Paracelsus' works, and he has succeeded in bringing some to light which were previously unknown. Whether the subject deserved such long-sustained effort is matter of opinion. Fifty years ago, Dr. Robert Watt, no stinter of labour, said, " To enumerate the immense number of German treatises (for he understood no other language) which have been published under his name, would be bestowing pains upon them which they certainly do not deserve." But in fifty years opinions change, and Dr. Mook has bestowed the pains. With regard to the execution of this, the chief part of the monograph, it has to my knowledge never been so fully done before. The amount of information collected by direct personal inspection of the books themselves is very great, and there is much besides in appended notes about editions which the author has failed to see, but descriptions of which he has found in other writers.

Full, however, as this part of the work is, it is not quite satisfactory. By comparison with a small collection of Paracelsian works, and with one or two common bibliographical books of reference, I have found about thirty titles which the author has overlooked or omitted. Most of these are of English translations, and are not of first-rate importance, but the fact of their absence suggests the possibility of other omissions or oversights. Defects of a different kind are too frequent: for instance, typographical errors, misstatement of dates and cross-references, misspellings of proper names, alterations of the titles of books by omissions, change of spelling, and so on. Such errors arise from carelessness, but they render the catalogue imperfect, and shake our confidence in the author.

In the third section, in which the tests of authenticity were to be applied to the works, we are favoured with certain general conclusions which may be stated in brief as follows :—(1) As no original MSS. of Paracelsus remain, test (1) is not applicable. What, then, can have become of all the MSS. used by Huser at the end of the sixteenth century? (2) The works published by Paracelsus during his lifetime are genuine. There are fourteen of these: five medical, six containing "Prognostications," and three reprints, or second editions. (3) Huser's reprints of these genuine works are so exact, that (4) he is quite to be trusted when he says that he printed a work from Paracelsus' MS. Mook, however, fails to specify the works so described by Huser. (5) Respecting works passing under Paracelsus' name, the origin of which cannot be so exactly determined as in the previous case, and the authorship of which is to be decided by internal evidence, Mook leaves the decision to the critics of the future. Thus, precisely the place where directions were most required to prevent the traveller from going astray has been left without a finger-post.

To conclude. The title is a misnomer: the monograph is not a critical study of Paracelsus, but a bibliography of his works, which the reader may find critical, but which is imperfect and inaccurate. The inaccuracies are such that when Mook ascribes errors to other writers, as he does not unfrequently, Mook's mere assertion is not sufficient evidence that an error has actually been committed. To make the work the important addition to medical bibliography which it might be, it would require thorough revision to remove inaccuracies, to complete titles, and to supply deficiencies, and especially to state what in the author's opinion are really Paracelsus' works. It is much to be regretted that, after all the years and labour spent in collecting materials, after the opportunities for comparing editions which the author has had, we should hardly be a step nearer the knowledge of Paracelsus' genuine works—the one thing for which it was worth while taking the trouble he has taken, the one thing indispensable, according to the author himself, for ascertaining what Paracelsus thought, and thereby of determining what sort of man he was.

III.

PARACELSUS (*c.* 1490–1541). It seems now to be established that Paracelsus was born near Einsiedeln, in the canton Schwyz, in 1490 or 1491 according to some, or in 1493 according to others. His father, the natural son of a grand-master of the Teutonic order, was Wilhelm Bombast von Hohenheim, who had a hard struggle to make a subsistence as a physician. His mother was superintendent of the hospital at Einsiedeln, a post she relinquished upon her marriage. Paracelsus' name was Theophrastus Bombast von Hohenheim; for the names Philippus and Aureolus good authority is wanting, and the epithet Paracelsus, like some similar compounds, was probably one of his own making, and was meant to denote his superiority to Celsus. In 1502–3 his father, taking his family with him, removed to Villach in Carinthia; and he resided there in the practice of the medical art till his death in 1534. In one of his works, dedicated to the magistracy of the town, Paracelsus refers to the esteem in which his father was held, and expresses his own gratitude for it.

Of the early years of Paracelsus' life there is hardly anything known. His father was his first teacher, and took pains to instruct him in all the learning of the time, especially in medicine. Doubtless Paracelsus learned rapidly what was put before him, but he seems at a comparatively early age to have questioned the value of what he was expected to acquire, and to have soon struck out ways for himself. As he grew older he was taken in hand by several distinguished churchmen, although it has been objected that dates will not warrant the idea of actual personal instruction. This, however, is not correct, for all the men Paracelsus mentions were alive in his lifetime, though he was so young that he could hardly have profited by their lessons, unless on the supposition that he was a quick and precocious boy, which it is very likely he was. At the age of sixteen he entered the university of Basel, but probably soon abandoned the studies therein pursued. He next went to Trithemius, the bishop of Sponheim and Würtzburg, under whom he prosecuted chemical researches. Trithemius is the reputed author of some obscure tracts on the great elixir, and as there was no other chemistry going Paracelsus would have to devote himself to the reiterated operations so characteristic of the notions of that time. But the confection of the stone of the philosophers was too remote a possibility to gratify the fiery spirit of a youth like Paracelsus, eager to make what he knew, or could learn, at once available for practical medicine. So he left school chemistry as he had forsaken university culture, and started for the mines in Tyrol owned by the wealthy family of the Fuggers. The sort of knowledge he got there pleased him much more. There at least he was in contact with reality. The struggle with nature before the precious metals could be made of use impressed upon him more and more the importance of actual personal observation. He saw all the mechanical difficulties that had to be overcome in mining; he learned

D

the nature and succession of rocks, the physical properties of minerals, ores, and metals ; he got a notion of mineral waters ; he was an eye-witness of the accidents which befel the miners, and studied the diseases which attacked them ; he had proof that positive knowledge of nature was not to be got in schools and universities, but only by going to Nature herself, and to those who were constantly engaged with her. Hence came Paracelsus' peculiar mode of study. He attached no value to mere scholarship ; scholastic disputations he utterly ignored and despised,—and especially the discussions on medical topics, which turned more upon theories and definitions than upon actual practice. He therefore went wandering over a great part of Europe to learn all that he could. In so doing he was one of the first physicians of modern times to profit by a mode of study which is now reckoned indispensable. In the 16th century the difficulty of moving about was much greater than it is now ; still Paracelsus faced it, and on principle. The book of nature, he affirmed, is that which the physician must read, and to do so he must walk over the leaves. The humours and passions and diseases of different nations are different, and the physician must go among the nations if he will be master of his art ; the more he knows of other nations, the better he will understand his own. For the physician it is ten times more necessary and useful to know the powers of the heavens and the earth, the virtues of plants and minerals, than to spend his time on Greek and Latin grammar. And the commentary of his own and succeeding centuries upon these very extreme views is that Paracelsus was no scholar, but an ignorant vagabond.

He himself, however, valued his method and his knowledge very differently, and argued that he knew what his predecessors were ignorant of, because he had been taught in no human school. "Whence have I all my secrets, out of what writers and authors? Ask rather how the beasts have learned their arts. If nature can instruct irrational animals, can it not much more men?" In this new school discovered by Paracelsus, and since attended with the happiest results by many others, he remained for about ten years. He had acquired great stores of facts, which it was impossible for him to have reduced to order, but which gave him an unquestionable superiority to his contemporaries. So in 1526 or 1527, on his return to Basel, he was appointed town physician, and shortly afterwards he gave a course of lectures on medicine in the university. Unfortunately for him, the lectures broke away from tradition. They were in German, not in Latin; they were expositions of his own experience, of his own views, of his own methods of curing, adapted to the diseases that afflicted the Germans in the year 1527, and they were not commentaries on the text of Galen or Avicenna. Unfortunately they attacked, not only these great authorities, but the German graduates who followed them and disputed about them in 1527. They criticized in no measured terms the current medicine of the time, and exposed the practical ignorance, the pomposity, and the greed of those who practised it.

The truth of Paracelsus' doctrines was apparently confirmed by his success in curing or mitigating diseases for which the regular physicians could do nothing. For about a couple of years his reputation and practice increased to a surprising extent. But at the end of that time people began to recover themselves. Paracelsus had burst upon the schools with such novel views and methods, with such irresistible criticism, that all opposition was at first crushed flat. Gradually the sea began to rise. His enemies watched for slips and failures; the physicians maintained that he had no degree, and insisted that he should give proof of his qualifications. His manner of life was brought up against him. It was insinuated that he was a profane person, that he was a conjuror, a necromancer, that, in fact, he was to be got rid of at any cost as a troubler of the peace and of the time-honoured traditions of the medical corporations. Moreover, he had a pharmaceutical system of his own which did not harmonize with the commercial arrangements of the apothecaries, and he not only did not use up their drugs like the Galenists, but, in the exercise of his functions as town physician, urged the authorities to keep a sharp eye on the purity of their wares, upon their knowledge of their art, and upon their transactions with their friends the physicians. The growing jealousy and enmity culminated in the Lichtenfels dispute; and, as the judges sided with the canon, to their everlasting discredit, Paracelsus had no alternative but to tell them his opinion of the whole case and of their notions of justice. So little doubt left he on the subject that his friends judged it prudent for him to leave Basel at once, as it had been resolved to punish him for the attack on the authorities of which he had been guilty. He departed from Basel in such haste that he carried nothing with him, and some chemical apparatus and other property were taken charge of by Oporinus, his pupil and amanuensis. He went first to Esslingen, where he remained for a brief period, but had soon to leave from absolute want. Then began his wandering life, the course of which can be traced by the dates of his various writings. He thus visited in succession Colmar, Nuremberg, Appenzell, Zurich, Pfäffers, Augsburg, Villach, Meran, Middelheim, and other places, seldom staying a twelvemonth in any of them. In this way he spent some dozen years, till 1541, when he was invited by Archbishop Ernst to settle at Salzburg, under his protection. After his endless tossing about, this seemed a promise and place of repose. It proved, however, to be the complete and final rest that he found, for after a few months he died on the 24th of September. The cause of his death, like most other details in his history, is uncertain. His enemies asserted that he died in a low tavern in consequence of a drunken debauch of some days' duration. Others maintain that he was thrown down a steep place by some emissaries either of the physicians or of the apothecaries, both of whom he had during his life most grievously harassed. In proof of this, surgeons have pointed out in Paracelsus' skull a flaw or fracture, which could have been produced only during life. Authorities, however, are not agreed on this point, and it may be simplest to suspend belief until more evidence is got. He was buried in the churchyard of St. Sebastian, but in 1752 his bones were removed to the porch of the church, and a monument of reddish-white marble was erected to his memory.

In making the attempt to ascertain what was Paracelsus'

character, and what were his philosophical and medical opinions, a very considerable difficulty presents itself at the outset. Of the voluminous writings which pass under his name, what are really his work, and what, if not actually composed by him, express his ideas? To this question no complete critical reply has as yet been given, though many opinions have been expressed. Dr. Marx, for example, will admit only ten treatises as genuine. Dr. Haeser allows seventeen for certain, a considerable number—some twenty-four—as doubtful, and the rest— he enumerates eleven—as spurious. Dr. Mook does not accept these estimates, or the criteria by which the genuineness of a treatise is ascertained. But neither does he give altogether convincing criteria of his own, and, what is still less satisfactory, he does not apply them— such as they are—to decide the numerous doubtful cases. The only thing Mook has done is to draw up a list of the different editions of Paracelsus' so-called works. This list is not complete in the enumeration of editions, and it is quite imperfect in bibliographical description, but with these and other serious defects it is the fullest at present extant. The first book by Paracelsus was printed at Augsburg in 1529. It is entitled *Practica D. Theophrasti Paracelsi, gemacht auff Europen*, and forms a small quarto pamphlet of five leaves. Prior to this, in 1526-27, appeared a programme of the lectures he intended to deliver at Basel, but this can hardly be reckoned a specific work. During his lifetime fourteen works and editions were published, and thereafter, between 1542 and 1845, there were at least two hundred and thirty-four separate publications according to Mook's enumeration.

The first collected edition was made by Johann Huser in German. It was printed at Basel in 1589-91, in eleven volumes quarto, and is the best of all the editions. Huser did not employ the early printed copies only, but collected all the manuscripts which he could procure, and used them also in forming his text. The only drawback is that rather than omit anything which Paracelsus may have composed, he has gone to the opposite extreme and included writings with which it is pretty certain Paracelsus had nothing to do. The second collected German edition is in four volumes folio, 1603-5. Parallel with it in 1603 the first collected Latin edition was made by Palthenius. It is in eleven volumes quarto, and was completed in 1605. Again, in 1616-18 appeared a re-issue of the folio German edition of 1603, and finally in 1658 came the Geneva Latin version, in three volumes folio, edited by Bitiskius.

The works were originally composed in Swiss-German, a vigorous speech which Paracelsus wielded with unmistakable power. The Latin versions were made or edited by Adam von Bodenstein, Gerard Dorn, Michael Toxites, and Oporinus, about the middle of the 16th century. A few translations into other languages exist, as of the *Chirurgia Magna* and some other works into French, and of one or two into Dutch, Italian, and even Arabic. The translations into English amount to about a dozen, dating mostly from the middle of the 17th century. The original editions of Paracelsus' works are getting less and less common ; even the English versions are among the rarest of their class. Over and above the numerous editions, there is a bulky literature of an explanatory and controversial character, for which the world is indebted to Paracelsus' followers and enemies. A good deal of it is taken up with a defence of chemical, or, as they were called, "spagyric," medicines against the attacks of the supporters of the Galenic pharmacopœia.

The aim of all Paracelsus' writing is to promote the progress of medicine, and he endeavours to put before physicians a grand ideal of their profession. In his attempts he takes the widest view of medicine. He bases it on the general relationship which man bears to nature as a whole ; he cannot divorce the life of man from that of the universe ; he cannot think of disease otherwise than as a phase of life. He is compelled therefore to rest his medical practice upon general theories of the present state of things; his medical system—if there is such a thing—is an adaptation of his cosmogony. It is this latter which has been the stumbling-block to many past critics of Paracelsus, and unless its character is remembered it will be the same to others in the future. Dissatisfied with the Aristotelianism of his time, Paracelsus turned with greater expectation to the Neo-platonism which was reviving. His eagerness to understand the relationship of man to the universe led him to the Kabbala, where these mysteries seemed to be explained, and from these unsubstantial materials he constructed, so far as it can be understood, his visionary philosophy. Interwoven with it, however, were the results of his own personal experience and work in natural history and chemical pharmacy and practical medicine, unfettered by any speculative generalizations, and so shrewd an observer as Paracelsus was must have often felt that his philosophy and his experience did not agree with one another. It was doubtless a very great ideal of medicine which Paracelsus raised; but when it came to realizing it in every-day life he could hardly do else than fail. During the three hundred years which have elapsed since his time knowledge both of the macrocosm and of the microcosm has increased far beyond what Paracelsus could have understood, even had it all been foretold him; the healing art has advanced also, though perhaps scarcely at the same rate, but it would be as hard for us as for him to apply any cosmogony, however rational, to curing disease. We are not one whit nearer the solution of the problems which puzzled Paracelsus than he was; the mystery of the origin, continuance, and stoppage of life is, perhaps through the abundance of light shed on other phenomena, even darker than it may have seemed to Paracelsus. If this be so it is no matter for surprise, or blame, or ridicule that he missed constructing a theory of the universe which at the same time would be a never-failing guide to him in the practical work of alleviating the evils which a residence in this universe seems to entail.

Some of his doctrines have been already alluded to in the article MEDICINE (q.v.), and it would serve no purpose to give even a brief sketch of his views, seeing that their influence has passed entirely away, and that they are of interest only in their place in a general history of medicine and philosophy. Defective, however, as they may have been, and unfounded in fact, his kabbalistic doctrines led him to trace the dependence of the human body upon outer nature for its sustenance and cure. The doctrine of signatures, the supposed connection of every part of the little world of man with a corresponding part of the great world of nature, was a fanciful and false exaggeration of this doctrine, but the idea carried in its train that of specifics. This led to the search for these, which were not to be found in the bewildering and untested mixtures of the Galenic prescriptions. Paracelsus had seen how bodies were purified and intensified by chemical operations, and he thought if plants and minerals could be made to yield their active principles it would surely be better to employ these than the crude and unprepared originals. He had besides arrived by some kind of intuition at the conclusion that the operations in the body were of a chemical character, and that when disordered they were to be put right by counter operations of the same kind. It may be claimed for Paracelsus that he embraced within the idea of chemical action something more than the alchemists did. Whether or not he believed in the philosopher's elixir is of very little consequence. If he did, he was like the rest of his age; but he troubled himself very little, if at all, about it. He did believe in the immediate use for therapeutics of the salts and other preparations which his practical skill enabled him to make. Technically he was not a chemist; he did not concern himself either with the composition of his compounds or with an explanation of what occurred in their making. If he could get potent drugs to cure disease he was content, and he worked very hard in an empirical way to make them. That he found out some new compounds is certain; but not one great and marked discovery can be ascribed to him. Probably therefore his positive services are to be summed up in this wide application of chemical ideas to pharmacy and therapeutics; his indirect and possibly greater services are to be found in the stimulus, the revolutionary stimulus, of his ideas about method and general theory. It is not difficult, however, to criticise Paracelsus and to represent him as so far below the level of his time as to be utterly contemptible. It is difficult, but perhaps not impossible, to raise Paracelsus to a place among the great spirits of mankind. It is most difficult of all to ascertain what his true character really was, to appreciate aright this man of fervid imagination, of powerful and persistent convictions, of unbated honesty and love of truth, of keen insight into the errors (as he thought them) of his time, of a merciless will to lay bare these errors and to reform the abuses to which they gave rise, who in an instant offends us by his boasting, his grossness, his want of self-respect. It is a problem how to reconcile his ignorance, his weakness, his superstition, his crude notions, his erroneous observations, his ridiculous inferences and theories, with his grasp of method, his lofty views of the true scope of medicine, his lucid statements, his incisive and epigrammatic criticisms of men and motives.

A character full of contradictory elements cannot but have had contradictory judgments passed on it; and after three hundred years the animus is as strong and the judgments are as diverse as ever.

[NOTE.—For the Article on MEDICINE referred to on p. 57, see *Encyclopædia Britannica*, 1883, Vol. xv., p. 808.]

Lightning Source UK Ltd.
Milton Keynes UK
UKHW020401081118
331957UK00009B/806/P